7395

£16

WITH
CHURCHILLS
TO
WAR

Plate 1   Colonel G.H. Brooks, who commanded the 48th for longer than any other CO (John Mennell)

WITH
CHURCHILLS
TO
WAR

48TH BATTALION ROYAL TANK
REGIMENT AT WAR 1939–45

PETER GUDGIN

SUTTON PUBLISHING

First published in 1996 by
Sutton Publishing Limited • Phoenix Mill
Thrupp • Stroud • Gloucestershire • GL5 2BU

British Library Cataloguing in Publication Data
A catalogue record for this book is available from the British Library

ISBN 0-7509-1239-1

Typeset in 10/12pt Times.
Typesetting and origination by
Sutton Publishing Limited
Printed in Great Britain by
Butler & Tanner, Frome, Somerset.

Contents

Acknowledgements ix

Lineage of 48th Battalion RTR xi

List of Plates xiii

List of Maps xvii

Abbreviations xix

Introduction xxi

Chapter 1 CLAPHAM AND SANDERSTEAD (1939–40) 1

Chapter 2 COLCHESTER AND SALISBURY PLAIN (1940) 25

Chapter 3 WICKHAM MARKET AND SCOTLAND (1940–43) 34

Chapter 4 ALGERIA AND TUNISIA (1943–44) 72

Chapter 5 ITALY (1944–45) 110

Postscript 160

Appendix A ORGANISATION AND EQUIPMENT OF THE INFANTRY
TANK BATTALION 165

Appendix B SQUADRON NOMINAL ROLLS 168

Appendix C HONOURS AND AWARDS 175

Appendix D ROLL OF HONOUR 176

Appendix E   Tank Markings and Names   177

Appendix F   25 Army Tank Brigade Technical

                  Intelligence Summary No. 1: PzKpfw IV Tiger 180

Bibliography   182

Index   185

This book is dedicated to
the memory of the late
Ken Reed,
sometime commander of 7 Troop and Recce Troop
and long time Chairman of the
48 RTR Association,
and to all the other former members of
this great battalion who have passed to the
'Green Fields Beyond'.

Acknowledgements

Although it is my name that appears on the cover as the author of this work, in reality it could not have been written without the generous and unstinted help given to me by many of the former members of the 48th Battalion Royal Tank Regiment and members of the 48th RTR Association.

With so many individuals deserving a personal mention it is invidious to select some for special mention from the alphabetical list of names, but none deserves it more than Leslie Burnham, MBE, erstwhile member of the Recce Troop and the Light Squadron and currently (as for many years past) the Hon Sec of the 48th RTR Association, whose own contributions, as well as his efforts to drum up documents, reminiscences and photographs from association members on my behalf have been tireless, as well as successful.

Especial thanks are also due to Col (Retd) John Mennell, OBE, TD, both for lending me his personal diary, his draft history of the battalion and his photographs, as well as for his checking of the early chapters of the draft typescript; to Don Hoad, former 2IC of C Squadron, for the loan of various nominal rolls of the squadron, as well as his personal photographs; to former LCpl and journalist Geoff Thomason, for the loan of a complete set of the *B-Line* magazine; to former regimental policeman and Recce Troop member Reg Heard for the loan of his personal diaries covering Penthièvre and Italy.

My thanks go also to Tom Gorringe, former A Squadron troop leader and battalion adjutant, for drawing the excellent maps; to Maj (Retd) Tony Kingsford, MBE, MC, former troop leader, B Squadron 2IC and battalion adjutant, for his contribution of photographs and documents, as well as for the checking of the final chapter, and to the following former members of the 48th, listed in alphabetical order rather than in order of size of contribution, who so willingly provided personal recollections, insignia, documents and photographs, many at the expense of stripping treasured personal photo albums: Barry Archer, 'Brownie' Baker, Bill Bayly, George Benfield, Roger Blankley, Gerry Brooks, Ned Cook, Arnold Cummins, Cyril Edwards, Don Faulkner, Dennis Gable, Alan Gilmour, Fred Harrison, Peter King, Maurice Ladd, Gerry Letchford, Ian More, Glyn Morrey-Jones, Peter O'Flynn, Henry Palmer, Eric Potter, Ken Reed, Jack Rockliff, Pat Russell, Arthur Spackman, Geoff Thompson, John Walker and Jackie Wykes.

The help of the Tank Museum at Bovington Camp and of the Imperial War Museum in giving permission for the use, free of charge, of photographs from their extensive archives and in giving the author access to various War Diaries and other documents is gratefully acknowledged. Thanks are also due to Mr Michael Hurlock, owner of Glevering Hall, for photographs of the hall and permission to reproduce extracts from his brief history of the hall, to Suffolk Record Office, to Dumfries and Galloway Regional Library for information relating to Hoddom Castle and to Nicholas Long, the Hon Sec of the Clapham Antiquarian Society, for photographs and details of the former Clapham High School for Girls.

Peter Gudgin
Leamington Spa, 1995

LINEAGE OF 48th BATTALION RTR

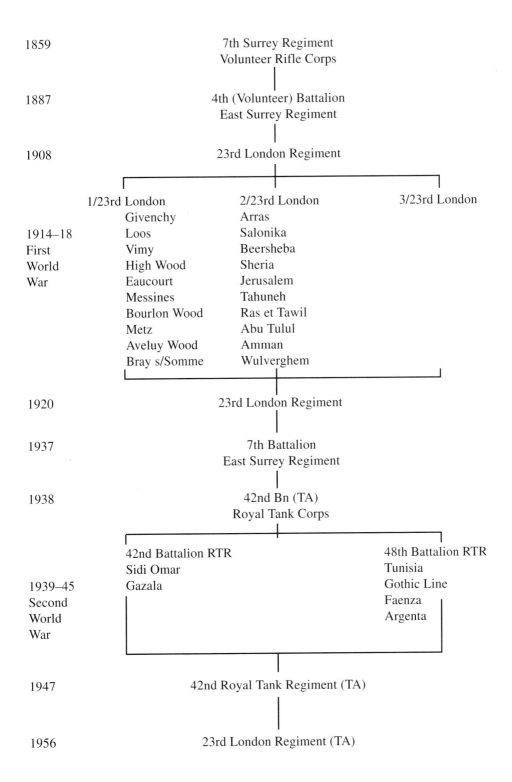

1859   7th Surrey Regiment
Volunteer Rifle Corps

1887   4th (Volunteer) Battalion
East Surrey Regiment

1908   23rd London Regiment

1/23rd London	2/23rd London	3/23rd London
Givenchy	Arras	
Loos	Salonika	
Vimy	Beersheba	
High Wood	Sheria	
Eaucourt	Jerusalem	
Messines	Tahuneh	
Bourlon Wood	Ras et Tawil	
Metz	Abu Tulul	
Aveluy Wood	Amman	
Bray s/Somme	Wulverghem	

1914–18
First
World
War

1920   23rd London Regiment

1937   7th Battalion
East Surrey Regiment

1938   42nd Bn (TA)
Royal Tank Corps

42nd Battalion RTR	48th Battalion RTR
Sidi Omar	Tunisia
Gazala	Gothic Line
	Faenza
	Argenta

1939–45
Second
World
War

1947   42nd Royal Tank Regiment (TA)

1956   23rd London Regiment (TA)

List of Plates

Frontispiece

1	Col G.H. Brooks.

CHAPTER 1

2	63, South Side, Clapham Common.
3	Lt Col W.J. Wykes MBE, TD.
4	Medium Tank Mk I of 2nd Battalion RTR at Farnborough, Hants.
5	Lt Col Wykes dismounting from a 2nd Battalion Light Tank Mk VIB.
6	Officers at annual camp, Aldershot, in August 1939.
7	Warrant officers and sergeants of the battalion at the 1939 annual camp.
8	A Company, 48th Battalion RTR, at annual camp, 1939.
9	B Company, 48th Battalion RTR, at annual camp, 1939.
10	C Company, 48th Battalion RTR, at annual camp, 1939.
11	B Company lines at the August 1939 annual camp.
12	Wireless instruction on an early tank wireless at annual camp.
13	Tanks in the tank park at Purley Beeches, 1939.
14	2Lt C.A. Joss commanding a Light Tank Mk IV.
15	Territorial Army call-up notice, 1939.
16	Officers' Mess, Sanderstead.
17	'Diabolo' formation sign of 21st Army Tank Brigade.
18	Medium tanks at Purley Beeches.
19	Programme for Battalion Christmas Pantomime 'Babes in the Wood'.
20	Infantry Tank Mk II (Matilda).

CHAPTER 2

21	C Squadron Medium tank at Colchester.
22	DR Troop at Higham, Essex, June 1940.
23	Lt Bell commanding a C Squadron Valentine on exercise in SE England.

CHAPTER 3

24	Glevering Hall, near Wickham Market.
25	Valentine I of 3 Troop, A Squadron, on Exercise Talisman, 1940.
26 – 27	Battalion tanks taking part in a propaganda film, 1941.
28	Tank crews take a break during filming.
29 – 30	War workers' tattoo, 31 August 1942.
31	Battalion orders group on Exercise Bumper.
32	Valentine of Battalion HQ Troop on Exercise Bumper.
33	A Squadron Churchills in the tank park at Glevering Hall.
34, 35 & 38	Amphibious training on the Isle of Wight in June 1942.
36	C Squadron Churchills being loaded on to war flats for the move to Scotland.

37	Formation sign of 4th (Mixed) Division, officers' uniform pattern.
39–42	Officers' ID card photographs, late 1942.
43	Hoddom Castle, Ecclefechan.
44	Churchill II of 12 Troop, C Squadron, at Hoddom, in July 1942.
45	Rota-trailer.
46	Churchill IV *Tessa* of 4 Troop leader, A Squadron.
47	Subalterns outside their hut at Hoddom Castle in February 1943.
48	Valentine V.
49	Dingo scout car and crew at Hoddom Castle.
50	Crew briefing at dawn.
51	The battalion Christmas card for 1942.
52	The white Allied recognition star on a Churchill turret roof.
53	Cover of *B-Line* souvenir final edition.

CHAPTER 4

54	Battalion baggage on quayside at Bône, March 1943.
55	Airgraph letter.
56	Airgraph letter for a special occasion.
57	PzKpfw III with 50mm gun.
58	PzKpfw III with short 75mm howitzer.
59	PzKpfw IV (Mark IV Special).
60	Churchills of A Squadron HQ and 4 Troop zeroing guns prior to first action, April 1943.
61	OC A Squadron and 4 Troop leader, April 1943.
62	PzKpfw VI Tiger Model E.
63	A Squadron attack on Djebel Djaffa on 21 April 1943.
64	Captured Tiger in original position at Djebel Djaffa, 22 April 1943.
65	The Tiger in Tunis, being inspected by Winston Churchill, June 1943.
66	The Tiger in England, at the Fighting Vehicle Proving Establishment.
67	Tpr R.W. Nicoll MM of B Squadron.
68	*Toledo* and crews of 14 Troop, C Squadron, April 1943.
69	Allied propaganda leaflet.
70	Battalion orders group in Tunisian cornfield, 5 May 1943.
71	German surrender on Cap Bon peninsula, May 1943.
72	Battalion A vehicles moving back to Penthièvre in Algeria, May 1943.
73	C Squadron officers, Penthièvre.
74	HM King George VI inspecting the battalion at Penthièvre, 18 June 1943.
75	Battalion Christmas greetings airgraph for 1943.
76	Lt Col J.W.R. Loveday, 16th/5th Lancers.

CHAPTER 5

77	Brig David Dawnay DSO, commander of 21st Tank Brigade 1944/5.
78	Typical M4 Sherman tank.
79	Turreted and turretless Honeys of Recce Troop, with crews.
80	New formation sign of 21st Tank Brigade, summer 1944.
81	Lt Col E.H. Tinker, 13/18th Hussars.
82	Battalion orderly room staff at Spoleto, August 1944.
83	C Squadron Churchill IV (NA75) and crew.

84	Dug-in Panther tank turret, part of the Gothic Line defences.
85	Part of the Gothic Line, showing trees felled and buildings demolished to clear fields of fire.
86	Battalion HQ officers at Presenzano, summer 1944.
87	Churchill V (CS) of B Squadron HQ Troop.
88	Capt Tom Bruce, 2IC of B Squadron, beside Squadron HQ sign, 1944.
89	Churchill Crocodile flame-thrower tank and trailer.
90	Jeep and driver of C Squadron commander in 1944.
91	C Squadron fitters and their half-track, 1944. (Photo: Don Hoad)
92	Lt Col P.W.D. Sturdee RTR.
93	Churchills of the 48th Battalion RTR parked up in Piazza del Popolo, Faenza, Christmas 1944.
94	NA75 Churchill IVs firing across the Senio, winter 1944.
95	Churchill VII.
96	Churchill IV (NA75).
97	Churchill bridgelayer.
98	Sherman 'dozer.
99	Churchill IV (NA75) of 48th Battalion RTR crossing the Senio over two Churchill ARKs.
100	Churchill ARK.
101	German SP 88mm anti-tank gun *Nashorn* (Rhinoceros).
102	*Daily Sketch* cutting about Sgt Catchpole.
103	Allied safe-conduct leaflet.
104	Sherman Duplex Drive (DD) tank.
105	Officers of B Squadron at Lungo Brenta, May 1945.
106	Churchill ARV I of B Squadron, with crew, at Lungo Brenta, May 1945.
107	B Squadron gondola crew in Venice, May 1945.
108	Brig Dawnay and Lt Col Sturdee at the farewell parade, Rimini.
109	Other ranks' discharge certificate.

POSTSCRIPT

110	Gradara War Cemetery of the Commonwealth War Graves Commission.
111	48th Battalion RTR Roll of Honour.
112	Glevering Hall as it is today.
113	San Maria Scacciano, after the war.

Maps

Map No.	Subject
1	Battalion moves in the United Kingdom
2	Battalion moves in French North Africa
3	Northern Tunisia
4	The squadron attack on Djebel Djaffa
5	Battalion moves in Italy
6	Breaking the Gothic Line
7	The capture of Rimini
8	The advance to the River Senio
9	Forcing of the Argenta Gap and the advance to the River Adige

Abbreviations

A/(rank)	Acting, e.g. A/Maj. acting major
'A' Vehs	Armoured vehicles
ABD	Army base depot
AP	Armour piercing
APDS	Armour piercing, discarding sabot
ARK	Armoured ramp carrier
ATS	Auxiliary Territorial Service
AVRE	Armoured vehicle, Royal Engineers
'B' Vehs	Soft-skinned vehicles
BD	Battledress
BEF	British Expeditionary Force
Bn	Battalion
BTA	Battalion technical adjutant
CO	Commanding officer
CS	Close support
CSM	Company Sergeant Major
DCM	Distinguished Conduct Medal
DD	Duplex drive (amphibious)
DR	Despatch rider
DSO	Distinguished Service Order
EME	Electrical & Mechanical Engineer
FDS	Field dressing station
FFI	Free from infection
GRTD	General Reinforcement & Training Depot
GSGS	General Staff Geographic Section
HE	High explosive
HMT	His Majesty's Transport (troopship)
HQ	Headquarters
in	inch
intercomm	intercommunication
IO	Intelligence officer
KD	Khaki drill (tropical uniform)
LAD	Light aid detachment (REME)
LCT	Landing craft, tank
LIAP	Leave in addition to Python
LILOP	Leave in lieu of Python
LO	Liaison officer
M & V	Meat and vegetable
MC	Military Cross
MG	Machine gun
ML	Motor launch

MM	Military Medal
mm	millimetre
MO	Medical officer
MP	Military Police(man)
NAAFI	Navy, Army & Air Force Institutes
NCO	Non-commissioned officer
'O' Group	Orders group
OC	Officer commanding
OCTU	Officer Cadet Training Unit
OP	Observation post
OR	Other rank
ORQMS	Orderly Room Quartermaster Sergeant
ORS	Orderly Room Sergeant
pdr	pounder (gun size, from weight of shot)
PIAT	Projector, infantry, anti-tank
POW or PW	Prisoner of war
PzKpfw or PzKw	*Panzerkampfwagen* (German for tank)
QM	Quartermaster
QMS	Quartermaster Sergeant
QMS(T)	Quartermaster Sergeant (Technical)
RAC	Royal Armoured Corps
RAP	Regimental aid post
RASC	Royal Army Service Corps
RCAOC	Royal Canadian Army Ordnance Corps
Recce	Reconnaissance
REME	Royal Electrical & Mechanical Engineers
RP	Regimental Police(man)
RQMS	Regimental Quartermaster Sergeant
RSM	Regimental Sergeant Major
RTC	Royal Tank Corps
RTR	Royal Tank Regiment
SHQ	Squadron headquarters
SMG	Sub-machine gun
SP	Self-propelled
SQMS	Squadron Quartermaster Sergeant
SSM	Squadron Sergeant Major
T/(rank)	Temporary, e.g. T/Maj. temporary major
TAB	Para-typhoid A & B (inoculation)
Tet Tox	Tetanus Toxoid (inoculation)
WE	War Establishment
WO	War Office, or Warrant Officer
2IC	Second-in-command

Introduction

The British invention and introduction of the tank, and the creation of the Corps which used it, played a very large part in the winning of the First World War. The tank itself, with its ability both to cross the trenches and barbed wire entanglements which had strangled battlefield mobility, and to withstand the murderous machine gun fire with which these obstacles were covered, provided the mechanical means to regain both battlefield mobility and the tactical initiative. The organisation built up to operate this weapon in battle gathered a wealth of specialist experience in the tactical handling of the tank; experience unrivalled amongst both the Allies and their enemies. Britain ended the war with a head start over the rest of the world in both the design of tanks and their employment in battle. The repository for this knowledge was the Tank Corps, formed out of the Heavy Branch, Machine Gun Corps, in 1917 and consisting of 25 battalions by the end of the war in November 1918.

As had so often been the case after previous wars, however, this advantage was soon lost, thanks to a combination of too rapid demobilisation, jealousy of the new Corps on the part of the older arms of the Service, particularly the cavalry, and a lack of understanding, amounting in some cases to an active dislike, of things mechanical among the senior ranks of the Regular Army. To these were added a parsimonious Treasury, which failed to make the necessary funds available for defence, a succession of governments to whom a strong defence after a war to end war appeared an unnecessary expense, and an industry which was unwilling to re-tool to produce small numbers of tanks for a War Office which could not make up its mind what it wanted. By 1935, what had now become the Royal Tank Corps consisted of only six battalions (one of which was a light battalion), five armoured car companies and three light tank companies.

The design advantage held by the British at the end of the First World War was frittered away; the tank had no civilian counterpart, so that industrial design and manufacturing expertise was rapidly diverted to the manufacture of civilian products. In addition, the pool of officers with knowledge of tank design requirements had been either dispersed throughout the Army or demobilised; this, together with the similar dispersal of those officers with detailed knowledge of how tanks were best employed tactically led to uncertainty within the War Office as to what, if any, the requirements for future tanks might be.

In the period after the First World War, the War Office could not make up its mind as to the types of tank it required. British military thought on the subject at the end of that war saw a need for two categories: a fast tank (the Whippet or Vickers Medium) for exploitation, and a heavy tank for cooperation with the infantry. For the future, however, a need for lighter, smaller tanks capable of higher speeds and greater manoeuvrability was foreseen.

At that time most countries, with the exception of Britain, regarded tanks purely as a supporting arm for the infantry. Britain, however, considered that different tanks for differing rôles should be developed to meet the varying tactical situations likely to be encountered on the battlefield. This policy led eventually to the development of three distinct types: the light tank, as a reconnaissance vehicle; the Medium (or cruiser) tank, as a vehicle sufficiently mobile to maintain the fluidity of modern warfare; and, rather later, the heavy (or infantry) tank for close cooperation with infantry in the assault. One of the attractions of such a mix of types to a War Office starved of funds was that it could build large numbers of light tanks and fewer personnel would be required to man and maintain them. The disadvantage of this policy, of course, lay in the logistics of production, training, repair and spares supply.

The result of these unfortunate circumstances was that, as the war clouds again started gathering over Europe in the late 1930s, Britain lagged far behind the rearming Germany, both in the size, the equipment and the tactical employment of its armoured force. Neither was the equipment available to cover the expansion of this force when expansion was finally, and belatedly, ordered. By the outbreak of war in September 1939 there were 59 regiments in what had now become the expanded Royal Armoured Corps (RAC); this consisted of the mechanised cavalry and yeomanry regiments and the battalions of the renamed Royal Tank Regiment (RTR). To equip these units there were only some 2,000 tanks available, of which 300 were completely obsolete while most of the remainder were light tanks of little combat value. The 8,000 tracked carriers available had to be shared with the infantry, while of the 200 or so armoured cars at least half were between 10 and 20 years old.

As on the many previous occasions when the country was threatened, the part-time volunteers came to the rescue of a country which had been criminally careless of its defence; in this case it was the Territorial Army (TA), successor to the fencibles and militia of earlier scares, the Royal Naval Volunteer Reserve and the Royal Auxiliary Air Force. This is the story of one TA tank battalion, the 48th Battalion, Royal Tank Regiment, formed at Clapham Junction, SW London, in April 1939 and disbanded seven years later in Italy. It shows how, fighting the muddle caused by shortages of equipment, instructors and accommodation resulting from years of short-sighted War Office policy, government parsimony and industrial lethargy, this typical cross-section of the male population of south London finally overcame these obstacles to become a close-knit team and an efficient fighting unit of the Royal Armoured Corps, which played a full part in the victorious campaigns in Tunisia and Italy, as well as earlier in the defence of the United Kingdom.

Finally, it is worth mentioning here that the official history of the RTR (*The Tanks* by Capt B.H. Liddell Hart) is strangely silent on the subject of the formation of the second batch of TA battalions of the RTR in 1939; however, this is only one of the many omissions and errors concerning the 48th Battalion in that history. In a vague and inaccurate paragraph on page 401 of volume one, the formation is mentioned of only seven out of the twelve of the new TA RTR battalions, ending with the 46th Battalion; there is no mention of the other five, including the 48th. This reluctance to mention the 48th continues up to the time of the final victory in North Africa, when an error-strewn page 254 in volume two confuses the 21st and 25th Army Tank Brigades and the battalions of which they were composed. These errors are repeated on page 278, where a completely erroneous breakdown of 25th Army Tank Brigade alleges it to have contained both 12th and 48th Battalions RTR as well as the 51st; a correct breakdown of 21st Army Tank Brigade is, however, given only three pages later on page 281. A further error occurs on page 287, where 40th Battalion RTR instead of the 48th is shown as belonging to 21st Army Tank Brigade. These errors and omissions are unfortunate, to say the least, and tend to lessen one's faith in what purports to be the definitive history of the RTR; to correct them is, however, only one of the reasons for writing this present work.

CHAPTER I

Clapham and Sanderstead

(1939–40)

With Adolf Hitler's accession to power in Germany in 1933, it soon became apparent to all but the most blinkered observers that a resurgent Germany had aggressive intentions in its search for more living space. Unfortunately, the blinkered observers included the successive British governments of the time, until eventually the unacceptable truth was made blindingly obvious even to them.

It is difficult at first glance to understand the reluctance of the British government to react to Germany's repudiation of the military clauses of the Treaty of Versailles and her subsequent rearmament. It must be remembered, however, that although, as a result of the First World War, the British public had been brought up to believe no good of the Germans, they had also been brought up to believe that the First World War had effectively ended the risk of a future war in Europe; they were therefore as loth as was their government to think that Germany would risk provoking another war after having been so decisively defeated in 1918. The British public did not wish their comfortable peace to be disturbed again by war; both they and their successive governments therefore preferred to look the other way as Germany annexed first the Saar, then the Rhineland, followed by Austria in March 1938 and Czechoslovakia in March of the following year. The indications of German rearmament were largely ignored by the British public in favour of domestic events such as the King's Silver Jubilee celebrations, his funeral, and his son's accession and subsequent abdication, followed by the coronation of King George VI. They placed their faith in the authority of the League of Nations to prevent war, at little cost and little risk.

The League was put to the test in 1935 and failed, but, because the test was incomplete and few people could bring themselves to face the alternatives, wishful thinking meant that faith in the League survived for some time longer. Reinforcing this evasion of responsibilities was the pacifist movement. The roots of such widespread pacifism were in the trenches of the war to end all wars. The whole of British society had been revolted by the devastation and sheer number of casualties caused by the First World War, and this revulsion led to a powerful lobby against war and a despairing faith in the institutions set up to prevent it. By the middle of 1936, the Peace Pledge Union had 100,000 members and was appealing for a similar number of women members. Peace societies flourished at all the universities, and the great Peace Ballot, the result of which was announced in June 1935 and in which more than 11,000,000 people took part, was the high water mark of inter-war pacifism.

It was against this background, therefore, that the government had to begin, quietly, reluctantly and tentatively, to face the problem of Germany's rearmament by beginning the process of rearming Britain, while maintaining belief, as a keystone of its foreign policy, in collective responsibility for peace through the League of Nations.

Britain's rearmament was made official policy in 1935; policy was put into practice in 1936, but at a leisurely pace until the Munich crisis in 1938. It started with the RAF, and continued with the Royal Navy; the Army came a very low third on the priority list, and it was not until 1937 that increases in the strength of the Regular Army were authorised. Only two out of the five Regular Army divisions had been fully equipped by October 1938, and it was only in the same year that the Army finally obtained its full peacetime complement of wheeled vehicles. Even then, the chief effort in the Army's re-equipment was devoted to the anti-aircraft defences of Britain; and even had it not been, the Army's conception of tank design and tactical employment was many years out of date, with even the new tanks on the drawing board being inadequately armed and those in service having relatively poor mobility and reliability compared to those of the Germans.

The rearmament was programmed to cause minimum disturbance to British industry, and aimed to have the armed services ready for war by the summer of 1940; equipment for the remaining three Regular divisions was planned to be ready by September 1939. The Munich crisis spurred the introduction of increases in the Territorial as well as the Regular Army and, as part of these, six Territorial infantry battalions were converted into battalions of the Royal Tank Corps in 1938. One of these, the 42nd (TA) Battalion RTC, was the London battalion, formed from the 7th (TA) Battalion East Surrey Regiment (23rd London Regiment), and had its headquarters at St John's Hill, Clapham Junction. Alan Gilmour, a pre-war journalist and later a tank driver member of 7 Platoon (later Troop) of B Company (later Squadron), recalls:

> I was attracted to the Royal Tank Corps by the display of a light tank on the forecourt of Charing Cross Station, installed by the 42nd Battalion RTC (TA). So, for some months, I belonged to the 42nd, training at Clapham. . . . At Clapham we were initiated into the mysteries (and stoppages) of the water-cooled Vickers machine gun, the fundamentals of the internal combustion engine and, although still not in uniform, taught how to salute.

The occupation of Czechoslovakia by Germany in March 1939 lent even greater urgency to the need to increase Army strength, and the decision to double the size of the Territorial field force was announced by the Prime Minister, Neville Chamberlain, in the House of Commons on 29 March. As a result of this decision, a further six TA battalions were formed of what had by then, with the formation of the Royal Armoured Corps, become the Royal Tank Regiment. Again London had its share, in this case the 48th Battalion RTR (TA), which was formed out of the 42nd Battalion at Clapham Junction on 26 April 1939. Alan Gilmour continues:

> We were introduced to the medium tank on training weekends outside London. The training sessions ended in convivial meetings in a pub on St John's Hill, Clapham, and these were, perhaps, the beginnings of the remarkable camaraderie that developed during the war, and has persisted.

The training weekends took place at Farnborough, Hants, in the barracks of the 2nd Battalion RTR.

The 48th was to be an infantry (I) tank battalion forming part of the 21st Army Tank Brigade; it in fact remained in this brigade for the entire duration of the war, the only battalion to do so. This brigade had itself only been formed earlier that year, its first commander being the recent commander of the newly re-formed 7th Battalion RTR and veteran of the Battle of Cambrai, Brig A.G. (Kench) Kenchington.

By now, the majority of the British public had recognised Germany's actions as aggressive and expansionist, and was at last in favour of taking action to put a stop to her aggression. A reborn patriotism began to assert itself, and the newly formed TA battalions were soon swamped with volunteers willing to be a part of the force to do this; most of the staff's time seemed to be devoted to swearing them in! In January 1939 the government had issued to every household in the United Kingdom its *Guide to National Service,* in which everyone was urged to volunteer for service of some sort, and this no doubt played a part in deciding so many young south Londoners to volunteer for the 48th Battalion RTR; they came from all ranks and walks of life, and represented a true cross-section of young male Londoners of the time.

The 42nd Battalion RTR, having been formed only the previous year, had problems of its own, but at least it had a proper TA drill hall for its HQ, training and the housing of its equipment; there was not enough room there for two battalions, however, although the 48th did initially carry out some of its training there, as well as in the local Express Dairy depot and in Battersea Town Hall. The 48th was therefore compelled to find its own premises before it could get down to serious training. Eventually, a suitable HQ location was found in the premises of the Clapham High School for Girls (see **Plate 2**) at No 63, South Side, Clapham Common, immediately opposite the Windmill pub; this school was closed in 1938 by the Girls' Public Day School Trust, owing to changes in the population of the district.

There was neither enough equipment nor trained instructors; a nucleus of only five officers and 20 other ranks could be provided by the 42nd from which to form the 48th. This nucleus came initially under the command of Maj George Rogers, who called his first conference to bring the battalion into being on 26 April 1939. The first Adjutant was a Regular officer, Lt Gerald Strong, who was often to be seen exercising his recalcitrant black Labrador on Clapham Common; he was with the battalion for only a very short time.

Accommodation and equipment were the main worries of this team, with the provision of instructors high on their list of priorities. As we have seen already, however, equipment was in short supply even for the Regular Army, and would continue to be so for some time to come; the situation for the Territorial Army was much worse and in fact it was not until September 1940, a year after the outbreak of war, that the 48th first received its full wartime

Plate 2   The former Clapham High School for Girls at 63 South Side, Clapham Common, the battalion's first HQ (Eric Smith Collection)

establishment of tanks. The volunteers reported to Battalion HQ twice weekly for training in the rudiments of soldiering; after training, they would adjourn upstairs to the canteen or out to the local pub, where discussion continued. Instruction at this time was basic, mainly in the Vickers machine gun and in driving; not many could drive in those days. As Roger Blankley of Cumbernauld, an early recruit, remembers:

> Little equipment was available, and it was not until just before the Annual Camp in August that almost every man was issued with a strange and mostly ill-fitting new uniform called Battle Dress [BD]. Even then many went to Camp with only an issue of brown overalls.

The annual camp was under canvas at Rushmoor, Aldershot, near the famous tattoo arena, from 6 to 20 August 1939, in a camp taken over from the 42nd Battalion RTR. By then, Lt Col W.J. (Jackie) Wykes (**Plate 3**) had assumed command, with Capt D.W.N.F. ('Tug') Wilson, a very excitable officer, as his Adjutant. Lt Col Wykes recalls that other personalities included Lt A.S. Carr (MO), Revd H. Deighton (Padre), Maj A.B. Woodgate, DSO, MC (Quartermaster) and Capt S.S.A.B. Rackow, a reservist and former member of the 23rd London (East Surreys). Photographs of the officers and of the WOs and sergeants of the battalion, taken during the camp, are reproduced in **Plates 6 and 7**; similar photographs of the assembled A, B and C Companies, taken at the same time but unfortunately without names, appear in **Plates 8, 9 and 10**.

Plate 3 Lt Col W.J. Wykes MBE, TD, the battalion's first commanding officer (Author's collection)

Plate 4   A Medium Tank Mk I of 2nd Battalion RTR at Farnborough, Hants., used by the officers of the 48th for weekend training in 1939 (John Mennell)

Plate 5   Col Wykes dismounting from a 2nd Battalion Light Tank Mk VIB during weekend training at Farnborough (John Mennell)

Plate 6 The officers of the battalion at annual camp, Aldershot, in August 1939. Back row, left to right: 2Lt F.W. Webb, Lt A.G. Arnold, Lt W.J. Heavey, 2Lt C.A. Joss, 2Lts A.H. Harland, G.A. Smith, M.P. Ladd, P. Barnett, RAC Loader: Centre row: Revd H.S. Deighton (42nd Bn RTR), 2Lts J.S. Mennell, J.H.A. Newcombe, A.W. Norrish, Lt R.S. Strachan MM, 2Lts R.H. Radcliff, C.P. Hughes, E.F. Stevens, G.G. Bell, C.H. Crowther, Lt S.A. Carr. Seated: Capts D.B. Edwards, P.C. West, N.N. Watney, D.W.N.F. Wilson (Adjt), Lt Col W.J. Wykes (CO), J.O. Clark (2IC), J.E. George, Capt S.S.A.P. Rackowe, Maj A.B. Woodgate DSO MC (QM) (John Mennell)

Plate 7   The warrant officers and sergeants of the battalion at the 1939 annual camp. Back row, left to right: Sgts R.H. Bushell (PSI), W. Atkins, J.H. Jones, L.C. Larcom, W.A.J. Greer, C. Noyes, N. Syrett, L.H. Merton, H. McIver, A.W. Godfrey, J. Furnival, A. Cummins, C. Dawson, G. South, J.E. Sergeant. Centre row: Sgts J.R. Nash, E. Didd (PSI), C/Sgt F. Shapter (PSI), CQMS T.B. Gale, C/Sgt J. McKenner (PSI), CQMS D. Oliver, W. King, Sgts E. Stephens, F. Esdale, R. Smaldon, J. Garner, E.L. Latreille. Seated: CSMs W. Clift, W.A. Paice MM, RSM W.J. Lockwood (PSI), Maj J.O. Clark (2IC), Lt Col W.J. Wykes (CO), Capt D.W.N.F. Wilson (Adjt), RQMS F.G. Miles, CSMs A.W.F. Warwick MBE, G.H. Charlton (Jackie Wykes)

Plate 8   A Company, 48th Bn RTR, at annual camp, 1939 (Roger Blankley)

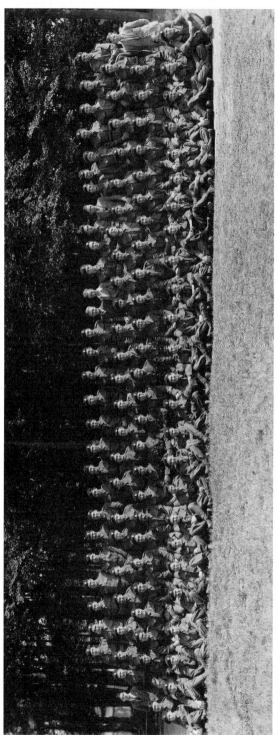

Plate 9 B Company, 48th Bn RTR, at annual camp, 1939 (48 RTR Assn)

Plate 10   C Company, 48th Bn RTR, at annual camp, 1939 (Don Hoad)

John Hancock, the first Orderly Room Sergeant, recalls:

During those early days between the formation of the 48th and the outbreak of war, the Orderly Room was presided over by a civilian clerk, Jack Love, an old Army man, ex-Warrant Officer (Guards, I believe) who could recite King's Regulations backwards in his sleep. With a pint of beer in his hand and a few more under his belt he would recount past campaigns and Army history from the relief of Gordon at Khartoum, so interesting and descriptive that the truth was not an issue. The RSM . . . and Jack Love conducted a never-ending war, which Jack invariably won. There were a number of permanent staff instructors, amongst whom I can remember CSM McKenna and Sgts Bushell, Shapter and Acker Stevens; Bushell and McKenna were to leave us soon after the outbreak of war, as, of course, was Jack Love, and I took over as Orderly Room Sergeant.

With only a limited amount of equipment available, training had perforce to consist mainly of individual training. Vehicles were a hotch-potch of old trucks, some ancient Vickers Medium tanks and a variety of motorcycles hurriedly obtained and still in the original makers' liveries. Driving instruction took place on Long Valley, Aldershot, still used to this day by the Ministry of Defence for the cross-country testing of prototypes of new armoured fighting vehicles. RYPAs, those machines that reproduced, for gunnery training, the roll, yaw and pitch action of a moving tank, were used for the first time, and even a wireless set was seen.

Almost immediately after the battalion's return from its first and last annual camp, and after Germany and the USSR had signed their non-aggression pact, the Battalion Key Party, consisting of Lt Col Wykes, Maj J. Eden George (a veteran of the 7th East Surrey (23rd London) Regiment), Maurice Ladd, John Mennell and one or two others, was called up on 25 August and made its HQ in the former girls' high school on Clapham Common. The Adjutant was still Capt 'Tug' Wilson, with 2Lt C.A. (Bill) Joss as his assistant and 2Lt John Mennell as Battalion Intelligence Officer and Messing Officer. They spent their time getting ready to receive, accommodate and feed the men of the battalion when they were called up. The Battalion War Diary was started on this day.

Plate 11   B Company lines at annual camp, August 1939 (Pat Russell)

The Germans invaded Poland on Friday 1 September, and on the same day Britain ordered full mobilisation and a nationwide blackout. An awestruck duty officer at Battalion HQ received a telephone message from HQ 44th Division saying: 'Clive Plumer Roberts. The TA will embody.' However, all was ready in the Orderly Room; within half an hour the embodiment notices had been sent out and the small Key Party sat back to await the avalanche. John Walker, a stalwart of Recce Troop and the Light Squadron and now of Stowmarket recalls:

At the time of the mobilisation I was on holiday with my then fiancée at Sheerness, in the local cinema, when the call-up came on the screen. Incidentally, we were watching *The Four Feathers*. So we left hurriedly and returned to London, and I reported to Clapham Common on the Sunday morning. My call-up notice [reproduced in **Plate 15**] was never handed in; I often wonder if the MPs are still looking for me!

The Key Party had not long to wait; within two hours, at seven o'clock that evening, Sgt Smaldon of A Company reported. He was the first of the many, and all night long they continued to arrive. Some had come straight from work without food, some came in uniform, some brought luggage, others came as they stood.

Initially they were accommodated in the girls' school, but this soon became overcrowded and the overflow had to be found billets in other houses nearby. The next morning brought the problem of feeding an ever-increasing number of men; however, Carpenters of Clapham,

Plate 12 Wireless instruction on an early tank wireless at annual camp (Pat Russell)

who for so long had fed the Houses of Parliament, came to the rescue and somehow managed to feed the hungry throng. Later that day the stream of arrivals became a torrent, and the officers, most of whom had by now arrived, were put on to the task of finding billets for them; by evening the heavens had opened, the thunder crashed and the lightning broke the newly-imposed blackout, irregularly illuminating long lines of quiet, rain-soaked men, still cheerful as they waited patiently to be put into their billets.

Cyril Edwards, now of Thorpe Bay, has vivid memories of the medical inspection after mobilisation:

This consisted of saying 'Aah' and '99', plus a body check for scars. After dressing, the whole gathering was assembled in the Drill Hall and addressed from the platform by a doctor in civilian clothes who read out a long list of medical complaints and called for anyone suffering from any of these to put his hand up; nobody did, and en masse we were proclaimed A-1.

There was no RASC organisation for the supply of rations, so the Messing Officer had to make further arrangements with Carpenters, the local caterers, for the feeding of the battalion. Respirators (such few as were available), steel helmets and other impedimenta

11

Plate 13   Battalion Medium Tanks in the tank park at Purley Beeches, 1939 (Pat Russell)

were issued on the following day. Cyril Edwards recalls that, when he reported to Clapham on mobilisation, '. . . the only personal kit for issue appeared to be steel helmets (didn't fit), so we were told to get, or to have sent from home, toilet and sewing kit and overcoats'.

In the meantime, the unit had been warned that it was to move on the following day, Sunday 3 September, to Sanderstead: the Key Party had already carried out some preliminary reconnaissance and arrangements were made to billet everyone on the civilian population of this attractive dormitory area for Croydon, on the wooded Surrey North Downs. The move took place on the day war was declared; while on parade, the battalion could hear Neville Chamberlain's broadcast declaration of war at 11.15am. This was immediately followed by the first air raid warning of the war, during which everyone sheltered in a cellar.

After the 'All Clear' was sounded, the battalion moved off to Sanderstead in relays of lorries and vans requisitioned from local builders, coal merchants, greengrocers and other tradesmen. Cyril Edwards goes on:

As the Prime Minister had just made his announcement that we were at war, the good people of South London cheered this motley collection of vehicles, which they believed were rushing their passengers south to face the Hun, and showed their appreciation by throwing packets of cigarettes and money into the open vehicles. Most of us had mixed feelings of relief and shame when the convoy halted in Sanderstead, and we were allocated billets in homes that made us welcome for several months, homes of a

Plate 14   2Lt C.A. Joss commanding a Light Tank Mk IV (Pat Russell)

standard many of us had not been inside before. I hope the cheering crowds along the route never found out that some now had maids and great comfort!

He continues: 'Early parades were something special when the cold weather broke out' due to the variety of civilian overcoats worn.

The battalion soon settled into its comfortable billets in Sanderstead; the Officers' Mess, initially installed in a pub in Purley, then moved to occupy the much more comfortable, and suitable, Purley Downs Golf Club. John Hancock continues:

The top brass and HQ Company were housed in Llandaff House on Sanderstead Hill; the Quartermaster's department was next door in 'Woodlands'. The tank and vehicle park was in a local beauty spot, Purley Beeches, and the Purley Downs golf course became the battalion training area; the local church hall was occupied by the other ranks' mess hall.

To begin with, and again in the absence of an adequate RASC organisation, arrangements had to be made for the catering to be carried out by a local department store, in this case Grant Bros of Croydon, which ferried meals in daily. Although the food was more of wedding reception standard than normal Army fare, the Messing Officer still managed to make a handsome profit for battalion funds on the messing account; unfortunately, in his

Army Form E.518

RESERVE AND AUXILIARY FORCES ACT, 1939.
TERRITORIAL ARMY.

CALLING OUT NOTICE.

To—

Name ...... *Walker J. C.*

Rank...... *Trooper* ...... Army Number *421168*

48th Bn. Royal Tank Regiment,

Regt. or Corps...... 63, South Side, Clapham Common......

In pursuance of directions given by the Secretary of State for War in accordance with an Order in Council made under Section 1 of the above-mentioned Act, you are hereby notified that you are called out for military service commencing from

forthwith 19 , and for this purpose you are required to join the

......

at...... **48th Bn. Royal Tank Regiment,** ......on that day.
63, South Side, Clapham Common

Should you not present yourself on that day you will be liable to be proceeded against.

Capt. and Adjutant,
48th Bn. R. T. Regt.

Stamp of Officer Commanding Unit.

Place......

Date ...... *Sept 1st 1939*

You should bring your Health and Pensions Insurance Card and Unemployment Insurance Book. If, however, you cannot obtain these before joining you should write to your employer asking him to forward these to you at your unit headquarters. If you are in possession of a receipt (U.I. 40) from the Employment Exchange for your Employment Book bring that receipt with you.

You will also bring your Army Book 3, but you *must not fill* in any particulars on page 13 or the "Statement of family" in that book, and the postcards therein *must not be used.*

[5/39] (393/2397) Wt. 21114 750M 7/39 H & S Ltd. Gp. 393 (2242) Form E518/1

Plate 15 Territorial Army call-up notice, 1939 (John Walker)

Plate 16   Lts Bill Webb (left) and Charles Crowther outside the Officers' Mess, the club-house of the Purley Downs Golf Club, Sanderstead (John Mennell)

absence on a course, his successor managed not only to dissipate this but also to build up a large debit balance which took the incumbent, on his return, several months of virtually starvation rations for the battalion to work off. A Court of Inquiry was held in May to investigate the loss on the messing account. Eventually the battalion established its own cookhouse, which did not please most of the troops as the caterers' food had been so much more varied and palatable.

The battalion's experiences at Sanderstead gave a somewhat distorted view, to say the least, of Army life in wartime: civilian billets, good and plentiful food, the proximity of well-stocked shops, good cinemas and live theatres, pleasant pubs (such as the White Lion at Warlingham, the Red Deer at Purley Oaks, the Railway at Purley, the Purley Arms at Sanderstead with its plentiful shove-ha'penny boards, the Red Lion at the bottom of Sanderstead Hill and the Greyhound, Green Dragon and Swan & Sugarloaf in Croydon), together with its nearness to home and the good bus, tram and train connections combined to make life reasonably comfortable. Roger Blankley recalls one memorable episode when the WOs' and Sergeants' Mess decided to visit, en masse, the Croydon Empire, a theatre where a strip show was being staged. The girls would strip down to one minimal item, but, as they finally removed this, the stage lights would go out. Not ones easily to be defeated by petty restrictions on their freedom to contemplate the unclothed female form, the WOs and sergeants had gone prepared, equipped with powerful torches and spotlights with which, when the stage lights were extinguished, they flooded the stage and the exposed female flesh

Plate 17 The diabolo formation sign of 21 Army Tank Brigade, 1940 to 1944 (Author's collection)

with light. They were asked to leave, but they were satisfied that they had achieved their objective. Blankley mentions in passing that the CSM of A Company was George Charlton, but whether or not this has any relevance to the Croydon Empire escapade is not clear. The other CSMs at this time were: C Company Freddie Warwick (the Army lightweight boxing champion), Don Simpson (B) and A/CSM Wally Creagh (HQ); Paddy Ryan took over from Creagh later, not for any shortcomings on the latter's part but because the battalion had an excess of warrant officers on its strength at the time.

While stationed at Sanderstead the troops were in receipt of a weekly allowance of 5s per man for providing their own messing and personal kit, plus 7s 6d for providing their own overcoats. With a high proportion of professional and business men in the battalion, private transport outnumbered military vehicles, and the joke about troops being asked to move their vehicles so that the company commander could park his bike was not far from the truth. Prominent among them was Cpl 'Gunner' Green in his Bentley; he was fairly well breeched and a (probably apocryphal) story about him tells how, when up before the CO for having damaged a 15cwt truck and being told that such vehicles were expensive, he is alleged to have pulled out his cheque book, asked the vehicle price and offered to write a cheque for two of them for the battalion. The CO's reaction is not recorded!

According to John Hancock:

The Orderly Room consisted of myself as ORS, Cpl Tobias, whose main function was the production of Part Two orders and who had an amazing memory and who could (and did) quote the Army Number of every member of the Battalion on sight, George Adamson, 'Piggy' Piggot and Tpr Hopkinson. George Adamson lived with his parents at the top of Sanderstead Hill and had worked with me pre-war. We were in urgent need of a good shorthand-typist, so when he asked me if there was any chance of joining the Battalion I took him immediately to 'Tug' Wilson. 'Tug' acted at once; rules or no rules, we had George in uniform working in the Orderly Room and he was to remain with the Battalion to the end. Another member of the Orderly Room came later; Len Swain, Orderly Room runner. Len had been licensee of the Cock at Ide Hill, near Sevenoaks. When the Officers' Mess became disenchanted with their Mess caterer, Sgt Law, I recommended Len to 'Tug' Wilson and the rest is history; Tpr Swain, runner, became Sgt Swain, Mess Caterer, which he was to remain until invalided home from North Africa.

The good people of Sanderstead were, on the whole, remarkably tolerant, and rallied round to help. Many good and lasting friendships were made, although incidents such as the following, recounted by Gerry Letchford of Poole, must have sorely tried their patience at times:

. . . our guard room was the kitchen of a house called 'Woodlands' on Sanderstead Hill. One night in the winter of 1939/40 we had set the sentries, but somebody unknown had left a tin of pilchards on the stove, one of the old type of black-leaded kitchen stoves; blankets were unrolled and all bedded down for a couple of hours before the guard change came round, forgetting about the pilchards. The tin exploded at about 2.00 am, the guard turned out and everybody thought the Germans had come until we looked round the guardroom, pilchards scattered in every direction. We were employed most of the next day getting it off the walls and ceiling and generally cleaning the place up for the next guard that evening.

Cyril Edwards goes on to describe his billet:

My billet was No 1 Edgar Road, where a kindly couple, Mr and Mrs Blow, took in five of us and treated us as their own family. Mrs Blow would not allow any of us with a cold to leave the house for morning parade, and sent Orderly Corporals and Sergeants looking for absentees very quickly away with a flea in their ear. Sunday lunch was very good too, so there was very little commuting home at weekends; in fact, my parents used to come and visit and were made equally welcome. All in all (it was) a very gentle introduction to soldiering.

Not all the locals took kindly to having armed soldiers in their midst, however; a local cleric with pacifist views preached weekly against both the war and the presence of the 48th in Sanderstead.

Shortages of equipment and instructors, however, continued to make meaningful training difficult; much of the time was spent on individual training, while many personnel were sent away to attend appropriate training courses, particularly on wireless, driving and maintenance and gunnery at the AFV Schools at Bovington and Lulworth. At the AFV Schools, the transition from peace to war had been swiftly effected and the output of instructors to the 48th and to other TA battalions soon began to reach a steady flow.

On 9 September 1939, the battalion received its first light tank, No MT9675, from the

42nd Battalion RTR; a 2pdr anti-tank gun, two Medium tanks and two Dragons followed on the 11th and two Mk I Vickers Utility Tractors on the 15th.

At this point, it might be helpful to the uninitiated to give some description of these tracked vehicles and others, all of pre-war design and of various degrees of obsolescence:

Light Tank

Various marks of this pre-war tank came at various times into the possession of the 48th and of most other RAC regiments and battalions. Weighing between 3.5 and 5 tonnes, according to mark, the light tank was designed by Vickers and first produced in 1929. Early marks were armed with a single Vickers machine gun, later ones with coaxial 0.5in and 0.303in machine guns, in a turret with 360 degrees of traverse. Crew was two or three men, depending upon the armament. Armour protection was minimal, ranging from 14mm down to 4mm in thickness. Maximum speed was about 30mph. Its main faults were the tendency to 'reverse steer' when the vehicle was over-running the engine, and the fragility of the tracks. Typical vehicles in the light tank series are shown in **Plates 5 and 14**.

Medium Tank

Two main marks of this tank were produced: the Mark I and the Mark II, each with several sub-divisions according to the modification state of the vehicle concerned. Again mostly designed and produced by Vickers after the First World War, these vehicles ranged in weight from 12 to 16 tonnes and carried a crew of five men. The first production vehicle made its appearance in 1924. These tanks were armed with one 3pdr gun and a coaxial 0.303in Vickers machine gun in a turret with all-round traverse, as well as two or three Vickers machine guns in the hull. The Medium tank had a maximum speed of about 15mph and its armour thickness was about 8mm. Typical versions are illustrated in **Plates 4 and 18**.

Dragon

The original Dragon was a tracked artillery load carrier and prime mover, consisting basically of a turretless, open-topped Medium tank. Dragons were useful for the training of tank drivers when too few tanks were available. A photograph appears at **Plate 13**. Later, lighter types based roughly on the light tank chassis were known, unsurprisingly, as Light Dragons; they were the forerunners of the range of light infantry/weapons carriers known by the generic term 'Bren Gun Carrier' and employed in large numbers throughout the Army in the Second World War.

On 29 September, twelve private cars arrived; these were intended for driving instruction, but it was decided instead to disguise them as tanks to give training some semblance of reality. Luckily, five Commer commercial trucks were issued shortly afterwards which were more easily converted; the private cars then reverted to their intended function. These acquisitions considerably lightened the load of the Transport Sergeant, Sgt Bill Cheesewright. In addition to these vehicles, the battalion now also had some Bren carriers and a miscellaneous collection of requisitioned vehicles. Petrol rationing for civilians was introduced on 23 September, but this did not greatly affect the owners of the private cars which so outnumbered the War Department vehicles in the battalion. In October, two Medium tanks Mk II*, Nos T121 (built by Vickers under a contract dated September 1924) and T146 (built by the Royal Ordnance Factory at Woolwich under a contract dated July 1925), were received from the 5th Battalion RTR; one of these, however, was badly damaged by fire on 9 November.

At this time, HQ 21st Army Tank Brigade, now commanded by Brig G.P.L. Drake-Brockman, recently CO of the newly-reborn 8th Battalion RTR, was stationed at nearby Warlingham. Brig Kenchington had departed for the War Office, where he was now the Deputy Director of Staff Duties (Armoured Fighting Vehicles) DDSD(AFV). The 42nd Battalion RTR was also stationed at Warlingham, to which village the officers of the 48th went fortnightly to be lectured on the tactical doctrine of the Army tank brigade as expounded by the brigade commander (and his Alsatian dog!). Without much equipment, however, and with little immediate prospect of getting any more, it all seemed a bit remote.

Officers continued to be posted in to the battalion in a steady trickle; 2Lt B. (Barry) Archer arrived from the 57th Training Regiment RAC at Warminster on 6 November, 2Lt V.R.B. ('Chips') Smallwood from the Inns of Court OCTU on the 29th, Maj L.P. ('Pip') Crouch, MC, a Regular RTC officer who had earned his MC on the North-West Frontier of India and who had been Army lightweight boxing champion in 1921 and middleweight champion in 1922, from the 55th Training Regiment RAC on 10 December and, on the 28th in exchange for Capt Foley and one other rank, Capt J.D. ('Stylo') Styles from the 4th Battalion RTR, part of the British Expeditionary Force (BEF) in France. Maj J.O. ('Joe') Clark was appointed second-in-command of the battalion at this time.

Armistice Day on 11 November was made memorable by the performance of the battalion trumpeters; these were the pride of RSM W.J. (Bill) Lockwood, a cavalryman from the 14/20th Hussars, who lavished much of his time on them. Their croaking practice calls could be heard almost all day coming from Purley Beeches, the local park which was now the battalion parade ground. Their end was sad, however; one day, the battalion was due to be visited by the brigade commander and a trumpeter was to play the General Salute. The best

Plate 18   The battalion's Mediums on the tank park at Purley Beeches (Pat Russell)

player was selected, but on the day he proved unequal to the occasion and only a broken croak emerged; the trumpeters were disbanded. RSM Lockwood was posted to France in February 1940 and was involved in guiding survivors to the exits and the boats in the ill-fated RMS *Lancastria*, which was sunk during the evacuation of the BEF; he had saved the lives of several men by his bravery. His successor was WO1 (RSM) Freddie ('Pinocchio') Payne.

The first Cambrai Day was marked by a full battalion parade in Purley Beeches; in the absence of the CO on a course, the battalion was addressed by the second-in-command. After a march past the remainder of the day was a holiday. An eventful year was drawing to a close, but no mention of Christmas would be complete without some reference to the battalion pantomime 'Babes in the Wood'; the book, music and production were entirely the work of the battalion, although some of the fair sex of Sanderstead lent their assistance. The efforts of the Demon King and his gallant band of assistants were, to say the least, outstanding! **Plate 19** shows a reproduction of the programme. It was a characteristic of the TA battalions that, no matter what was required, an expert in it could be found from within the battalion's ranks; the 48th was no exception, with stockbrokers, bankers, lawyers, signwriters, poets, musicians, composers, playwrights, journalists, sportsmen, photographers, artists and most other trades and professions represented among its members.

The battalion received its first Matilda tank (Infantry Tank Mk II) on 22 December; Tpr W.M.S. (Mike) Jeffrey, later Colonel and Regimental Colonel of the RTR, was the lucky man chosen as its driver.

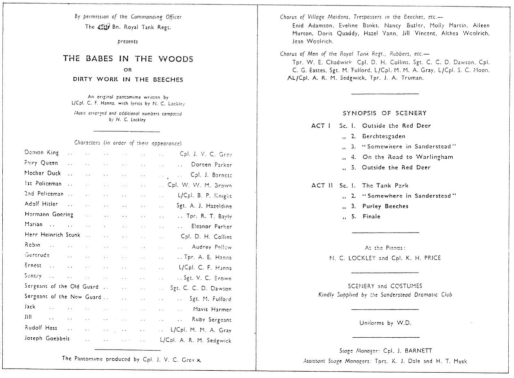

Plate 19   The programme for the battalion's 1939 Christmas pantomime 'Babes in the Wood' (48 RTR Assn)

The Army had stated a requirement for infantry tanks in 1934 and, as they were in the medium weight class, this necessitated the renaming of the existing Medium tanks as cruiser tanks; the three British tank categories, therefore, were now light tanks, cruiser tanks and infantry (or 'I') tanks. The Infantry Tank Mk II (Matilda) was the latest thing in 'I' tanks at this time and, apart from its inadequate 2pdr gun main armament, was ahead of anything the Germans could field as far as armour protection was concerned. Designed by the Mechanisation Board and built by Vulcan Foundry in 1939, it was produced in considerable numbers in the early days of the war; although popular, however, it could not be produced quickly, as its cast armour and complicated hydraulics did not lend themselves readily to mass production. It was powered by two petrol or diesel engines of standard commercial type, each with an output of 174bhp (AEC diesels) or 190bhp (Leyland petrol); these drove the tracks via a Wilson pre-selective gearbox, gear-changing being assisted by air servo. The Matilda weighed 26.5 tonnes and had a maximum speed of only 15mph with a road range of only 60 miles. It was armed with a 2pdr gun and coaxial 7.92mm Besa machine gun in a turret with all-round hydraulic power traverse, and carried a crew of four. It is illustrated in **Plate 20**.

The battalion reassembled in the New Year to find two new acquisitions: snow and the Autodrome. The first was cleared as a matter of course but the second was more durable and more important. The population of Croydon was more fortunate in many respects than many, but particularly so in having within the town's boundaries a completely self-contained driving training ground called the Autodrome. Owned and designed by the local Ford dealer, Hubert Dees Ltd, it contained several miles of concrete roads, complete with hills, hairpin bends, roundabouts, traffic signs and Belisha crossings, on which the training of learner drivers could be safely carried

Plate 20   The Infantry Tank Mk II (Matilda) (Author's collection)

out without danger or inconvenience to other road-users and the residents of Sanderstead. This was requisitioned by the War Department and taken over by the battalion on Boxing Day; apart from being used to house the vehicle park and the technical stores, it also provided properly equipped classrooms for instruction in driving and maintenance. The tech stores were under the control of the QMS(T), WO2 Bill Paice, and his number two, Sgt Barton. D & M and Driver Mechanic classes were organised and practical maintenance under the experienced eye of Capt Styles became a reality as opposed to mere words on the training programme.

So started the New Year; on 1 January, Lt E. (Eric) Jupp arrived from 1st Heavy Armoured Brigade and on the 2nd the battalion was inspected by the commander of 21st Army Tank Brigade, Brig Drake-Brockman. On the 8th the battalion received three cavalry carriers to add to its tracked vehicle strength, and on the same day food rationing was introduced for the civilian population; at first, only bacon, ham, sugar and butter were rationed. 2Lt John Mennell was promoted to acting captain as Battalion LO and OC of HQ Company; his 2IC was Capt 'Ollie' Collins, and others promoted included Lt G.G. ('Ding-Dong') Bell. January and February of 1940 came and went, as did an outbreak of measles; training dragged on and, on 19 March, CSM Payne was promoted to acting RSM on the posting to France of RSM Lockwood. But, if the truth be known, the battalion was by now becoming a little stale and soft. It had been too near London for too long, the war was in the 'phoney war' stage and nothing much seemed to be happening; the troops needed a shock, or some real soldiering, to remind them that they were really in the Army and that there was a war on.

It did not have long to wait. Early in April, the unit was shaken to hear that Norway had been invaded by Germany; here at last, it seemed, was a chance to do something. Maj Crouch, only recently promoted to second-in-command, left to take part in the action but soon returned full of stories of 'bombs as big as grand pianos', as well as of the accuracy of the anti-aircraft fire (mostly Bren light machine gun) which, 'if it had reached 20,000 feet higher would have brought the lot down'. To those who had not yet realised just how painfully short of equipment the British Army was, it was a sober awakening.

However, life for the battalion at Sanderstead proceeded pleasantly on its way, although billets were now more difficult to find as the natives were becoming just a shade less friendly – with some justification if the episode of the tin of pilchards was anything to go by! – and slight discomfort resulted from the TAB and Tet Tox inoculations which the battalion had to undergo on 28 April. The Adjutant, still Capt Wilson, went to France on an attachment to the 13/18th Hussars, little thinking how it would end; 2Lt C.A. ('Bill') Joss replaced him temporarily as Adjutant on 15 April. On the 22nd, Lt Heavey was replaced by Capt Bell as Battalion Technical Adjutant (BTA), and on the 26th the battalion celebrated its first birthday.

On 10 May, the battalion arrived at breakfast to learn that the war had now really started; Germany was overrunning Holland and Belgium and the BEF was on the move. Even in Sanderstead the war started to intrude, although only slightly at this stage, when a message was received from HQ London District cancelling all leave for operationally vital personnel. It was soon followed by another, placing the whole battalion at eight hours' notice; for what, they wondered? At that time they had not heard the stories of clouds of parachutists descending on Dutch airfields and the forts, such as Fort Eben Emael, on the River Meuse. A steady stream of further orders from HQ London District told the battalion, among other things, to immobilise all transport when not in use, to treat all parachutists as enemy, to place itself on a war footing and to carry respirators at all times.

Two days later, on the 12th, the CO issued orders that one company would be at 10 minutes' notice to move each night and would stand-to for one hour before last and first light. In addition, all officers were to be armed with a revolver and ammunition and carry a rifle and ammunition when on duty in a vehicle. The vehicles ready for action were one Light Mk IV, one Medium Mk II and one Matilda Mk II! This mobile column, with its tactical transport, was maintained at the Autodrome; its rôle was airfield protection at nearby Croydon, Kenley and Biggin Hill airfields. A few days later, on 14 May, this striking force was strengthened by the arrival of two Light Mk VICs from the factory and two Bren gun carriers from the 8th Battalion RTR; the following week it was further reinforced by the arrival of a brand-new 'I' tank Mk IIA Matilda and, on 17 May, by a section of three 'I' tanks from the 8th Battalion RTR, commanded by a 2Lt Attwood. The daily routine for the Duty Squadron at the Autodrome was:

Parade at 7.00pm
Stow tanks with ammunition
Meal
Check guns and wireless net
Stand-to at 9.00pm (including much crew drill under Capt Styles)
Man the tanks round the Autodrome
Stand-to at 05.00am
Unload vehicles
Fall out

The battalion's rôle was subsequently reduced to the protection of Kenley and Biggin Hill only. Both were reconnoitred by the CO accompanied by the LO, Capt Mennell; on one social visit to Kenley they encountered Winston Churchill who, in addition to being Prime Minister, was Hon Air Commodore No 615 Squadron, RAuxAF, the fighter squadron then stationed there. A practice turn-out to Kenley aerodrome took place on 23 May, and a wireless link to Biggin Hill aerodrome was established.

A few days later the Adjutant, Capt Wilson, returned from France, where his BEF attachment had come to a sudden end. He had an exciting, if sobering, tale to tell; apparently the situation was very much grimmer than the somewhat rosy picture painted in the British press and on the radio. The British Isles faced a very real threat of invasion; the Local Defence Volunteers (LDV), renamed Home Guard in July, was formed, and the 48th supplied the local units with instructors. On 26 May convincing reports of enemy parachutists landing at Hawkinge aerodrome in Kent came in from RAF Kenley between 01.15am and 03.30am; luckily these were later proved to have been false but, in the excitement, the Adjutant pulled the trigger of a rifle in the Orderly Room, narrowly missing the Assistant Adjutant, Bill Joss. The battalion stood-to in the Autodrome, but it all fizzled out eventually.

During the evening of 1 June, telephoned orders were received from HQ London District for the battalion to move to the Essex coast in an anti-invasion rôle. Early the next morning the Advance Party, under the command of Maj A.B. Woodgate, DSO, MC, the Quartermaster, was on its way. The following day the CO, accompanied by the LO (Capt Mennell), and the squadron ('companies' were now renamed 'squadrons') commanders (Maj J.O. Clark, A Squadron, Maj J.D. Styles, B Squadron and Maj J. Eden George, C Squadron) left for Colchester to carry out his reconnaissance. He learned that his task would be to relieve both the 16/5th Lancers and the 17/21st Lancers in support of 45th Infantry Brigade; these regiments were holding a stretch of the Essex coast from Weeley in the south to Harwich in the north. Battalion HQ and the administrative elements were to be located in Sobraon Barracks, Colchester, to be taken over from 17/21st Lancers; the squadrons would be mainly dismounted, guarding road blocks. On 19 June, the government issued a leaflet, prepared by the Ministry of Information, setting out rules for the guidance of the civilian population in the event of invasion; obviously, the threat was being taken very seriously.

The battalion main body moved by road on 3 June. To the wondering eyes of the many Sanderstead inhabitants who turned out to wave it goodbye, there appeared a convoy the like of which can seldom have been seen in British military history. The few War Department vehicles the battalion possessed were hopelessly outnumbered by the multitude of civilian vehicles and private cars of all ages, shapes and sizes, which stretched as far as the eye could see; it was an unforgettable sight. Slowly but surely this convoy wound its way through London and the Blackwall Tunnel to Colchester, where it arrived safely by the evening. The 'A' vehicles left by train at 2.00pm the following day from Purley station, arriving at 10.00pm. On this day, evacuation of the remainder of the BEF from the beaches of Dunkirk was completed; unfortunately, almost all its heavy equipment, including precious Matilda tanks, was left behind. This boded ill for the chances of the 48th being re-equipped with modern tanks and vehicles in the near future!

The Battalion Rear Party left Sanderstead a week later, on 11 June, thus finally ending a happy, if militarily unsatisfactory, nine months, during which both the war itself and a sufficiency of warlike equipment with which to fight it had successfully eluded the battalion.

CHAPTER 2

Colchester and Salisbury Plain
(1940)

In Colchester, the battalion experienced its first taste of barrack life. It took over Sobraon Barracks from the 17th/21st Lancers on 5 June; the Lancers had only recently returned from India and were looking very smart in their boots and breeches. The take-over of vehicles from both 16th/5th Lancers and the 17th/21st was carried out on the following day; of the 12 Light Mk IIs received from the 17th/21st, only four were in fighting order. On the same day, 6 June, the battalion was visited by the commander, brigade major and staff captain of 21st Army Tank Brigade, and on the 9th seven Vickers Medium tanks taken over from the 16th/5th were sent to the 54th Training Regiment RAC at Perham Down.

The battalion mobilisation force now consisted of:

> Two Matilda Mk IIs
> Eleven Medium tanks
> Seven Light tanks (two Mk VICs and five Mks IIA and IIB)

The battalion was now deployed into its first operational positions: A Squadron was on the right, with 2Lt Harland holding the right flank; B Squadron on the left, with two troops and Squadron HQ comfortably installed in a pub; and C Squadron in mobile (sic) reserve in the rear. Battalion headquarters was also comfortably, if not gallantly, ensconced in Colchester. The battalion was operationally under command of 45th Infantry Brigade, part of 15th (Scottish) Division.

On 10 June, the surrender of 51st (Highland) Division took place at St Valéry; the final surrender of the French Army was not far off, and the German Army was now on the Channel and North Sea coasts of the mainland of Europe, opposite the battalion's positions in the mud flats of Essex. The Dunkirk evacuation was repeated, with larger vessels, on 17/18 June at Brest, Cherbourg, St Malo and St Nazaire, when a further 136,000 British and Canadian and 20,000 Polish troops were brought safely back to Britain. British military involvement on the Continent had thus ended for the time being, leaving it free for the Germans to consolidate and prepare for Operation Seelöwe (Sealion), the invasion of Britain.

After the long spell of billet life in Sanderstead, the battalion enjoyed the change to a more operational rôle, with its guard duties and 'stand-tos' at first and last light; it was therefore to everyone's regret when the battalion was withdrawn, after only five days' 'active service', into mobile reserve in Colchester. Obviously, however, a tank battalion could not be left for long to carry out the rôle for which the LDV had been created and the 45th Infantry Brigade was more suited. To increase the battalion's mobility, it had been allocated ten 30-seater buses to carry the dismounted personnel; these had previously been owned by Messrs Tympson, so they inevitably became known as 'Tympson's Horse'. About 250 mounted 'infantry' were raised and placed under the command of the 2IC, Maj 'Pip' Crouch; the practices that were held, if not of much military value, were at least highly amusing. On 10 June the battalion had its first 'flap', which resulted in C Squadron being moved at short

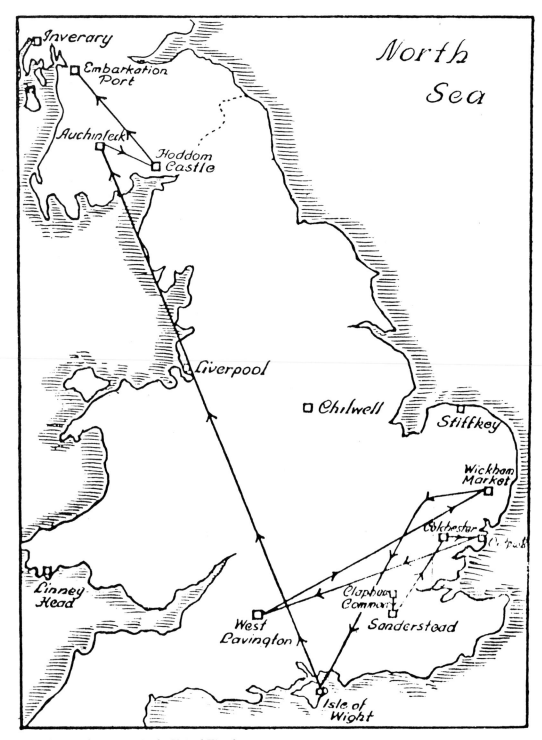

Map 1   Battalion moves in the United Kingdom

Plate 21   A Medium Mk I of C Squadron on the tank park at Colchester (Roger Blankley)

notice during the night to HQ 45th Infantry Brigade at Wivenhoe Park; when morning came all was normal again, and the squadron returned with nothing worse in the way of casualties than a deficiency of two wireless watches. However, Winston Churchill had drawn the attention of the Secretary of State for War to the misemployment of soldiers on static defence works in a minute dated 25 June, and the battalion's change of rôle could well have resulted from this: he was particularly sensitive to the training, equipment and employment of tank units.

The Germans were now beginning in earnest the air reconnaissance of the east coast, and occasionally bombs fell. Nearly every night the air raid warning sounded and all troops were made to stand-to. Vehicles were dispersed outside the town, and so much sleep was lost, and the daily routine so interfered with as a result, that the personnel of the battalion were ordered to take three hours' compulsory sleep during daylight hours every day.

In its new rôle it was possible for the battalion to relax a little, as well as to carry out some tank training. A suitable area for tank driving was found, and some of the light tanks were diverted from their operational rôle for this purpose. The Matildas were also declared non-operational so that a training course on this tank could be run. Tactical exercises without troops (TEWTs) were run by everybody and in fact the battalion was almost back to normal; however, in addition to usual guard duties extra guards had to be mounted on Martlesham Heath airfield.

The War Diary tells us that the new identity cards for officers (AF B2606) were received on 19 June, and were issued as fast as the officers could be photographed. Of these photographs, those that survive are reproduced in **Plates 39 to 42**. On the 22nd, twelve unarmoured Light Dragons were received, useless for operations but useful for driver training. SSM 'Buck' Ryan arrived in B Squadron, where he was to stay until posted to C Squadron three years later, and SSM Don Simpson moved to HQ Squadron. Lt Caldwell was in charge of the despatch riders (also known for short as DRs or, from the phonetic alphabet then in use in the Army, Don Rs), that intrepid bunch of motorcycle messengers who could put to shame the modern moto-cross rider or city messenger-boy. Fortunately he preserved them for posterity in the photograph at **Plate 22**, taken at Higham, Essex, in June 1940. At that time, the DRs doubled as regimental policemen (RPs), with the job of ensuring that the battalion's vehicles were given right of way over civilian traffic on the roads; in this rôle, they wore red and black armbands bearing the letters 'RP' and white plastic slip-on sleeves, while as DRs the distinctive dress consisted of the goggles and gauntlets seen in the photograph.

Colchester could now be investigated in earnest and was found to be very good value, catering for every taste; the battalion settled down to enjoy its first operational station and, to the accompaniment of air raid warnings red, yellow and white, the month of June passed. On the 28th there was a call for volunteers for the Parachute Regiment, which had just been formed: a number of men volunteered.

The roll of battalion officers on 30 June was as follows:

Battalion HQ

CO Lt Col Wykes	IO 2Lt Collins
2IC Maj Crouch	BTA Capt Bell
Adjt Capt Wilson	QM Lt Warwick
Asst/Adjt Lt Joss	MO Lt O'Flynn RAMC
LO and OC HQ Sqn Capt Mennell	Chaplain Capt Shorten RAChD

A Squadron		B Squadron	C Squadron
OC	Maj Clark	Maj Styles	Maj Eden George
2IC	Capt West	Capt Crowther	Capt Edwards
	Lt Heavey	Capt Watney	2Lt Ladd
	2Lt Barnett	2Lt Simmonds	2Lt Smith
	Lt Jupp	2Lt Smallwood	2Lt Cardwell
	Lt Radcliffe	2Lt Loader	2Lt Harland
	Lt Newcombe	2Lt Ericson	2Lt Spencer-Smith
		Lt Rawlins	
		2Lt Archer	
		2Lt Hughes	
		2Lt Leggett	

The battalion was not, however, to be allowed to enjoy its pleasant surroundings for much longer; on 9 July, a warning order was received from HQ 21st Army Tank Brigade for the unit to prepare to move to a brigade concentration area on Salisbury Plain. Before leaving the fleshpots of Colchester, however, the battalion had one last fling; also on 9 July, orders were received to move at once to Martlesham Heath airfield in an anti-parachutist rôle. The 48th moved very quickly, and by nightfall the complete unit was in position, but again nothing came of the 'flap'.

On 12/13 July the battalion moved to the area of West Lavington in Wiltshire, the tracked vehicles entraining at Ipswich on the 12th and the main body on the 13th. For the first time

Plate 22   The DR Troop at Higham, Essex, in June 1940, photographed by the troop commander, Lt Caldwell. Left to right: Tprs Pollard, Thorne, Tothill, Baker, Sumner, Flynn, R. Norman, Kerwood, Alan Gilmour, Ned Cook, L. Norman and LCpl Wilson (Ned Cook)

since its annual camp the previous August the unit found itself again under canvas, and, for the first time since 21st Army Tank Brigade had been formed, the whole brigade was concentrated. The 48th found itself alongside the other two 'I' tank battalions in the brigade, its progenitor, the 42nd Battalion RTR (now commanded by Lt Col A.C. ('Ant') Willison, DSO, MC), and also the 44th Battalion RTR from Bristol, under its commanding officer, Lt Col H.C.J. Yeo, DSO. As the junior battalion in the brigade, the 48th had the unit code number '175'. The members of the 48th much regretted the loss both of independence and of the more glamorous operational rôle on the east coast, although the concentration of the brigade tank battalions was undoubtedly wise. It was now going to be possible to get down to some serious training. While on the subject of training, Capt Mennell returned from an Intelligence course at Swanage on 14 July and, on the 25th, 2Lt M.P. (Maurice) Ladd departed on a course at the London, Midland and Scottish Railway tank factory at Horwich.

As it grew light on the battalion's first morning under canvas, all ranks peered eagerly out of their tent flaps to see in what sort of a place they had landed; Salisbury Plain proved much as expected, with low, dreary ridges covered in heather, broken here and there by scattered clumps of trees, stretching as far as the eye could see, and no sign of human habitation. Colchester, with its superfluity of pubs and cinemas, seemed even more desirable. Neither was the keen breeze, which whipped across the plain even in July, a very cheering portent for the autumn and winter months to come. The prospect appeared rosier, however, once the creature comforts of Warminster and Devizes had been discovered. The battalion was located near to the then busy little village of Imber; Roger Blankley recalls:

It was there that we used to drink the local pub dry in about two days flat. One evening, despite the fact that I was supposed to be on wireless watch, I went along with others to Imber; beer ran out early, but a local farm foreman invited several of us to visit his home and sample his collection of home-made wines. This we did only too well, and none of us awoke until dawn. Finally returning to camp, we found that it had been the night of the great invasion scare.

With the threat of invasion growing steadily, the brigade's first priority was to organise itself on an operational footing. Bearing in mind that the tank battalions were all below strength in tanks at this time (the 48th, for example, had only two proper tanks, both Matildas, on strength), the brigade commander decided to pool the brigade's resources to form two composite battalions. These were known as the 99th Battalion RTR and the 100th Battalion RTR, neither of which is mentioned in Liddell Hart's history *The Tanks*. In this connection, it is interesting to mention that several other RTR battalions were officially formed in the Second World War but were 'notional', in that they were the titles of dummy units used, in the Middle East and Italy, to deceive German Intelligence; these also are omitted from the Liddell Hart history of the RTR, and include the 38th, 39th, 60th, 62nd, 65th, 101st, 102nd and 124th Battalions RTR. All these units published Part I, II and III Orders, and compiled war diaries which are still in existence; their equipment consisted, however, only of dummy tanks, and their personnel were mainly Royal Engineers, generally of only company strength.

However, we digress. Initially the 48th supplied No 3 Squadron of the 99th Battalion RTR, under the command of Maj Styles; later, as more equipment arrived, it supplied the headquarters and squadrons of 100th Battalion RTR. With this reorganisation, realistic collective training at troop, squadron and battalion level was at last possible.

Slit trenches were dug by all ranks of the battalion soon after their arrival, and then filled in again as, in traditional Army fashion, the battalion's site within the brigade area was changed. By 21 July, however, the new site was occupied and the interior economy complete; to mark the occasion, a brigade church parade was held, at which Brig Drake-Brockman took the salute. This was the only occasion in the brigade's history on which all the battalions of the brigade paraded together. It was also, as it turned out, the last occasion on which Brig Drake-Brockman was to take a parade as the commander of 21st Army Tank Brigade.

On 31 July, the battalion was visited by Maj Gen George Lindsay, then the Representative Colonel Commandant of the Royal Tank Regiment. On 3 August, an even more earth-shaking event in the history of the battalion occurred – the arrival of its first Infantry Tank Mk III, the Valentine. Lt Col Wykes and the BTA, Capt Bell, hurried to the station to inspect it, and the CO himself drove it on its maiden journey from the station to the tank park; it was soon an object of wonder, and visitors, including Brig Drake-Brockman on 4 August, arrived from near and far to gaze upon it. It was the first arrival of many; two more arrived on the 6th, 16 from the 7th Battalion RTR at Gleneagles on the 14th and two on 19 August. On the same day, three light tanks were handed over to the 43rd Battalion RTR. A limited amount of leave was authorised on 4 August, the first since 10 May.

The Tank, Infantry, Mk III (Valentine) was a 17-tonne tank designed by Vickers Armstrong Ltd in 1939 and put into production in 1940. According to one school of thought, it derived its name from the talented Vickers tank designer whose Christian name it was. Another school attributes it to the fact that the tank was accepted by the War Office on or about St Valentine's Day. Yet another states that 'Valentine' was an acronym of the initial letters of Vickers Armstrong Limited, Elswick, Newcastle-upon-Tyne. Which is correct is anybody's guess at 60 years' remove; the least likely is surely the 'Valentine's Day' theory, while the acronym is probably too clever. The most probably true is the version that has the tank named after its chief designer, who died tragically before the tank was put into production. In production, it eventually ran to 11 marks before being replaced, of which all except the Valentine I (which had an AEC petrol engine) were powered by diesel engines. Main armament of the Valentine Mks I to VII was a 2pdr gun, of the Valentine Mks VIII, IX and X a 6pdr gun and of the Valentine Mk XI, a 75mm gun. The Valentine had a crew of three men, except for Mks III and V, which had a three-man turret and a total crew of four; its maximum speed was 15mph and its armour thickness 65mm maximum. The 48th was equipped initially with the Valentine I (see **Plates 23 and 25**) in August 1940, the Valentine II in April 1941 and the Valentine V (**Plate 48**) in November 1942.

In the officers versus sergeants football match, held on 11 August, the ORS, Sgt Hancock, broke his leg in his enthusiasm to guide the sergeants to victory. On the 17th the brigade commander carried out his annual inspection of the battalion's vehicles; this went well, and the BTA, Capt Bell, who had personally contributed very little towards this result, got a pat on the back from the brigadier. The Home Forces Commander-in-Chief, Lt Gen Sir Alan F. Brooke, visited the battalion on 24 August and lunched in the Officers' Mess; the lesser fry were excluded from the Mess for lunch but not from the ante-room tent, in which Sir Alan's red hat was lying. Capt Mennell saw it and thought to try it on, but unfortunately the great man chose that moment to return to the ante-room for his handkerchief. History does not relate what, if any, penalty Capt Mennell had to suffer for this piece of lèse-majesté.

Plate 23   Lt G.G. Bell commanding a C Squadron Valentine on exercise in south-east England (Pat Russell)

Possibly the Valentines, or their crews, brought with them the scarlet fever which now spread like wildfire through the whole battalion, isolating it from the rest of the brigade and, worse still, stopping the pitifully small flow of men going on leave. Now that it had its own tanks, however, the battalion had in any case ceased to be involved in the 99th and 100th Battalions RTR, and gladly handed over to the 42nd Battalion RTR the two Matildas. Another plague, this time of earwigs, struck the battalion in its tents as the beautiful summer weather continued. Air activity had increased by this time, and there was a constant drone of RAF fighters in the skies above the battalion lines. About this time the battalion had its first taste of action when the air raid alarm was sounded one morning; everybody took to the slit trenches, complete with gas capes and respirators, standing there for about an hour. Just as time was beginning to drag, an aircraft ducked out of a low cloud, instantly identified by Lt Rawlins, the battalion aircraft recognition expert, as 'one of ours – a Blenheim'. As someone later remarked, it was then guilty of extreme carelessness as it dropped three bombs in the direction of the officers' slit trenches. Luckily, however, no damage was done, and some minutes later the camp anti-aircraft machine guns burst into life, accompanied by derisive cheers from the troops.

Training continued despite sundry alarums and excursions, and, as more tanks arrived, the battalion was able to use the Plain to more advantage. Fourteen more Valentines arrived on 14 September, bringing the unit up to its War Establishment strength in 'I' tanks for the first time since its formation. Summer was drawing to a close, however, and the nights under canvas were becoming decidedly cool. Thoughts began to turn to billets when word came that the battalion was to winter in the Warminster area; a reconnaissance was carried out on 16 September, and work was begun to make the allotted quarters habitable.

Before this, however, late on the night of 7 September, came the warning that everyone had been awaiting yet somehow nobody had expected: the code-word 'Cromwell', signifying that an enemy invasion was about to be attempted. The battalion was placed at one hour's notice to move, for what would be the first battle against foreign troops on British soil since the Battle of Fishguard in the 18th century, when a small force of French troops landed in Pembrokeshire and was rounded up by another regiment of volunteers, the Pembrokeshire Yeomanry. It would be idle to pretend that the emergency found the battalion completely ready and prepared; in fact, it would be more correct to say that it could scarcely have been more unprepared. Capts Mennell and Archer were despatched to reconnoitre a forward concentration area at Minterne Magna, near Cerne Abbas in Dorset, on a lovely day on which war could not have seemed more distant; a suitable avenue of trees was found for the battalion, which today Capt (now Colonel, retired) Mennell passes about once a fortnight. 21st Army Tank Brigade reported a mass of enemy shipping moving south of the Isle of Wight and a line of ships seven miles long moving north, 25 miles off Portsmouth. The battalion was stood-to for the next three days, but luckily nothing came of the reports and the 'flap' passed.

News of the air raids on London was having a bad effect on the morale of a London-based battalion, as there were several heart-rending tales from wives, parents and sweethearts. Enemy air activity over the plain was fairly continuous about this time, and bombs fell in the battalion area at least twice. One enemy aircraft was shot down within the area and another some distance away, but visible. It was the shooting-down of a Heinkel He111 bomber in the area which resulted, shortly afterwards, in the removal of Brig Drake-Brockman for an assault on enemy aircrew captured in the area. His farewell inspection of the battalion took place at West Lavington on 17 September, prior to the start of a Southern Command exercise on the 24th; he was replaced on the 25th by Brig R. Naesmyth, on a temporary basis, pending the outcome of a court martial over the incident. Brig Drake-Brockman was later reduced to the ranks, left the British Army and emigrated to Canada, where he joined the Canadian Army and quickly rose to the rank of major.

When the shouting and excitement of the invasion scare had died down, the battalion returned to its normal training routine and continued its preparations for the move into winter quarters. It took part in a brigade exercise against the Queen's Bays on 8 October. On 1 October, however, the move into Warminster had been postponed; as the weather was by now becoming really cold, it was not unusual to find the whole battalion in bed by dusk. On the 10th, the reason for the postponement became clear; a warning order from brigade ordered the battalion to be ready to move to Glevering Hall, a country house and estate near Wickham Market in Suffolk, under the command of 21st Army Tank Brigade but under 11th Corps, 15th (Scottish) Division and 165th Infantry Brigade for certain rôles.

On 17 October, the battalion thankfully bade farewell to Salisbury Plain, with its cold winds, earwigs and noisy night-flying Harvard trainer aircraft; in some respects it had been an uncomfortable experience, but it had seen the battalion fully equipped with up-to-date tanks and moulded into the semblance of a fighting unit. Now it was bound for its second stint in East Anglia, again in the same anti-invasion rôle in support of 15th (Scottish) Division, the beach division.

CHAPTER 3

Wickham Market and Scotland

(1940–43)

The move to Wickham Market was carried out by rail, with the tanks on war flats; many of the personnel of the battalion made the 12-hour journey, by day and night, in a train without corridors which did not stop at a station for the whole journey. They arrived, dog-tired, at 01.00am in a thick mist at Framlingham, where they were met by a posse of senior officers demanding a demonstration of the new ramp-loading wagon! This wagon enabled tanks to be loaded on to rail flats when no loading platform was available and was a very useful device; it was scarcely the time to ask for a demonstration, however, particularly as this would be the first time that the battalion would have used it.

The rest of the journey to Wickham Market was carried out as a slow six-mile road march through the sweet-smelling but misty Suffolk lanes, until the vehicles were eventually guided into their new tank park at 03.30am. Then, and only then, were the crews allowed to sink wearily to sleep. Morning brought recovery, however, and everyone was eager to see the sort of place at which they had arrived.

The battalion was camped, again under canvas, in the grounds of Glevering Hall (**Plate 24**), a medium-sized 18th century country house set in fine parkland and situated about one mile from Wickham Market, five from Framlingham and six from Woodbridge; it was to remain there for 18 months, a very long time for an operational tank unit to remain in one place in wartime and in fact the longest ever spent by the battalion in one location throughout its life. Apart from the officers, who were accommodated in the hall, it was to remain under canvas through the next three winter months, bell tents being the men's only protection against the cold east winds and the snow. Conditions were hard but, despite ice in the shaving water, cracked cylinder heads in the tanks and broken tank tracks, Christmas was made tolerable, if not comfortable, under canvas by tank cookers, candles and other illegal devices.

Over the four days after moving in, the battalion was on the receiving end of visits from the commanders of Eastern Command, 11th Corps, 15th (Scottish) Division and 165th Infantry Brigade. It transpired that the battalion was the only armoured unit in 11th Corps, and was to be in mobile reserve in support of 15th (Scottish) Division, then commanded by Maj Gen Sir Oliver Leese, Bart, in its anti-invasion rôle.

The rear party arrived from Lavington on 28 October 1940. On the 30th, three Dornier Do17s flew over at tree-top height, presumably on a recce as they did not attack, and on the 31st Brig Drake-Brockman officially relinquished command of 21st Army Tank Brigade. The assumption of command by Brig Naesmyth was confirmed on 8 November. On the 16th, 2Lt C.A. Foss was appointed Battalion Gunnery Officer and on the 17th a dogfight took place, very low and near the battalion location, in which a Hurricane from Martlesham Heath was shot down; Capt Mennell later met the pilot, apparently none the worse, in the Bull at Woodbridge. The following day there was a brigade signal exercise near Sudbury, in which Battalion HQ was lower control. On the 24th, Capt J.C. ('Olly') Collins was appointed Adjutant in place of Capt 'Tug' Wilson, who had been posted at his own request on the 19th to 101 OCTU at the Royal Military College, Sandhurst. Capt Edwards also left, and it was

Plate 24   Glevering Hall, near Wickham Market, Suffolk, during its occupation by the 48th (John Mennell)

learned subsequently that he had retired. Cambrai Day was suitably celebrated on the 20th, including an all-ranks dance in the village hall, which went well.

The battalion soon settled into its rôle, which was not too different from its previous one in East Anglia. Martlesham Heath airfield again figured largely in its plans, the battalion being responsible for counter-attacking should it fall into enemy hands. Many rehearsals and practices were held, and much liaison with the RAF took place throughout what was otherwise a long, fairly uneventful, stay at Wickham Market, the war again managing to keep out of the 48th's way. Although in theory the threat of invasion was still present, in reality the time was now past when such an operation could have succeeded; less attention was therefore paid to it than had been the case in the summer. This is not to say that the higher command was ignoring its responsibilities in this connection; on the contrary, all conceivable contingencies had been considered and prepared against, but suitable tides and weather were unlikely to be available again that year. In addition, military preparedness was now much further advanced in the United Kingdom than had been the case earlier in the year and was improving by the week.

The battalion had its excitements during its stay: the first was the annual firing at Linney Head, Castlemartin, in south Wales. A Squadron was the first to suffer the 36-hour rail journey and the mud, Atlantic gales and other discomforts of this bleak spot, from 14 to 22 December. B Squadron followed on Boxing Day, returning on New Year's Day 1941, and C Squadron's turn came on 2 January. Alan Gilmour, a tank driver of B Squadron, recalls:

> . . . the mud at Linney Head firing range, where, once a track was shed, it was difficult to locate in the morass, where the ruts worn by succeeding vehicles were so deep that tanks steered themselves.

By the time they had all returned, their hutted accommodation at Wickham Market had been completed by Pioneer Corps labour, so that the rest of the winter could be spent in somewhat greater comfort and warmth.

Brig Naesmyth, still commanding 21st Army Tank Brigade, inspected the battalion on 27 January, prior to its taking part in 11th Corps Exercise No 12 in the area of Bury St Edmunds on the 28th/29th. Army tank brigades, as the name implies, were intended to be independent formations coming directly under an army's command; as such, vehicles belonging to their subordinate units carried their unit tactical numbers on front and rear, in white numerals on a brown rectangle, with a white line at the bottom. On wheeled vehicles, they also appeared on the rear axle differential housing, where they were illuminated at night by the vehicle convoy light. The three tank battalions in 21st Army Tank Brigade carried the numbers '173' (for the most senior battalion), '174' (for the next senior) and '175' (for the junior battalion). Army tank brigades also had a formation sign in the shape of a diabolo, that of 21st Army Tank Brigade being dark blue; it was carried by all vehicles, usually on a front mudguard and on a convenient flat surface at the rear, and by all ranks on the left upper sleeve of battledress (BD) and service dress below the epaulette.

11th Corps was at this time commanded by a former RE officer, Lt Gen G. le Q. Martel, who had played such a prominent part in Tank Corps HQ as Brigade Major in the First World War, in British tank development between the wars and who, later in this same month, was appointed Commander, Royal Armoured Corps in the War Office.

Plate 25   A Valentine I of 3 Troop, A Squadron, on Exercise Talisman in 1940. Note the tactical number '175' and the diabolo brigade formation sign on the lower nose plate of the hull. The Y on the turret side denotes that this was an 'enemy' vehicle on the exercise (Author's collection)

Maj 'Pip' Crouch, the battalion second-in-command, was loaned to the Australian Government as chief instructor to its AFV school, and departed for Australia on 5 February; Maj Cameron, a Regular officer, was posted in to replace him as 2IC. On the 25th the battalion received a telegram ordering it to mobilise immediately for service overseas in a tropical climate. This was only the first of several such orders received by the battalion before it finally went overseas; an amending signal was received on 18 April changing the 'service overseas' to 'home service' and the battalion relaxed with a sigh. The original order did, however, have the effect of changing the brigade's composition, as both the 42nd and 44th Battalions RTR actually left for the Middle East theatre, as 'I' tank battalions in 1st Army Tank Brigade, landing in Egypt on 13 June 1941. They thus became the first two Territorial units of the RTR to take the field, leaving the 48th for a time as the sole battalion in 21st Army Tank Brigade. Because of this, the 48th's unit tactical number changed briefly to '173' as it was now the senior battalion. Later, the 43rd Battalion RTR joined the brigade for a time and subsequently the 12th Battalion RTR also, to bring it up to strength again; the 48th's unit tactical number therefore changed back to '175'. The 43rd was later replaced in the brigade by the 145th Regiment RAC (Duke of Wellington's), and this remained the final shape of 21st Army Tank Brigade for the greater part of the war. As the junior battalion, 145th Regiment RAC took the tactical number '175' from the 48th, whose own number changed in consequence to '174'.

2Lt F.A. (Freddie) Haigh arrived on posting to the battalion on 28 February and 2Lt A.O. (Alan) Lott on 3 March; on the same day RQMS 'Eggy' Eggleton was commissioned as a lieutenant (QM), remaining in the battalion as Quartermaster until he met with an unfortunate accident in Italy immediately after the war. Also in February, the battalion was honoured by a visit from Gen Martel in his new capacity of Commander of the Royal Armoured Corps.

The battalion took part in 11th Corps Exercise No 13, in the area of Thetford, from 3 to 5 March; on the 13th, the battalion's new 'B' vehicles arrived and were issued. The commanding officer, Lt Col Wykes, departed on a course on 31 March.

The battalion's petrol-engined Valentine Is were withdrawn on 10 April and replaced with the Valentine II which had a diesel powerplant. Twelve Valentine Is were handed over to the North Irish Horse of 25th Army Tank Brigade on the 13th. The Valentines had given nothing but trouble since their arrival in the battalion, and the problems had worsened in the cold weather experienced since the unit had arrived in Wickham Market; it was almost impossible to move from the tank park without some 30 per cent of the tanks breaking their tracks. Exercises became a nightmare, as they always involved leaving some unfortunate crews, broken down and stranded, to hobble home as best they could, often days after the exercise had ended. Various types of track were tried, with varying success; eventually, a manganese steel track was produced which largely overcame the problem. At the same time, the tanks had experienced a series of cracked cylinder heads, which further disheartened the battalion, but the change to the Valentine II, with its diesel powerplant, more or less cured this problem.

On 13 April orders were again received for the battalion to mobilise for overseas service in a tropical country; embarkation leave began on the 15th. A War Office telegram received on 18 April, however, warned the battalion that it was, after all, to mobilise for home service only; all embarkation leave was therefore cancelled. On 21 April, Lt Col Wykes was struck off the battalion strength, having been away for 21 days; Maj Cameron, the 2IC, briefly assumed command in his stead. As part of the unit's mobilisation, an influx of junior officers occurred on 23 April: 2Lts E.A. (Alan) Harvey, A.F. (Tony) Kingsford and J.C. (Jack) Dunn arrived from the 55th Training Regiment RAC and Lt C.C. ('Po-Po') Chambers joined on appointment to a commission, being posted initially to B Squadron on 1 May. On 29 April, the battalion represented an enemy panzer division on Eastern Command Exercise Thunderbolt.

Lt Col Wykes was posted out on 1 May, after having commanded the battalion since the month following its formation. It had been decided that a battalion mobilising for war should be commanded by a Regular officer, but, although this decision could not be criticised, the battalion was sorry to see Jackie Wykes go. He it had been who had borne the responsibility of training and leading the battalion in the first disorganised months and had set it on the road to success; it was hard that he had to leave when the way was becoming easier. In his place, the battalion welcomed from the 45th Battalion RTR Lt Col G.H. (Gerry) Brooks RTR, a 44-year-old veteran of the First World War, whose stay was to be a long and popular one – longer in fact than that of any other commander of the battalion. Nobody could have gained and retained the affection and respect of all ranks more than Gerry Brooks, who combined a happy extrovert character with firmness and loyalty to his men in just the right proportions. He was the ideal commanding officer for the 48th, no easy unit to command as it consisted of so many volunteers of such varied experience and background. Maj Cameron reverted briefly to 2IC on Col Gerry's arrival.

Scarcely had the battalion recovered from the excitement of its first mobilisation when it was ordered to provide a complete squadron, completely re-equipped with light tanks and a few part-worn Valentines, two or three Dingo scout cars and six Bedford trucks, to move to an undisclosed destination forthwith. For a battalion which was itself in the process of fully mobilising, and which had already lost many of its best NCOs to commissions, this was a body blow. Maj Cameron was appointed to command the squadron, known officially as A Special Service Squadron RAC but unofficially as the Light Squadron, and was given great freedom in the selection of personnel to man it. Capt Tommy Jupp was 2IC, with Lts Hughes and John Simmons commanding the two Valentine troops and Lts Jimmy Cardwell and Paul Barnett the two light tank troops. The cream of the battalion was taken, including the Medical Officer, Capt Peter ('Paddy') O'Flynn RAMC, leaving gaps which took many months of training to fill.

The A Special Service Squadron left Wickham Market amidst great secrecy in the middle of one May night, going first to Melrose in Scotland, where it became part of 29th Independent Brigade, together with B and C Special Service Squadrons. From there it went for training in landing craft to Inverary, where the personnel were very comfortably billeted in the Polish liner *Batory*. After completing this training, all ranks were paraded and inspected by Winston Churchill, the Prime Minister, before departure. Alas, their high hopes of adventure were never realised; after hanging about in the UK for several weeks, they finally reached Freetown, on the shores of West Africa, in September 1941 after a three-week voyage in a vessel that, in the words of Dennis Gable, '. . . rolled like hell in the rough seas, but fortunately I didn't suffer from sea-sickness'. The squadron remained in the area of Freetown until March 1942, training with the Royal West African Frontier Force in a desultory fashion and carrying out tank training as best it could in such unsuitable tank country. They never did find out what their intended purpose had been, although it seems probable that Madagascar could originally have been their intended objective: one of the other special service squadrons of 29th Independent Brigade, formed round the 10th Hussars and equipped with Tetrarch light tanks, did take part in the Madagascar operation. Maj Cameron was posted away half-way through their stay in Freetown, leaving Capt Jupp to command the squadron for its move back to the UK and for the remainder of its existence as a separate entity. After disembarking at Wemyss Bay on the Clyde, the squadron moved by tank train to Hoddom Castle, where it arrived on St Patrick's Day, 17 March 1942; it then moved to Auchterarder, where it remained until its disbandment in August of that year. The majority of the ORs, but none of the officers, returned to the 48th in the following month.

With the appointment of Maj Cameron to the command of the Light Squadron, Maj J.O. ('Joe') Clark had been promoted to battalion 2IC from the command of A Squadron. Capt John Mennell was promoted to T/Major to command A Squadron in his place and at about the same time Maj Charles Crowther took command of C Squadron. The new battalion MO to replace Paddy O'Flynn was Capt J.H. ('Doc') Moir RAMC, who arrived complete with his newly-acquired wife and was therefore considerably, if temporarily, accommodated by the unit in a nearby hostelry. A consultant anaesthetist by profession, he was unused to general medical practice, particularly in an Army unit, and tended to pronounce as fit any patient who was still warm. His size 14 feet helped to distinguish him from the crowd, while his height necessitated his having to sit for 'Freedom From Infection' (FFI) inspections.

On 10 May, the battalion sent two Valentine IIs to take part in the Saxmundham War Weapons Week, one of a series of such 'weeks' to take place around the country to keep alive the public's interest in the armed forces and their equipment. At about this time, rumours of a new, bigger and better infantry tank were rife; these became fact later in the year, when the battalion was ordered to send some officers and other ranks on a course being run by Vauxhall Motors Ltd. The new tank was then called 'David', for reasons now lost in the mists of time but possibly a cunning ruse to deceive any German spy getting to hear of it into thinking that it was smaller than the real Goliath which it in fact was. Funnily enough, the code-name 'David' had also been used, in 1923, to describe the prototype close support version of the Medium Tank Mk I. The new tank was referred to with bated breath; compared to the Valentine it seemed enormous, but it still only had a 2pdr gun as its main armament and its tracks were very noisy. However, the battalion did not start to receive it until October 1941, by which time it was called the Churchill, or Infantry Tank Mk IV.

In the field of training the stay at Wickham Market was undoubtedly extremely beneficial; on Salisbury Plain the battalion had learned how to drive its tanks and to carry out simple troop and squadron manoeuvres. In Suffolk it became aware of the more complex problems of a tank battalion under active service conditions. Its members learned that an efficient administrative, recovery and maintenance organisation is just as important as tactics in battle; to be unaware of the importance of maintenance was to spend a cold and cheerless night out of doors. In this connection, Alan Gilmour remembers, at a time when Lt Ken Reed was commanding 7 Troop, B Squadron, one particular night exercise:

> . . . on a desolate area of Suffolk used by the RAF to jettison their bombs, when, about midnight, the leading tank of the troop disappeared down an enormous bomb crater, resting with both tracks off; the second tank also fell down and mounted the rear deck of the first, while the third vehicle swayed on the lip of the crater. Rain came down in torrents as the crews laboured with crowbars and sledgehammers (in complete darkness of course), while overhead returning bombers throbbed low, preparing, we feared, to jettison their loads. But all tanks were mobile and on the road by 04.00am.

The battalion gradually moulded itself into a fighting organisation, all of which took time. It was lucky in having training areas close at hand on which the whole unit could exercise. The most popular area was Sutton Common, situated some five miles from the camp. Everyone who was in the battalion at the time will recall the endless attacks from 'Long Plantation' to 'Gobblecock Hall' (where light refreshments might be had), which were varied from time to time by attacks from 'Gobblecock Hall' to 'Long Plantation'. In addition to training locally, the battalion took part with increasing strength and skill in all the exercises organised by corps and division, which were very numerous indeed. It would be difficult to count how many times the battalion attacked across the River Lark and exploited 'in the general direction of Thetford', or how many bloodless battles were waged for the possession of Brandon Bridge; they all served their purpose, however, and each one taught something fresh.

No mention of training would be complete without some reference to the Thetford Training Area, where each squadron was able to spend two weeks entirely on its own, carrying out training of its own choosing. This gave the squadron commanders the opportunity of really getting their squadrons together under their own hand; it also gave the commander of 21st Army Tank Brigade, now Brig Thomas Iver-Moore MC (Brig Naesmyth had left to command the AFV Schools at Bovington), the chance of testing each squadron individually in what was known as the 'Eagle Squadron Competition'. The trophy was won by B Squadron on the only occasion on which it was completed, although A Squadron were twice victors in the tactical exercises. Finally, of course, a great deal of individual training was carried out.

Recreation at Wickham Market included cricket, football, tennis and swimming. Churchmans of Ipswich very kindly put its sports club at the battalion's disposal and was most lavish with its hospitality. The White Hart and other hostelries in the village were the scenes of unforgettable conviviality, which reached their peak on Friday evenings, while Ipswich, Framlingham and other neighbouring towns and villages were the object of often hilarious expeditions. Facilities for quiet recreation were provided by the local British Legion club, and there were frequent dances in the local village hall. Other activities during the battalion's stay included help in the making of a propaganda film (see **Plates 26, 27 and 28**) in conjunction with the War Office Film Unit, under the direction of the late Sir David Lean, and participation on Sutton Common on 31 August in a War Workers' tattoo, in which the unit gave demonstrations of mounted drill and a mock battle, as well as giving joy-rides on the tanks. Maj John Mennell gave the commentary over the public address system and Col The Hon Walter Elliott MC, MP the opening address (see **Plates 29 and 30**). The battalion also lent its tanks and crews for a similar demonstration in Colchester; both ventures were great successes, for which the battalion was commended by the daily Press.

In the second half of September the battalion took part in Exercise Bumper, the biggest ever organised in Britain up to that time; the unit was part of 11th Corps, which represented an enemy force attacking towards London. The concentration area was south of Newbury, Berks, to which the battalion made its way by tank train; there it remained for some days while anxious officers wrestled with the reams of paper which had to be digested before the battle commenced. Then began a long approach march in the general direction of Bedford, harbouring towards dark in the drive leading to Woburn Abbey, with Battalion HQ in one of the lodges. John Mennell, then commanding A Squadron, recalls:

> I called there [at Battalion HQ] during the evening to find a bit of a party in progress; Gerry [Brooks] had just heard that a son [George] had been born to him, and he and the Battalion umpire, a Lt Col Ted Hooton, were in fine form. I reported all my squadron in, less one tank, and was promptly told to b***** off and get it in. I didn't think this a very good idea, as there was the prospect of an early move the next day, but I went off into the night. I duly found my tank; the crew had moved into a nearby house and had their feet well under the table. There was nothing I could do as they were awaiting spares, so I returned to the lodge to find the two colonels in even better form. One slight

Plates 26 and 27   The battalion's tanks taking part in the making of a propaganda film, directed by David Lean, on Sutton Common near Woodbridge in the summer of 1941. (IWM)

Plate 28   Tank crews take a break during the making of the propaganda film (MOI)

bonus was that Hooton threw his beret into a large earthenware bowl of cream; I was rather pleased about that! The next two days consisted of forced marches, sometimes at speed. On one occasion, my tank skidded round a corner and neatly removed the side from a private car driven by a very irate doctor; he was left sitting in it, completely exposed to view. We found it funny, but clearly he did not; I can now see why, but at the time we were thoroughly enjoying ourselves, as we had never before had an exercise where we could go anywhere we liked within reason.

For six days the tide of battle flowed back and forth, and the tanks reached as far as Bletchley, Luton and Aylesbury; the 90-mile cross-country run between Newbury and Aylesbury was the longest continuous journey the unit performed in Valentines. The physical discomfort and fatigue experienced by the troops were equal to, if not greater than, any suffered in the months of actual campaigning which came later. At last it was over, and, after a due delay, the battalion returned to Wickham Market to digest the lessons learned.

From 13 to 25 October, the battalion was again in Merrion Camp, south Wales, for the second of the two visits which it made during its stay at Wickham Market for annual firing on the Castlemartin ranges; the cold was again indescribable, and the quarters not much

Plate 29   Brig T. Ivor-Moore MC, commander of 21 Army Tank Brigade, announcing the programme for the war workers' tattoo produced by the battalion in 1942. Maj J.S. Mennell is on the left (IWM)

better. In the meantime, the first of the Churchill tanks with which the battalion was to re-equip had started to arrive on the 20th, and a representative from Vauxhall Motors started a Churchill driving and maintenance course the following day.

Re-equipment with the new Churchill tank continued through November; by the 29th, only 10 Valentines remained on unit strength after 12 had been sent to 11th Armoured Division that day. On 30 November the battalion had 43 new Churchills on its strength. The Churchill was the 'bigger and better infantry tank' of which rumours had been circulating in the summer and which, then known as 'David', had been shown to those officers and other ranks who had attended the course at Vauxhall Motors' Luton plant. It had been renamed 'Churchill' as a tribute to the Prime Minister; the name also had the advantage of beginning with the letter C, which, since the Covenanter, had for some reason become the custom for British tank names.

The Churchill was officially known as the Infantry Tank Mk IV. It was bigger and heavier, at approximately 40 tonnes, than any British tank previously fielded in the Second World War, and was very much more thickly armoured, with thicknesses ranging from 100mm in the front down to 16mm on the hull roof. Powered by a Bedford twin-six engine with an output of 350bhp, the tank had a maximum road speed of 16mph and a road range, on internal tanks only, of 90 miles: this was later extended by the addition of an external jettisonable tank at the rear, used for approach marches. The first production model of the Churchill, the Churchill I, had as its main armament only the same 2pdr gun in the turret as the Matilda, the early Valentines and the cruiser tanks. It carried 150 rounds of ammunition for the 2pdr and also mounted in the front of the hull beside the driver a 3in howitzer, for which it stowed 58 rounds, and a 7.92mm Besa machine gun coaxially mounted in the turret.

Plate 30   Col Walter Elliott MP (in the turret) and Lt Col Gerry Brooks, commanding 48th Bn RTR (seated on the hull roof) on a Valentine of Battalion HQ Troop in the war workers' tattoo (IWM)

The Churchill II (**Plate 35**) was similar to the Churchill I except that the 3in howitzer in the hull was replaced by another 7.92mm Besa MG. The 48th received both types, the Churchill IIs being issued to tank troops and the Churchill Is to squadron headquarters for use in the close support rôle. The tank was later up-gunned, firstly mounting the 6pdr gun (Churchill III and IV), then the American M3 75mm gun (Churchill IV NA75) in a modification carried out by 21st Tank Troop Workshops in North Africa, the 95mm howitzer (Churchill V and VIII) and finally the British 75mm gun (Churchill VI and VII). The 48th was later equipped, in Scotland, with the Churchill III which had a welded turret (**Plate 68**) and IV which had a cast turret (**Plate 60**); in North Africa it received NA75 Churchill IVs (**Plate 83**) and, later still in Italy, with the Churchill V and VII (**Plates 87 and 95**). After the initial 'bugs' had been eliminated from the Churchill, it became one of the most reliable and most important British tanks of the war, running to some 19 marks and 22 variants for specialist RE and other uses, including the Crocodile (**Plate 89**), ARV (**Plate 106**), AVRE, ARK (**Plate 100**) and Bridgelayer (**Plate 97**). Altogether, 5,640 Churchills were built, all under the Vauxhall Motors design parentage. The tank was still in service, with the 7th Royal Tank Regiment, in the Korean War.

Plate 31 Battalion orders group on Exercise Bumper in the summer of 1942, with a C Squadron Valentine on its transporter in the background. In the foreground, from left to right are Capt G.G. Bell (BTA), Capt C. Crowther, Maj Styles, Maj J.S. Mennell (OC A Sqn) and Major J.O. Clarke (2IC) (IWM)

The battalion's initial experiences with the Churchill, however, were not encouraging. As earlier with the Valentine, the Churchill at first was extremely unreliable. Gearboxes, clutches, road wheels and suspension all failed in dismal succession and, as with the Valentine, troops had a hard task to reach harbour on account of mechanical troubles. It had, of course, been rushed into production off the drawing board and without adequate testing. The tank park became a mausoleum of dismembered monsters, but the problems were known to the powers-that-be, and a crash rectification programme was put in hand by Vauxhall Motors: before very long this had reduced the problem to manageable size. Capt 'Ding-Dong' Bell left the battalion on 15 November on posting to 145th Regiment RAC, one of the other two tank battalions in 21st Army Tank Brigade.

On 2 December, the battalion underwent the brigade commander's annual inspection and, from the 6th to the 8th, it took part in Eastern Command Exercise Scorch. On the 13th another influx of young officers occurred, consisting of 2Lts R.B. (Brian) Achurch from the 60th Training Regiment RAC, J.W.J. (John) Gage from the 53rd Training Regiment RAC and D. (David) Shillinglaw from the 57th Training Regiment RAC. A fourth arrived on the 29th in the person of Lt F.W. (Deric) Skey.

Lt W.M. (Robbie) Robson was posted in on 8 January 1942. On the 9th, Lts C.C.

Plate 32 A Valentine of Bn HQ Troop on Exercise Bumper; note the tactical number 175 on a brown rectangle with a white stripe at the bottom, the 21 Army Tk Bde diabolo on the lower nose plate of the hull, and the thickness of the HQ Sqn diamond on the turret side; squadron signs were later narrowed to a ½ in line width (IWM)

Chambers and V.R.B. Smallwood were granted the acting rank of captain, the former from 28 October and the latter from 15 March 1941. The Commander-in-Chief, Home Forces, visited the battalion on 21 January.

A month of combined operations training at the Combined Operations Training Centre at Inverary followed in February. B Squadron was the first to undertake the 32-hour rail journey to Dalmally in Scotland on the 6th; the weather was wintry, even the entraining at Wickham Market being hazardous owing to ice. On the journey north, M & V rations were doled out on a desolate stretch of permanent way in a snowstorm. From the railhead at Dalmally, as night fell, the squadron's Churchills did a 17-mile march over a treacherous and precipitous snow-covered route to Inverary, described by Alan Gilmour, then a driver with 7 Troop, as 'a hair-raising experience'. Here the squadron underwent a week's training on three rather decrepit LCTs (landing craft, tank); a night on board the SS *Ettrick*, which had to be boarded by scrambling up scaling nets and rope ladder from a launch in the dark, was included in the fun. The squadron started the return journey to Wickham Market on the 14th, leaving some tanks behind at Inverary, together with a maintenance party, for the use of other units in training. This party did not rejoin the squadron for three months. A Squadron left for Inverary on 14 February, returning on the 21st, and C Squadron left on the 21st, returning on 1 March. In the light of what the battalion learned later, this training was very amateurish,

Plate 33   A Squadron Churchills in the tank park at Glevering Hall, autumn 1942. The half-hearted camouflage reflects the lack of enemy air recce at this time (John Mennell)

but it fuelled much speculation at the time as to where the unit was to be employed. The majority of the training consisted of learning how to drive the tanks on to, and off the LCTs.

On 31 March the battalion received its first Churchill III; this was a much better-armed tank than the II, mounting a 6pdr gun in place of the 2pdr of the earlier vehicle, in a slab-sided welded turret that was bigger than the original cast turret.

With great regret, however, the battalion now had to leave its by now comfortable and familiar quarters at Wickham Market by road, train and tank train for Cumnock in Scotland; the main party left on 27 April. The camp it left was unrecognisable as the one to which it had come some 18 months earlier in October 1940; an open estate of grazing land had become covered with neat wooden huts with insulated walls, electric light, fires and other amenities. The tank bays were of concrete, and concrete tracks now ran through the camp as well. Many unit feet were under many local tables, and parting was a wrench.

On arrival Cumnock was found to be a pleasant little mining village, both picturesque and peaceful, situated in Ayrshire in the heart of Burns country in the Scottish lowlands, some 12 miles from Ayr and 40 from Dumfries. It was notable, it was soon discovered, for its pit-head baths, fish and chip shops and ice cream; it was also noticeably more difficult than it had been in England, particularly at weekends, to get a drink! The battalion was now camped, under canvas once again, amidst perfect surroundings on the estate of the Earl of Dumfries; the unit's address, with effect from 1 May, was the Dumfries House estate, Auchinleck, Ayrshire. Brigade HQ was at Lockerbie, with the other battalions at Hawick and Moffat.

Pleasant though the surroundings were, and however hospitable the natives, from the training point of view it must be admitted that there were snags to the area for a tank unit. The country was extremely boggy and this led to the revived use of the officers' ash-plant walking stick, or its equivalent, originally introduced in the First World War for prodding the ground to assess its suitability for tank 'going'. Every exercise saw some unfortunate Churchill stuck hard and fast, sometimes even up to the turret, and one wondered how anybody in authority could have chosen such an area for tank training. However, the battalion

Plate 34   Amphibious landing training on the Isle of Wight in June 1942, in preparation for the Dieppe raid. Titania, the Churchill I tank of 9 Troop commander, comes ashore under the eagle eye of the Royal Navy. Note that this and all other participating tanks now carry the red-white-red identification stripes on front, sides and rear (IWM)

soon mastered the art of recovering tanks from such situations and began to enjoy the changed surroundings.

On its arrival in Scotland, the battalion soon realised, from the number of other units in the area, that this had been no ordinary change of station. 21st Army Tank Brigade now became part of what had been 4th Infantry Division and was now, as a result of the substitution of a tank brigade for an infantry one, 4th (Mixed) Division. As a further result of this change, the brigade ceased to be Army troops and accordingly dropped the 'Army' from its title to become plain 21st Tank Brigade; at the same time, its component tank battalions changed their vehicle unit signs, deleting the white line under the code number (which denoted Army troops) and changing their unit numbers from the '170' series to the '60' series (the 48th becoming '68'). The battalion's vehicles now carried the 4th (Mixed) Division flash on one mudguard front and rear, and the 21st Tank Brigade diabolo in dark blue on the other. Similarly, personnel carried the divisional flash on the right sleeve of the battledress and the brigade flash on the left. 4th (Mixed) Division was part of 5th Corps, which was itself a part of the First Army.

This then was a striking force assembling in secret; for what, the battalion wondered? Certainly it could not be the 'Second Front' for which certain sections of the Press were

Plate 35   The Churchill II Talisman *of 3 Troop A Sqn attempts a more difficult landing, unsupervised by the Navy (IWM)*

calling, supported by various anonymous and ill-informed, but obviously pro-Soviet, graffiti artists, daubing slogans such as 'Strike Now in the West' and 'Second Front Now' in white paint on every available wall and bridge; the British forces could not be ready for such a large-scale operation for at least another two years, as those with more knowledge of the practical side of such operations knew full well.

The battalion was ordered in May 1942 to provide a squadron to train with the Guards on the Isle of Wight for a special and secret mission. B Squadron was selected to carry out this task, together with 3 Troop of A Squadron under the command of Lt Alan Lott (**Plates 34, 35 and 38**). In spite of severe bombing, the time spent on the island made a welcome change but while the main body of the squadron was thus engaged, 10 Troop was detached to the Lagonda Works at Slough, where experimental flamethrowers were fitted to their tanks. Training with these was carried out in Richmond Park, near the ATS camp; Arnold Cummins remembers this well:

One day I got a faceful of creosote, which was being used as the incendiary fuel, and

Plate 36   C Sqn Churchills being loaded onto war flats at Wickham Market for the move to Scotland. Note the name of the nearest tank (Tonbridge) and the tactical number 175 (John Mennell)

Plate 37   Formation sign of 4 (Mixed) Division, officers' uniform pattern (Author's collection)

was rushed up to the medics in the ATS camp to have my eyes washed out. The Brigadier [Richardson] in charge drove me in his staff car, and was much concerned about my eyes, fortunately without reason.

Luckily for B Squadron and the attached 3 Troop, the plans for the mission were changed and the squadron was released to return to the battalion in Scotland. It was only after the Dieppe débâcle that the squadron realised how lucky it had been; had the landing taken place on 4 July as originally planned, B Squadron would have filled the rôle ultimately played by the Canadian armour in the landing. According to Winston Churchill's account in Volume IV of his book *The Second World War*, the weather was unfavourable on the original date so the operation was postponed, first to 8 July and then to 17 August. In the landing, of the 5,000 men involved, the Canadians lost 18 per cent killed, with a further 2,000 men taken prisoner.

A War Office Urgent Memorandum dated 31 May was received on 3 June [was the Post Office that bad in those days?] again ordering the battalion to mobilise for overseas service, this time by 23 June. On the 6th the battalion, along with Brigade HQ, moved to Hoddom Castle, Ecclefechan, near Lockerbie, Dumfriesshire, a picturesque site at this time of the year with the fast-flowing River Annan running beside it. Originally one of the many Pele towers, private residences that could be defended in time of emergency, that were a feature of the Borders, Hoddom was destroyed by the English in 1570 and rebuilt shortly thereafter by Lord Herries, Warden of the Marches. The present building (**Plate 43**) dates basically from the late 16th century, two wings added in the 19th century having disappeared. After the union of

Plate 38   A rear view of a Churchill just come ashore, taken from the landing craft ramp. Note the external jettison tank on the rear, also the 21 Army Tk Bde diabolo on the nearside track guard (IWM)

England and Scotland, its purpose had virtually disappeared and its subsequent history had been uneventful. Before the Second World War, the castle had been a youth hostel and had also been used as the setting for the Robert Donat film *The Ghost Goes West*; now it rose, grey and stark, from its surrounding wooded grounds, glad to have reverted to a more military rôle.

The battalion shared the castle, which also contained the Officers' Mess, with HQ 21st Tank Brigade; the senior officers had rooms in the castle, but the junior officers and the men occupied wooden huts with the basics of electric light, stoves, beds and lockers. The senior officers in the castle suffered from a plague of mice in their rooms after 'lights out', which compensated the younger element to some extent for the spartan nature of their own quarters; this was more than offset by the friendly welcome of the inhabitants of nearby Annan, Lockerbie, Dumfries and Carlisle, to all of which regular recreational transport was run. Dumfries was a favourite, as the town had all the amenities and it was near enough for the return journey not to take too much out of one's free time in the town. Carlisle, being further away, required the use of the early-morning milk train for the return journey to Ecclefechan if a worthwhile time there was to be had, but it undoubtedly offered more in the way of shops and entertainment. The other tank battalions of the brigade were located in the same area, 12th Battalion RTR at Stobs Camp, Hawick, and 145th Regiment RAC at Langholm.

Early in July, further amphibious training was undertaken, in two separate forms: firstly, the squadrons cooperated in turn with units of 10th Infantry Brigade at a new Combined Training Centre at Toward Point on the Firth of Clyde and, secondly, exercises in landing operations were held near Ardrossan in Ayrshire. Crews were by this time well-practised in the art of waterproofing the tanks, which had been fitted with exhaust extensions and other devices to enable them to negotiate deep water. A third form of amphibious training was undertaken individually and involuntarily by one of the squadron commanders at Hoddom when his tank crashed through a bridge into the stream beneath, effectively damming it; thereafter he was known throughout the battalion as 'The Admiral'.

Shortly after the battalion's arrival at Hoddom it carried out an extensive trial of the Churchill tanks on behalf of the manufacturers, some 10 tanks completing a 1,000-mile run with only essential maintenance being done.

On 4 July, 2Lt Freddie Haigh was promoted to W/S lieutenant and became the Battalion Technical Adjutant; on the 13th Capt Bill Joss was promoted temporary major to command B Squadron in place of Maj 'Stylo' Styles, who took over as second-in-command of the battalion from Maj Joe Clark. RSM Freddie Payne handed over to RSM Fell of the King's Dragoon Guards.

From 26 July to 10 August, the battalion took part in Exercise Dryshod, a First Army exercise involving large-scale troop movements; on the 29th, for example, some of the Churchills accomplished no fewer than 91 miles. The tanks entrained at Annan station on the 26th. The 48th's participation took it over an extensive area between Lugton, near Glasgow, and Dumfries; in the course of this manoeuvre a tank harbour was formed in the grounds of Drumlanrig Castle, the seat of the Duke of Buccleugh. Heavy rain in the later stages of the exercise, however, rather dampened the enthusiasm of the participants. Various mementoes of the 48th's advance down the centreline were left behind, such as a pillar box rolling down the street, a gaping hole in a castle wall and a high tension pole swinging in the air. To even the score, there were several tank casualties in the 39-mile road march on 3 August. Our sufferings, however, were as nothing when compared to the Pioneers, who had to march 39 miles: as most of them were rejects from the infantry because of their feet, the results can be imagined.

Towards the end of August, presumably as a result of exercise experience, squadron signs (symbols and figures) on the tank turrets were repainted in the narrower width of half an inch; previously they had been much thicker and, being in yellow, more obvious to an enemy. During August Lt I.P. More arrived on posting from 144th Regiment RAC, and took command of 14 Troop in C Squadron, with Sgt George Catchpole as his troop sergeant. Also during August the new War Establishment for infantry tank battalions was implemented in the 48th and the Reconnaissance Troop was formed as part of HQ Squadron, with personnel partly from the Scout Car Troop and partly from the men of the recently-returned Light Squadron. Total personnel strength of the troop was 26 ORs and the Troop Officer, Capt Achurch; vehicle strength was 11 Bren gun carriers. The troop was organised into three sections, each of three carriers, under the command of a corporal, the section leader's vehicle having a crew of three and the other vehicles in the section each having a crew of two. The HQ section consisted of two carriers, each with a crew of three: commander, driver and wireless operator. The Troop Sergeant, Eric Potter, remained with the troop throughout the remainder of the war, as did several of the crewmen.

On 27 August, a team of 50 men from the Royal Canadian Army Ordnance Corps arrived to change the tank engines, to carry out modifications to the 6pdr guns and turret traverse motors and to fit splash guards and towing hooks for the Rota-trailers. The Rota-trailer (**Plate**

Lt Col G.H. Brooks (CO)

Maj J.S. Mennell (2IC)

Lt F.W. Skey (IO)

Capt R.B. Achurch (LO)

Plate 39 Officers' ID card photographs, late 1942 (John Mennell)

Capt B.H. Archer (Adjt)

Maj P.H. Clark

Capt G. Thompson (BTA)

Maj C.H. Crowther

Plate 39(a)

Maj W.M. Robson

Maj C.A. Joss

Capt Royston REME (EME)

Capt K.P. Reed

Plate 39(b)

Capt (QM) A.E. Eggleton (QM)

Capt J.H. Moir, RAMC (MO)

Capt W.F. Webb

Maj F.A. Haigh

Plate 40   Officers' ID card photographs, late 1942 (John Mennell)

Lt R.G. White (Signal Offr)

Capt M. Rand

Capt C.C. Chambers

Capt N.R.M. Chadwick

Plate 40(a)

Capt F.D. Hoad

Capt A.O. Lott

Lt M.C. Savage

Lt J. Barber

Plate 40(b)

Lt P.L. Gudgin

Lt T. Gorringe

Lt H.D. Palmer

Lt M. Goldby

Plate 41   Officers' ID card photographs, late 1942 (John Mennell)

Lt A.F. Kingsford

Lt M. Hunter

Lt J.W.J. Gage

Lt P.C. Reynolds

Plate 41(a)

Lt J.C. Dunn

Lt R.B. Webber

Lt I.P. More

Lt R.E. Wife

Plate 41(b)

Plate 42   Lt F.H. Spencer

45) was a two-wheeled armoured trailer carrying reserve fuel in the hollow wheels and reserve ammunition for the main armament and machine guns in the box body. On the 29th came a message from First Army HQ, ordering the battalion to prepare to move overseas to a tropical climate. Ten days' embarkation leave was granted, putting many men who had planned to get married during their next privilege leave in an awkward position; the tanks were, it was said, to be shipped by 4 September. The first tanks were waterproofed on the 3rd, but nothing more was heard of the move. Capt Barry Archer left A Squadron to take up the appointment of Adjutant on 1 September, Capt Don Hoad taking his place as 2IC of A Squadron. The rest of the month seemed to be occupied by senior visitors and inspections, including the GOC-in-C of 5th Corps on the 9th, the C-in-C of First Army the following day, the GOC of 4th (Mixed) Division, Maj Gen 'Ginger' Hawkesworth DSO MC, on the 12th and the brigade commander's inspection on 27 September. Also during September an interesting question was posed to the battalion: would it change its name to '4th Battalion RTR' in place of the original 4th, wiped out in Tobruk? Squadron commanders paraded their squadrons and put it to the vote, but the answer was a decisive 'no'; in A Squadron, only Sgt Basford, a Regular NCO who might have served with the 4th Battalion, voted in favour. Lt Col Brooks, who, as a Regular RTR officer, would naturally have liked to command a Regular battalion of the regiment, nevertheless accepted the battalion's decision with very good grace.

It had really begun to look as if the battalion was at last to get closer to the action,

Plate 43   Hoddom Castle, Ecclefechan (Dumfries & Galloway Regional Council)

particularly as, from its location near the main road north to Glasgow, it had been noticing towards the end of August the increase in the number of military convoys heading north, and the vehicle loading signs which they bore. By the middle of September, however, it became evident that the battalion's time had not yet arrived when there was still no news of its impending departure; it had been told to study desert warfare and the use of the sun compass, but the latter was difficult to practise in Scotland, where it seemed always to be raining. The CO and 2IC were called to London for, it was alleged, planning, but nothing came of it. Rota-trailers, carrying 40 rounds of 6pdr ammunition and eight boxes of Besa machine gun ammunition, together with fuel in the wheels, were issued on 21 September; these took much getting used to, particularly when reversing the towing tank, or when traversing rough cross-country.

On 20 October, Maj John Mennell relinquished command of A Squadron to T/Maj Robbie Robson, on being appointed 2IC of the battalion in place of Maj Styles; the latter left to command the First Army Reinforcement Unit (1 ABD), having held the 2IC appointment for only a short period after the departure of the previous incumbent, Maj J.O. Clark, to become 2IC of the 12th Battalion RTR. At the same time T/Maj Freddie Haigh replaced as commander of C Squadron Maj P.H. ('Pip') Clark, who left through ill-health, and Lt Geoff Thompson became BTA in his stead. On the same day, 2Lt A.F. (Alan) Holtorp and 2Lt P.L. (Peter) Gudgin (the author) arrived on commissioning from the RAC OCTU, Sandhurst, the former being posted to B and the latter to A Squadron, where he was lucky to be given immediate command of 4 Troop; the troop sergeant of 4 Troop, Sgt 'Plum' Warner, had been holding the fort since the previous troop leader, Lt Jack Dunn, had moved to C Squadron to command 11 Troop.

On 2 November, orders were received to hand in all the Churchills and to re-equip with Valentines and Crusaders; the Valentines were Valentine Vs (**Plate 48**) with a three-man turret and powered by a 138bhp GMC diesel engine in place of the AEC petrol engine of the earlier marks, but this still left the hull gunners from the Churchill crews surplus to

Plate 44   Churchill II of 12 Troop, C Squadron, and crew in the tank park at Hoddom, July 1942. Left to right: Jim Latimer, Tom Heron, 'Dumpy' Griffin, John Moffett, 'Jock' Wallace (Ken Stokes)

Plate 45   A Rota trailer, fully stowed (Tank Museum)

Plate 46 Churchill IV Tessa *of 4 Troop commander, A Squadron (Author's collection)*

Plate 47 Subalterns outside their hut at Hoddom Castle, February 1943. Left to right: Lts Peter Gudgin, Jim Truman, Alan Holtorp, John Barber, John Gage, Henry Palmer (Author's collection)

Plate 48   The Valentine V (Author's collection)

*Plate 49   Dingo scout car and crew at
Hoddom Castle; note the new tactical number
(68) on the front bin. The 4 (Mixed) Division
formation sign can also just be distinguished
in the original print under the central dark
camouflage patch (48 RTR Assn)*

Plate 50   Crew briefing at dawn: a tank commander briefs his driver prior to an exercise. Note the 68 tactical number and the red-white-red stripes on the hull front (IWM)

requirements. To convert back to Valentines from Churchills, with their thick armour and 6pdr gun, seemed a very retrograde step, particularly if the battalion was about to see action; its morale took a steep downward turn in consequence. The Rota-trailer stowage had, of course, to be changed as well, to take account of the change in ammunition calibre; 106 rounds of 2pdr ammunition could be carried compared to the 40 of 6pdr.

Re-equipment was complete by 14 November, a very creditable performance, and the guns were zeroed on the 17th, when some 15 rounds of 2pdr ammunition were fired. One of A Squadron's troop leaders well recalls driving his Valentine V for the first time, down the main street of Annan, lightly knocking each street lamp out of the vertical as he drove past having forgotten to make allowance for the extra width of the fuel jettison tanks on each side!

A flap arose in the middle of the month, as a result of which Maj Mennell spent five days in London as the battalion representative on a planning team from 4th (Mixed) Division for a secret operation involving a neutral country; we had to be ready to go on 23 November, equipped with Valentines, but luckily the operation did not come off.

Earlier in the month, the battalion had learnt of the North African landings on 8 November by First Army and the Americans in Operation Torch. Although itself a part of First Army, the battalion felt some disappointment at not being involved in a campaign which, it seemed from the early success of the landings and the push towards Tunis, would be over before they

With Every Good Wish

for

Christmas and the New Year

48th Bn. Royal Tank Regt.

Plate 51   The battalion Christmas card for 1942 (Author's collection)

could contribute anything; after all, Medjez-el-Bab was already in Allied hands. Little did the battalion imagine at that time that Medjez would still only just be in our hands when the 48th arrived in Tunisia some months later.

On 18 November the battalion received yet another warning order from HQ 4th (Mixed) Division warning it to be ready to move overseas to a tropical climate from 26 November; on the 26th, all personnel and vehicles of the battalion were placed on 10 days' notice to move. It was a very uncertain time, and nobody could really plan on anything. Despite, or perhaps because of this, a hearty Christmas was enjoyed by all; the officers versus sergeants mud match was bigger and better than ever, not even the Orderly Room Sergeant escaping unscathed. Neither was the CO lacking in the Christmas spirit, of which both he and the newest-joined subaltern were given very (some might say, as did the CO, excessively) large quantities when they visited the 12th Battalion RTR for Christmas Eve celebrations in its Mess at Hawick. The battalion Christmas card for 1942 is illustrated in **Plate 51**. At last, on 28 December, embarkation leave was ordered, half of the battalion to take it in the first half and the rest in the second half of January 1943.

Little of note happened in January, which is not to be wondered at with only half of the battalion present. The Revd Woodall was posted in as the Battalion Padre during the month, but he did not stay long; on the 18th the CO was called to London for a planning meeting, leaving the 2IC in command. On 19 February, 4th Division Preparatory Order No 1 ordered the battalion to prepare to move overseas to a tropical climate after 6 March; the previous

Plate 52 The white Allied recognition star painted on the top surface of all vehicles prior to the North Africa landings; this one is on a Churchill turret roof (Author's collection)

night, B Squadron had held a successful dance and social in Annan. On the 20th, orders were thankfully received to hand over the Valentines, and arrangements were made for the re-equipment of the battalion with Churchill tanks, to be sent direct to the port of embarkation from the Chilwell and Handforth Ordnance Depots. Parties were sent to these two depots to take over the new tanks. In the midst of all this, 2Lts B.W. (Bruce) Cottrell, D. (Dave) Thomas and W.J.S. Hutcheson were posted in from 111th Regiment RAC.

On 26 February the LAD vehicles left for the port of embarkation, followed the next day by three convoys of wheeled vehicles, all carrying a large white five-pointed star (**Plate 52**) on the bonnet or the cab roof for recognition from the air; they were loaded on to MT ships in ports as far apart as Bristol and Glasgow. Before leaving, LCpl Geoff Thomason of B Squadron, a professional journalist before the war, started a squadron magazine, *The B-Line*, to which all ranks from colonel to trooper contributed; it appeared monthly thereafter from 1943 until the end of the war, even under fire and beaten out on a captured typewriter, apart from a few interruptions from the enemy. Its contents showed a consistently high standard of literacy and erudition throughout its 30-month life. The cover of the final edition, designed by Squadron Commander Maj Bill Joss, and colour-printed in the UK, is reproduced in **Plate 53**.

That the battalion was at last about to move overseas was borne out when it was again inspected by the Divisional Commander, Maj Gen Hawkesworth, on 4 March; on the following day, HM King George VI honoured both the battalion and HQ 21st Tank Brigade with a farewell visit. Members of the battalion lined the drive up to the castle in a guard of

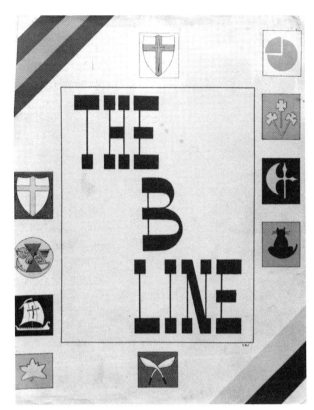

Plate 53 The cover of The B-Line *souvenir final edition. 4 (Mixed) Division's formation sign, as applied to vehicles, is at the top right (Geoff Thomason)*

honour, and the King spoke to the officers formed up outside the castle after taking lunch with the officers of Brigade HQ. He was cheered by the troops as he took his departure. Also on 5 March, Capt D.E.A. Scott-Gardner CF was posted into the battalion as unit chaplain in place of Padre Woodall; how lucky we were to get him was brought home to us over the coming months in North Africa and Italy, where his tireless and courageous work on behalf of the personnel of the battalion was justly rewarded by the award of the Military Cross.

The battalion's officers were now in the appointments they would hold when first going into action, and these were as follows:

Bn HQ

CO	Lt Col G.H. Brooks
2IC	Maj J.S. Mennell
Adjt	Capt B. Archer
IO	Lt F.W. Skey
LO	Capt R.B. Achurch
BTA	Capt G. Thompson
RSM	WO1 E.T. Fell
Bn Sig Offr & OC	
Bn HQ Tp	Lt R.G. White

HQ Squadron

OC	Maj C.H. Crowther
2IC	Capt M.P. Ladd
OIC Intercomm Tp	Lt T.S. Bruce
OIC Recce Tp	Capt K.P. Reed
QM	Lt(QM) A.E. Eggleton
RQMS	WO2 'Poky' Dye
EME	Capt D. Royston REME
MO	Capt J.H. Moir RAMC
Chaplain	Capt D.E.A. Scott-Gardner CF

A Squadron

OC	Maj W.M. Robson
2IC	Capt C.C. Chambers
Recce Offr	Lt E.A. Harvey
SSM	WO2 H. Vaughan
Tp Ldrs	Capt A.O. Lott
	Lt M.C. Savage
	Lt J.A. Truman
	Lt T. Gorringe
	2Lt P.L. Gudgin

B Squadron

OC	Maj C.A. Joss
2IC	Capt N.R.M. Chadwick
Recce Offr	Capt M. Rand
SSM	WO2 D. Simpson
Tp Ldrs	Lt A.F. Kingsford
	Lt M. Goldby
	Lt H.D. Palmer
	2Lt A.F. Holtorp
	2Lt B.W. Cottrell

C Squadron

OC	Maj F.A. Haigh
2IC	Capt F.D. Hoad
Recce Offr	Capt J.C. Dunn
Tp Ldrs	Lt R.E. Wife
	Lt P.C. Reynolds
	Lt M. Hunter
	Lt I.P. More
	Lt R.B. Webber

On the morning of 12 March, A and B Squadrons marched from Hoddom Castle to Ecclefechan station and entrained for the port of embarkation, Glasgow. The second personnel train left Ecclefechan for Glasgow on the following day. Both trainloads of personnel embarked at the port of Govan on HMT *Banfora*, and both 12 and 13 March were taken up with settling the troops into their mess decks and the officers into their cabins, and humping our considerable baggage aboard. All baggage had been stencilled before leaving Hoddom with the battalion's unit code, AA 16007, together with three brown and red colour-coded stripes; these can be seen in **Plate 54**. The rest of the day was spent on ship's final inspection and our first boat drill, in bright sunny weather.

The *Banfora* was a ship of about 10,000 tons displacement and rather more than 20 years old. It had been seized earlier in the war from the Vichy French at Madagascar, or so the story went; in any event, it was manned by Frenchmen, and the captain went by the reassuring name of Jean-Baptiste. It must be said that the ship was not ideal for the present job, having been designed primarily as a passenger/cargo boat, with the emphasis on cargo. The officers were housed quite comfortably in the passenger cabins, but the improvised troop decks in the cargo holds left much to be desired as far as ventilation, light and comfort were concerned; this of course only became really apparent when we were at sea and the weather became first rough, in the Bay of Biscay, and then hot, in the Mediterranean. The embarkation went smoothly, with only one absentee, a Cpl Stephenson who had been posted in from another unit and ran off the previous night. Lt John Gage also missed the boat because he had contracted jaundice, and would have to be replaced after arrival at our destination.

According to one battalion diarist, the officers' food on board was:

> . . . fantastically good. Menu at breakfast today:
>> Porridge or cereal
>> Haddock
>> Bacon and egg
>> White bread, butter and marmalade
> Lunch consisted of:
>> Soup
>> Macaroni au gratin
>> Steak and chips or Melton Mowbray pie
>> Sago pudding
>> Cheese and biscuits
> Quite incredible and I thought rather overdone. . . . Lack of drink has so far not proved a disadvantage though slightly irritating.

This last remark related to the fact that, because we were in an Allied convoy and our American allies were not allowed alcoholic drink on board, we too were 'dry', for probably the first time in British military history. We were surprised and rather hurt by this, as we had been looking forward to making free with the duty-free! However, even if the only drinks we could buy were ginger beer and lemonade, at least the abundance of good pre-war standard cigarettes at 4d for 10 was some compensation.

On the 14th, a very wet day, with everyone in high fettle and full of anticipation, we slipped our moorings and stole gracefully down the Clyde until we arrived off Gourock that evening. It was an interesting journey, for we passed all manner of ships on the way, from a battleship through aircraft carriers down to destroyers and even little MLs. All the way down the river we were cheered by the good people of Scotland, who must have realised that yet another unit was on its way to the melting pot of war. By the evening we had taken our station in Gourock Bay with the remainder of our convoy; this included HMT *Ormonde*, with Brigade HQ, the 12th Battalion RTR and the 145th Regiment RAC, now under the command of Lt Col A.C. Jackson RTR, aboard.

We now felt, perhaps for the first time, the loneliness of the soldier going to war as a boat came alongside to take away the last letter that we were able to post in Britain; somehow we felt more cut off by this logical action than by any other. The moment soon passed, however, and speculation then ensued as to when we would actually sail. We were not left long in doubt; when we came on deck the next morning it was to see the coast of Scotland slipping quietly past, as we had sailed at 05.00am on 15 March. By nightfall land was out of sight.

CHAPTER 4

Algeria and Tunisia

(1943–44)

We obviously sailed some way out into the Atlantic before turning south and then east, with many changes of course in between, to mislead any enemy reconnaissance aircraft or submarine as to our true destination; it certainly misled us, at any rate those of us not too sea-sick to bother. The weather had deteriorated and the sea had become very rough; conditions on the troop decks were appalling to begin with, and made worse by the vomit. Most of the battalion, with the notable exceptions of the CO and his 2IC, was struck down with sea-sickness of varying severity, which did not abate until the sea became calmer as we approached the Straits of Gibraltar. Two days previously we had been given the first official intimation of our area of destination when we were issued with a booklet entitled *Notes For Troops Bound For N. Africa*; the following day we were given maps of the area and had access to some intelligence summaries.

It was now obvious that we were bound for Tunisia, although we had no idea of our intended port of disembarkation. From the notes and maps we had been given it was apparent that the country varied greatly both in geography (see **Map 3**) and climate; along the north coast the scenery ranged from Scottish Highlands to English Lake District, although the climate was obviously very different from both.

In the north, the Medjerda river winds eastwards through Medjez-el-Bab to its mouth between Tunis and Bizerta, sometimes through narrow gorges and sometimes in a broad open valley up to 10 miles in width. This valley is, for the most part, cultivated, and lies on clay soil which becomes very glutinous after rain. The valley is intersected by many deep-cut tributary wadis, which are themselves tank obstacles whether wet or dry.

South and south-east of the Medjerda is the Tunis plain, inside a perimeter running roughly along a line from Tebourba, east of Medjez, through Goubellat, Bou Arada and Pont-du-Fahs. To the west and south of the plain, and extending north of the river, is an area, some 50 miles square, of high, irregular mountains and hills; it was for the possession of these hills – for example, Djebel Azag ('Green Hill'), Djebel Adjred ('Bald Hill'), Djebel el Almara

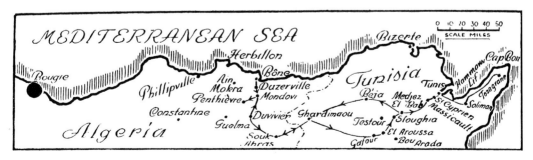

Map 2   Battalion moves in French North Africa

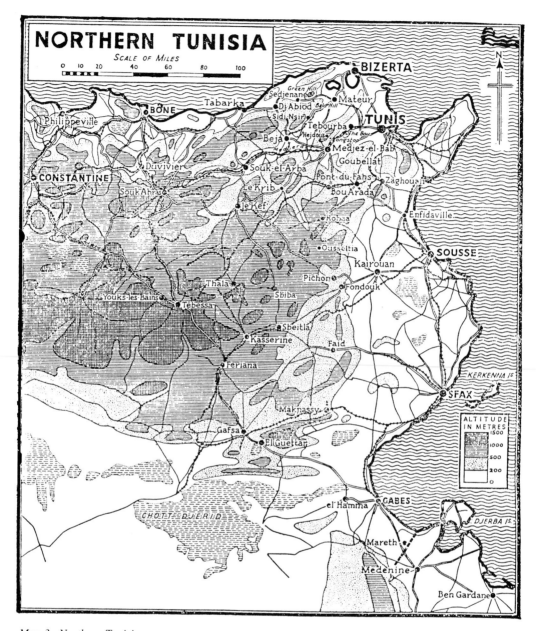

Map 3   Northern Tunisia

('Longstop Hill') and Djebel Bou Aoukaz ('The Bou') – that many of the decisive battles of the campaign were to be fought. On these commanding heights, a few defenders, properly dug-in among the rocks, could watch, hold up and take full toll of an attacking force much larger in size, while wide flanking movements round the hills were always difficult because the configuration of the country made it comparatively easy to forecast likely tank approaches and block them with mines and anti-tank guns.

The Eastern Dorsal, a high mountain ridge, runs southwards from Pont-du-Fahs for some 150 miles to Maknassy and then south-westwards for a further 50 miles to where, about 20 miles south of El Guettar, it joins the line of the great 'chotts' or salt lakes. Passes through the Dorsal are few (Maknassy, Faid, Fondouk, Kairouan and Karachoum), while the German Mareth Line in the south closed the gap between the chotts and the coast. The Dorsal thus made, with the chotts, a natural defensive barrier against an attacker from the east or the south. Between the Dorsal and the sea lies the coastal plain.

The number of good roads in Tunisia was small. Main roads were apparently metalled, with soft verges, but became slippery in wet weather; secondary roads were sometimes metalled but were more often little more than earthen tracks. After a few hours' rain many so-called roads became largely impassable to vehicles, while in dry weather the surface deteriorated badly and vehicle movement generated clouds of fine, choking dust.

In the coastal belt the rainy season normally lasts from December to February, but in 1943 spells of unusually heavy rain had continued up to the time of our disembarkation (and, as it later turned out, well into April), and adversely affected military operations by both sides. During these spells, which usually lasted for about a week, the lower parts of the country became a quagmire in which movement off the metalled roads often became quite impossible for both wheeled and tracked vehicles.

Apart from the restrictions on tank movement imposed by the weather, the areas in which armour could operate with any chance of achieving decisive success were limited to the area south of Pichon, the Goubellat plain and the Medjerda valley north-east of Medjez-el-Bab. The geography of the country favoured the side which held the dominating hills, and the initial British advance had been brought to a halt, by the end of December 1942, on the general line from Tebourba, west of Mateur through to Sedjenane.

Although we were going to war, the thought of entering a foreign country, hitherto unseen by us, with customs, dress, climate, religion, language and geography so different from our own was thrilling in its way. It must be remembered that, in those days, only a very small proportion of the British public had ever been outside Britain, and an even smaller proportion had been to Africa; our appetite had been whetted by the booklet with which we had been issued, and we were anxious to learn more about the continent to which we were sailing.

At last, late one evening, we sighted land on our starboard side: the blazing lights told us that it must be neutral Tangier, and quite close. We had passed the Straits at night for obvious reasons, so we were unable to see Gibraltar, shrouded in its blackout. However, it was good to see evidence of dry land again, although, now that we had entered the Mediterranean, we were going to be more likely to suffer enemy air and submarine attack before arriving at our destination. Before entering the Straits of Gibraltar the convoy had split, our part to continue through the Mediterranean and the other to go round the Cape.

On 23 March at about 03.30am our convoy was attacked by Italian torpedo-carrying aircraft, and the *Warwick Castle* was hit just aft of the bridge, causing several fatalities. She flew a red signal, dropped out of the convoy and had to be beached; fortunately, most of her passengers (some of them nurses) and crew were rescued, arriving at Algiers that afternoon jammed on the decks of two destroyers without clothes or equipment. She was the only ship in our convoy to be hit and the only one with women aboard! We docked about noon and disembarked the three reinforcement (R) squadrons of the brigade prior to going on to Bône, via Bougie and Philippeville, the following day. We expected an air raid that night, as the enemy must have known we were there and they made a habit of raiding Algiers with both aircraft and E-boats. However, we were spared this introduction to the theatre of war, although we would have liked to see the much-vaunted air defences of Algiers in action. By now we were beginning to notice the oppressive heat; we had not, of course, been issued with tropical uniforms (Khaki Drill, or KD for short) before leaving the UK, and our battledress was not intended for hot climates. We noticed also how quickly darkness fell compared to the UK; the sun seemed to fall to earth, and no sooner had it set than it was dark.

We weighed anchor early the following morning and, hugging the North African coast, reached Bougie about 3.00pm. We had one anti-aircraft alarm en route, which turned out to be a friendly aircraft although the Navy shot at it before it could be correctly identified. We found ourselves in a very pleasant little bay amid very attractive scenery, with high mountains running sheer into the sea and high white buildings climbing up the hill; there seemed little sign of war damage, apart from one or two masts of wrecks sticking up from the sea and the remains of several ships sunk in the original landings in the harbour itself. The crew was apparently not very happy about the next stage of the voyage, as Bône was supposed to be the hottest place on the coast for enemy attacks and we would have to pass through 'E-Boat Alley' to get there. In the event, however, the trip was entirely, and surprisingly, without incident, apart from one submarine alarm when a destroyer dropped some depth charges in our vicinity.

We arrived at dusk, about 6.00pm, on 25 March, and disembarked that night after an infuriatingly slow approach, in brilliant sunshine, to the dockside; it was almost as if the ship was reluctant to disgorge us on to African soil. Once alongside and tied up, the disembarkation began almost immediately, to the accompaniment of numerous and often contradictory orders over the PA system, and we started to leave the ship down a gangplank inclined at an alarming angle; as each man was loaded with full equipment, kitbag and sundry other cumbersome items of kit, the air was rich with curses, groans and threats. To make matters worse it was a particularly hot night, so that the faces of the men soon glistened with sweat in the glare of the arc-lights on the dock; the amount of light shown came as a great surprise after the strict blackout enforced in the UK and on board ship, especially as we were only some 60 miles from Tunis and less from the front line, well within range of enemy fighters and bombers.

We were destined for No 4 Transit Camp, so an advance party was quickly sent off to organise it; meanwhile, the battalion paraded on deck by squadrons and, as each was complete, it was sent off in the dark to follow the advance party. That march will stay for ever in the memories of those of us who had to undertake it; the strange smells and sounds of the country were what one noticed first, but the heat soon made itself felt too. Alleged, before we set out, to be some five miles distant, the transit camp in fact turned out to be some eight miles from the dockside, and everyone was exhausted when they finally arrived there at about midnight. We were almost too tired to notice that the camp consisted of a collection of stores tents, Nissen huts and marquees pitched haphazardly on the sand dunes. A welcome mug of tea was produced, and we lay down to sleep more or less as we were, as a welcome cool breeze sprang up.

The following day the sun rose at 06.30am and we woke refreshed and in a more cheerful frame of mind; the day was spent by the men in kit checks, sea bathing, PT and improving the partially-completed slit trench shelters, and by the officers in a seemingly endless round of squadron leaders' conferences. By daylight, Bône appeared to be a dirty little town by British standards, with an amazing variety of inhabitants; apart from British servicemen there were Arabs, Senegalese, white French and odd French colonials of all shades. Most appeared dirty, the children half naked and the men unshaven; buildings were mostly decrepit and filthy, with a fair amount of bomb damage, and flies were everywhere. However, the tiled floors of the houses, and the window shutters, combined to keep the interiors cool on even the hottest day. Despite the disadvantages and the little time available, several of the men managed to see a couple of English-language films, *South of Karanga* and *While New York Sleeps* at Le Majestic, the local cinema.

Rather sooner than we had been led to believe, the convoy carrying our tanks and other vehicles arrived in Bône, after an exciting three days of attack by aircraft and submarines, in which they had shot down six aircraft and accounted for one submarine. Unloading started on 28 March; unloading parties were detailed, and continued working 24 hours a day. The only delay was caused when a derrick on the SS *Artemus Ward* broke, being out of action for several days. Tank crews were accommodated in various requisitioned houses in the town while the tanks were taken out of preservation, de-waterproofed and their tools and kit unpacked, checked and stowed in order to make them battle-worthy; before leaving the docks, however, they had to be checked by Port REME. The wheeled vehicles were filled up with fuel and driven to an immediate assembly area, in the old phosphate works in the town. There they were sorted out by their units and taken to a unit vehicle harbour, in our case 'B' Harbour; the route was signed all the way and the system worked well.

The NAAFI ration came as a pleasant surprise, consisting of:

> One bottle of beer
> 50 cigarettes or one ounce of tobacco
> Two boxes of matches
> One bar of soap
> One razor blade
> One bar of chocolate
> One quarter-bottle of whisky per officer

As the tank ration packs also contained a tin of 50 cigarettes, we found it very easy and cheap to start the habit which would cause so many of us so much grief in later life. We were rationed at this time to one outgoing letter per week; this would improve later, as the supply of air letter cards improved and when the Airgraph microfilm photographic letter system was introduced in April 1943 (**Plates 55 and 56**).

On 2 April we had our first injection against typhus, followed by two others at weekly intervals; the first was a nasty one, and quite painful. The first convoy of tanks left Bône for Ghardimaou under the command of Lt Alan Harvey on 30 March on tank transporters, loading at Duzerville, south of Bône. Others followed by train, via Souk Ahras. The journey was very slow, but took us through some interesting country; Ghardimaou was the railhead and also, therefore, the dump for all unserviceable equipment, too heavy or bulky for road transport, being returned to base for repair or scrapping.

We had been preceded to North Africa by 25th Army Tank Brigade, also equipped with Churchills and Rota-trailers. This brigade had disembarked in the middle of February 1943, and we had heard of some of their exploits, notably a gallant action at the so-called Steamroller Farm by a squadron of the 51st Battalion RTR. Prior to reaching Ghardimaou, we had had every faith in the ability of the Churchill's very thick armour protection to keep out all but the luckiest enemy shot. This faith was severely shaken when we de-trained at Ghardimaou; facing us as we left the little station was a large collection of knocked-out Churchill hulks with all manner of holes punched right through them, many of them obviously burnt out. Our confidence took a very steep dive. We were also interested to see the large number of apparently undamaged Rota-trailers in the dump; it was obvious that 25th Army Tank Brigade had discarded them before going into action, and we accordingly did the same as soon as we could.

It might be appropriate at this point, before starting to recount the 48th's part in the

Plate 54 Battalion baggage on the quayside at Bône in March 1943; note the battalion embarkation code, AA 16007, painted on the crate (Author's collection)

proceedings, to recapitulate for the reader the state of the war in North Africa at the beginning of April 1943. It will be remembered that the Allied landings in French North Africa, Operation Torch, had taken place on 8 November the previous year and had successfully secured ports between Casablanca and Algiers; further landings on the 12th at Bougie were equally successful. Once a footing had been established ashore in Algeria, an attempt was made by First Army to push eastward with the small force available in an attempt to capture Tunis and Bizerta; elements of 78th Infantry Division pushed forward along the coast road and 'Blade Force', an armoured regimental group based on the 17th/21st Lancers of 6th Armoured Division, took the Constantine to Medjez-el-Bab road to the south.

At the same time, the British Eighth Army's breakout from El Alamein in Operation Supercharge had begun on 1 November, and Rommel's forces on the Eighth Army front were in retreat by the 4th. With the threat to Rommel's rear posed by the Allied landings in Algeria and the subsequent drive into Tunisia, Hitler took the decision both to occupy Vichy France and to form an Axis bridgehead around Tunis and Bizerta, within which a major force could be assembled both to oppose the Allied advance from Algeria and to protect the rear of Rommel's army.

The first Axis troops came pouring into the bridgehead by both sea and air, to no prearranged programme but with creditable speed; by the end of November Gen Nehring, who had arrived on 16 November to take command of the Axis troops in the bridgehead, expected to have under his command some 15,000 German troops with 50 medium tanks and 20 of the formidable new Tiger heavy tanks. The German medium tanks, the PzKpfw III and

Plate 55 *A typical airgraph letter (Author's collection)*

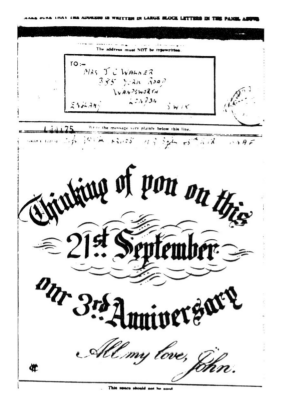

Plate 56   An airgraph letter for a special occasion, as drawn by the battalion calligraphist, Sgt Charles Warner (John Walker)

IV, were already well known; approximately equivalent to the British 'I' and cruiser tanks in weight, protection and mobility, they were, however, more reliable and better armed, the PzKpfw III (**Plates 57 and 58**) with either a short- or a long-barrelled 50mm gun or a short-barrelled 75mm howitzer, and the PzKpfw IV (**Plate 59**), with either the same 75mm howitzer or a long-barrelled high velocity 75mm gun (this version known by the British as the Mark IV Special); all of these weapons were provided with both HE and AP ammunition, whereas neither the British 2pdr nor 6pdr at this stage had a high explosive round. The Tiger heavy tank was a new beast, about which relatively little was then known; it will be described later.

First contact was made with Axis forces by the Allies in the hills east of Tabarka, and the Allied advance was finally brought to a halt on the general line Tebourba, west of Mateur to Sedjenane. It was at this point that the 48th, back in Hoddom and hearing that Medjez-el-Bab was in our hands, had feared that there might be nothing for the battalion to do by the time it arrived in North Africa, as mentioned in Chapter Three. The enemy, however, having the shorter lines of communication as well as air superiority at that time, was able to reinforce his force more quickly than the Allies and began a series of attempts to outflank Allied forces to the south. These thrusts were blocked and the Allied line extended south to Gafsa, but the arrival of exceptionally heavy rains made cross-country movement virtually impossible; stalemate was reached, until the Allied build-up and the ending of the winter rains could make the resumption of the Allied advance possible. In February, the enemy, reinforced by Rommel's army withdrawing from Tripolitania, launched a series of attacks against the

Plate 57 The German medium tank, PzKpfw III, armed with a 50mm gun, was used in the heavy Tiger battalion to give close support to the slow-moving Tiger tank (Wilhelm Hartmann)

passes through the Eastern Dorsal. All were repulsed, with the exception of that against Kasserine, where the enemy overran the American positions and reached Thala before 6th Armoured Division restored the position.

Coordination of the efforts of the British Eighth and First Armies had at last been achieved by the appointment in February 1943 of Gen Alexander to command 18th Army Group, incorporating both armies. In March, air supremacy had passed to the Allies and, when Eighth Army attacked the Mareth Line on the 21st/22nd, it did so in coordination with an attack by First Army's 9th Corps, which attacked the Fondouk Gap, and another by its 5th Corps in the north, which started an offensive on 7 April with the object of clearing the ring of hills north of Medjez-el-Bab. On 9 April, 9th Corps forced the Fondouk Gap and, on the 11th, captured Kairouan to link up with Eighth Army.

This then was the position at the time when we shook the dust of Ghardimaou from our feet, with Medjez-el-Bab still in Allied hands, but only just, and the hill features north and east of the town still firmly in enemy hands and preventing our advance on Tunis.

On 2 April, while the rest of the battalion was homing in on Ghardimaou, A Squadron was ordered by Ghardimaou's Town Major to move to the area of Bou Arada to relieve C Squadron of the 51st Battalion RTR in the line. A composite squadron of 14 tanks of A Squadron and four of B was accordingly loaded on to transporters and left at 2.00pm on the 3rd for Le Krib, where it arrived six hours later. From there it proceeded on its tracks through the night, arriving at its harbour area, recently vacated by B Echelon of the 51st

Plate 58   Another version of the PzKpfw III, armed with a short-barrelled 75mm howitzer, was also found in the heavy Tiger tank battalion for giving fire support to the Tigers (Author's collection)

Battalion RTR, in the area of Gafour, at 06.00am on 4 April. The crews spent that day preparing the tanks for action, pulling back the guns and zeroing them in a wadi nearby (**Plate 60**). They were joined by the squadron's A Echelon at 11.00am and by the B Echelon at 4.00pm; at 8.00pm a camouflage officer from HQ First Army arrived to arrange for the erection of dummy tanks in the harbour area to represent a second squadron. In the meantime, Maj Robson had been visiting Gen Monsabert at the French HQ, as well as the CO of the 51st Battalion RTR at HQ 25th Army Tank Brigade. On the following day, the 5th, all tanks had completed their zeroing and stowage, and Maj Robson received 3rd Infantry Brigade Operational Order No 5, as a result of which the tanks moved off at 8.30pm, without lights, up the line. 1 and 3 Troops moved under command of Capt Lott (3 Troop leader) to a leaguer at J630078, while the rest of the squadron continued on via El Aroussa and Bou Arada to harbour at J656986 (grid references refer to Sheet 34 of GSGS 1:50,000 map *Tunisia*, 1942 Edition); by 01.30am on 6 April the squadron was harboured, camouflaged and bedded down.

Further orders were received from HQ 3rd Infantry Brigade that morning, placing the squadron in support of Groupement Bouchier of the French Foreign Legion; 6 April was spent studying the ground over which we might have to operate, while the following three days were spent in accustoming the Foreign Légionnaires to riding on, and cooperating with, tanks, something about which they appeared to be completely ignorant, as well as in maintenance of the tanks and gun cleaning. We also managed to locate the BBC on our tank No 19 Wireless Sets, so managed to keep up with the news and other favourite programmes.

Plate 59 The PzKpfw IV was the other standard German medium tank, whose main armament was always a 75mm; in this version, known to the British as the 'Mark IV Special', the gun was a high velocity anti-tank weapon. Ten of these tanks were attached to the remnants of 501 and 504 Heavy Tank Battalions for Operation Lilac Blossom in April 1943 (Author's collection)

We devised a crude loudspeaker system by putting one earphone of the headset in a biscuit tin for the higher frequencies, and the other in a papier maché 6pdr ammunition container for the lower frequencies; it worked quite well!

On the 11th, with an 80mph sirocco blowing, the Squadron Recce Officer, Lt Alan Harvey, spent the day reconnoitring a tank approach to Arzoub-el-Hanesk, while the following day was spent by Maj Robson and Col Bouchier in plotting the minefields and passages through them in the area of Arzoub-el-Hanesk; the squadron passed this time in harbour. On 14 April, the squadron and units of 3rd Infantry Brigade stood-to on receiving reports of approaching enemy tanks and infantry in the Bou Arada valley; nothing came of this alarm, however, and the squadron rejoined the battalion in harbour at El Aroussa during the night of 18/19 April.

Meanwhile, having had its second and third typhus injections, the battalion had moved from Ghardimaou to El Aroussa on 10, 11 and 12 April; B Echelon had moved to the area of Sidi Ayed. In the absence of A Squadron on detachment, a squadron of the 51st Battalion RTR came under command of the 48th; on the 13th the battalion came under command of 46th Infantry Division, with a counter-attack rôle in the El Aroussa area. On the 18th, with the battalion complete once again, the detached squadron of the 51st Battalion RTR returned to its unit, we came on to the brigade command wireless net and the battalion came under command of 5th Corps. We moved to the Testour area the next day, a move which was not completed until 03.00am on 20 April; in the meantime, our B Echelon joined 21st Tank Brigade at Teboursouk and A Echelon harboured at Testour. We had now started taking our Mepachrine anti-malarial tablets and were suffering; nevertheless, at 11.00pm that night, the battalion was placed at one hour's notice to move from 03.00am on 21 April. At 04.45am,

Plate 60 Churchills of A Squadron HQ and 4 Troop zeroing their guns prior to their first action in April 1943 (Jack Rockliff)

orders were received for one squadron to move immediately to 21st Tank Brigade area, but these were countermanded an hour later. At 06.20am the whole battalion was ordered to move as soon as possible to the HQ 21st Tank Brigade area; B Squadron moved off at about 06.45am, the rest of the battalion at 08.00; all that morning, B Squadron waited behind a ridge at J573248, while A and C Squadrons remained further west in reserve in the Auchinleck Avenue area.

This crash move had been inspired by a German spoiling attack, carried out by elements of the Hermann Göring Division supported by a mixed tank force of Tigers, PzKpfw IIIs and PzKpfw IVs formed from the remnants of 501 and 504 Heavy Tank Battalions. This attack, known by the Germans as Operation *Fliederblüte* (Lilac Blossom), was launched against 1st Infantry Division and 4th (Mixed) Division, in the centre of the Allied front, on the night of 20/21 April. 5th Corps was about to launch its offensive on 21 April, starting with a series of attacks northwards on Longstop Hill and eastwards at the circle of hills north of Peter's Corner; the German attack was well-timed to take place while the British artillery was being deployed forward of our forward defensive locations (FDLs) and ammunition was being dumped at the guns, thus having the maximum disruptive effect. It very nearly succeeded, penetrating as far as 21st Tank Brigade headquarters and nearly reaching the HQ of 4th (Mixed) Division.

It was in the British counter-attack on 21 April that the 48th went into action for the first time. Operating under command of 10th Infantry Brigade, the battalion, less C Squadron, which was under command of 21st Tank Brigade, was tasked to enable the 1/6 East Surreys to capture two hill features, the Djebel-el-Mehirigar (J5823) and Djebel Djaffa (J5923), as

Plate 61   Maj W.M. Robson, OC A Squadron (second from left), and the author (on left) with A Squadron HQ crew, April 1943 (Jack Rockliff)

well as the saddle north-east of the latter, to which the German attacking force had withdrawn. The attack was to be carried out by A Squadron, supported from a flank by B Squadron in hull-down positions on the ridge behind which they had waited all morning (see **Map 4**).

At the orders group, held by Brig Hogshaw, the commander of 10th Infantry Brigade, at his headquarters, an incident occurred which was profoundly to affect the subsequent action: a few scattered shells burst near the 'O' group and caused its members to scatter. When the confusion had died down, the infantry battalion CO and his company commanders had departed, leaving unsettled the vital question of liaison between tanks and infantry. Our CO, Lt Col Brooks, immediately decided to send the commander of the Reconnaissance Troop, Capt Ken Reed, in a carrier to liaise and remain with the infantry battalion commander but, owing to the bad 'going', he could not make contact with the infantry advanced battalion headquarters; thus the wireless link between tank and infantry headquarters was never made.

The plan agreed before the 'O' group broke up was for the infantry to attack on one axis and the tanks on another. This was a recipe for disaster if ever there was one, especially with no liaison between tanks and infantry. And so, in the event, it proved. A Squadron's plan was to attack two troops up, with 4 Troop, commanded by Lt Peter Gudgin, leading on the left and 3 Troop, commanded by Capt Alan Lott, leading on the right; they crossed the start line, which lay in a field of waving corn, at J565232 (grid references refer to Sheet 27 of the GSGS 1:50,000 map *Tunisia*, 1942 Edition) at 2.30pm, moving north-east with the hill features on their right (see sketch map at **Map 4**). The first wadi running across their path

Plate 62   The PzKpfw Tiger Model E, first met by the Allies in North Africa, was the basic tank of the Heavy Tank Battalions. Weighing 56 tonnes and armed with a version of the formidable 88mm AA/ATk gun, it dwarfed and outgunned all the Allied tanks of the period (Wilhelm Hartmann)

had been reconnoitred and had been successfully negotiated but a second one, which had not been reconnoitred, was both steeper and deeper and the leading tank, that of the leader of 4 Troop, dug nose-in at the bottom. The Troop Sergeant, 'Plum' Warner, managed to tow him out and, at the same time, found a way round to the left of the wadi for the rest of the squadron; this did, however, mean that the whole squadron had to use the same gap. The first tank was across the second wadi at 3.00pm, by which time B Squadron had moved into its hull-down positions on the ridge (J580243) behind which it had spent the morning.

The infantry had little difficulty in capturing its first objective, the Djebel-el-Mehirigar, from where, with the help of 1 Troop, now on the right of A Squadron, a small party moved up on to the second ridge. In the meantime, Capt Lott had crossed a third wadi and was heading towards a small pimple just short of the defile when he suddenly saw, and engaged at short range, a PzKpfw III head-on to him. His first shot set it on fire, but immediately afterwards his own tank was penetrated by a 75mm shot through the turret ring below the 6pdr, and the tank immediately exploded in fire. Capt Lott and his operator were able to bale out, although very severely burned, but his gunner, driver and co-driver (LCpl William Aspinall, Tpr Bernard Marriott and Tpr Richard Smith) were unable to do so and were killed by the explosion. Immediately afterwards Lt Gudgin's tank was hit by the 88mm gun of a PzKpfw VI Tiger, the shot penetrating the hull Besa machine gun mounting, passing right through the tank between the wireless operator and commander into the engine and setting it on fire; simultaneously, the turret was hit on the right by a 50mm shot which lodged in the armour and on the left by a 75mm shot which glanced off; luckily the crew was able to bale out, although again it was the initiative of Sgt Warner in placing his own tank between them and the enemy, who were machine gunning them, that enabled the turret crew to free the

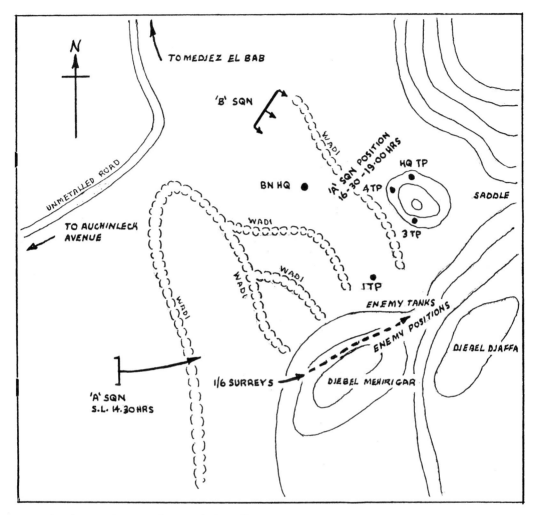

Map 4   The squadron attack on Djebel Djaffa in support of 1/6th East Surreys, 21 April 1943

driver and co-driver. The photograph (**Plate 63**) shows the objective as seen from Battalion HQ, with smoke from Capt Lott's burning tank rising in the centre and the author's tank beginning to smoke on the left of the middle ground.

A second tank of 4 Troop had a suspension unit smashed by another shot, and the tank of A Squadron's Recce Officer, Lt Alan Harvey, was also penetrated in the turret by another close-range shot from a Tiger's 88mm; in this case, however, the projectile did not explode but broke up, setting only the wireless and some stowage on fire. The crew managed to bale out with only superficial wounds, but then returned to the tank and extinguished the fire with hand extinguishers; the tank was later driven back to our lines under its own power. Appendix II to the Battalion War Diary for 21 April continues:

17.00 hrs approx. Another enemy tank appeared over the ridge to the rear and quickly moved down to the cover of the hillock where the other enemy tanks were. This may

Plate 63   The A Squadron attack on Djebel Djaffa on 21 April 1943, viewed from the start line. The smoke from the burning tanks of Capt Lott and Lt Gudgin can be seen in the centre with other squadron tanks dotted around the hillside (IWM)

have been a Mk VI 'Tiger'. Later another unidentified enemy tank appeared twice and received at least one hit from 3 Troop tanks. As dusk came, smoke was put down on Djebel Djaffa to enable our infantry to withdraw; they had been unable to capture it. At the same time A Squadron withdrew from their positions.

The following day it was possible to inspect the battlefield. One Mk III, burnt out, was close to the two Churchills, also burnt out. Further still, behind the shoulder of Djebel Djaffa, were another Mk III, a Mk IV and a Mk VI (Tiger). None of these appeared to be damaged at all seriously. Casualties: 3 ORs killed, 3 Offrs and 6 ORs wounded. Tanks 4Z [four written off].

Capt Lott sadly died from his injuries in hospital some two weeks later. This action was mentioned in the Allied communiqué that night. The commander of 4 Troop remembers:

We went into action that day with a feeling of unreality. We had no idea of the whereabouts or progress of our infantry, and our manoeuvres in the cornfield below the hill features occupied by the enemy, as we struggled to cross the wadis barring our route, must have looked very amateurish. I was leading on the left of the squadron, with Alan Lott on my right, and our progress up the stony slope of the Djebel greatly resembled some of our training exercises in Scotland the previous winter. The resemblance ceased abruptly when I saw Alan Lott's tank literally explode to my right, with two figures virtually blown out of the turret. I had seen nothing to cause this; neither had I seen the tank which he had engaged, but had no time to look more thoroughly before my own tank was hit. I had felt the shell pass my right leg as I stood on my commander's pedestal. As I ordered the crew to bale out we were hit twice more, but luckily by smaller-calibre projectiles which did not penetrate. On the ground we examined ourselves and found ourselves to be only slightly damaged; we were, however, being machine-gunned from the high ground. 'Plum' Warner, my troop sergeant, again came magnificently up to scratch by placing his tank between us and the enemy while we struggled to release LCpl Bob Fletcher, my driver, and his co-driver from the driver's compartment, in which they had become trapped when the 88mm shot had pushed in the front hull Besa mount.

After we had released them I went down to Alan Lott to help him and his operator back to our lines with my own crew; he was terribly burnt and must have been in agony, but he would not come with us without first trying to rescue his gunner, driver and co-driver. By this time his tank was a blazing inferno, with ammunition exploding to add to the flames and nobody could have got anywhere near it, let alone anybody inside still being alive; he was adamant, however, so I and my crew set out on the long and dangerous trek back to our lines, through former enemy trenches and minefields. I decided that the best cover would be obtained by using the former enemy trenches until we were out of sight of the enemy tanks on the Djebel, so, with my pistol at the ready, I led off. I was very startled, as I rounded the first traverse, to see two German parachutists apparently standing at the parapet; careful examination, however, revealed that they were only straw dummies in German uniform. After that alarm, our journey back to our own lines was uneventful, if tiring. The following day we drew another tank from the Forward Delivery Squadron and resumed our place in A Squadron; examination of the burnt-out wreck of *Tessa* later showed us to have been hit by the 88mm projectile of a Tiger tank in the hull Besa MG mount, and by the 50mm of a PzKpfw III on one side of the turret and the 75mm of a PzKpfw IV on the other. What hurt me most was the loss of my prized camera, specially loaded with Dufaycolor film before leaving the UK.

It was standard German practice for the Tigers in Tunisia to be accompanied by PzKpfw III medium tanks as close defence; in their heavy tank battalions, each Tiger platoon normally consisted of two Tigers and two PzKpfw IIIs. In this case, however, for Operation *Fliederblüte*, the enemy force consisted of 12 Company of Para Regiment 5 (by this time known as Jägerregiment Hermann Göring), supported by four Tigers and four PzKpfw IIIs of the combined 501/504 Heavy Tank Battalion, together with five attached PzKpfw IVs. This explains the mixture of gun calibres responsible for the strikes on A Squadron's tanks in this action, but there is no doubt that the ability of the 88mm gun to penetrate even the front armour of a Churchill, suspected when we had seen the pile of knocked-out hulks of 25th Army Tank Brigade at Ghardimaou, had been well and truly confirmed.

The German 88mm anti-aircraft gun, used in the anti-tank rôle in Libya, had already become legendary in the Eighth Army; the Tiger mounted the same gun with modified recoil gear, and additionally protected the crew with 100mm of armour. It could take on any Allied tank then in service, at any range, and knock it out while remaining proof against penetration by the Allied tank's own gun. The Allies had first learnt of the Tiger's existence from decoded intercepts of German signals between Rommel and the War Ministry in September 1942; from these we also learned that 10 Tigers would be shipped to North Africa in November and a further 10 in

December 1942. The British first reported contact with the Tiger in the attack on Djedeida on 28/29 November; the first Tiger to fall into Allied hands had been knocked out on 20 January 1943 by 6pdr anti-tank guns of A Battery, 72nd Anti-Tank Regiment RA, and it was from this vehicle, although badly damaged by fire, that our first technical assessment of the tank was made. A copy of the Technical Intelligence Report, dated 25 February 1943, which was circulated to all units as a result of this initial assessment, is at Appendix F. The abysmal performance against it of the British 2pdr and 6pdr guns is well illustrated.

It was all the more surprising, therefore, that we had managed to knock one out, armed as we were with 6pdrs, and to have captured one in virtually undamaged condition was a triumph probably not realised in A Squadron, which knocked it out, or the battalion. As soon as the battle had receded sufficiently to make it safe to do so, the Tiger, bearing the turret number '131' and the insignia of No 1 Company of 504 Heavy Tank Battalion, was examined thoroughly in situ and then recovered by 104th Tank Workshops REME. Apart from the odd damaged road wheel, the only damage that could have been responsible for its having been abandoned was a 6pdr scoop on the turret ring, which had prevented the turret from traversing, and another on the gun mantlet, which could have wounded the commander. It was found to be in running condition, so was refurbished with captured spares and, after the end of the campaign in North Africa, was put on show in Tunis for a short time; while there, and bearing the diabolo insignia of 21st Tank Brigade and the First Army shield, it was examined in June 1943 by Winston Churchill and HM King George VI, prior to being shipped to the UK for detailed examination and testing. Photographs of this tank (**Plates 64, 65 and 66**) show the position in which it was found, the vehicle in Tunis bearing its British

Plate 64   The Tiger of 504 Heavy Tank Battalion, knocked out by A Squadron on 21 April 1943, in the position in which it was captured, with a Churchill and Dingo in the background. This was the first Tiger to be captured in working order by the Allies and it was shipped to the UK for detailed examination (IWM)

Plate 65   The same Tiger on display in Tunis, now carrying the First Army shield and the 21 Tank Brigade diabolo, being inspected by Winston Churchill in June 1943 (Author's collection)

Plate 66   The same Tiger in England, at the Fighting Vehicle Proving Establishment (FVPE) in Chertsey, where it was undergoing automotive trials in 1943 (Author's collection)

insignia and at the School of Tank Technology at Chertsey. It is now in the Tank Museum at Bovington, where it is once again being refurbished to make it a runner.

This digression was felt to be worthwhile because of the hitherto little-known part played in the capture of this significant tank by the 48th Battalion RTR. Having put the record straight on that matter it is almost time to continue the story of the battalion, which we had left licking its wounds after the abortive attack on Djebel Djaffa. Before doing so, however, the comments of the official War Office Pamphlet *Notes from Theatres of War No. 16 - North Africa (November 1942–May 1943)* on that action are interesting, and were as follows:

> Liaison between tanks and infantry has not always in North Africa been sufficiently close. As an example of poor cooperation may be cited an attack made by one battalion of infantry and one battalion of tanks in the MEDJEZ-EL-BAB sector on 21 Apr 43. The two arms attacked on different axes, and the nature of the operation made a high degree of cooperation necessary if the tanks were to give the infantry the support wanted. No liaison was arranged, however, and the infantry battalion commander left the orders group conference without seeing the tank commander. The latter sent a reconnaissance officer with a wireless set in a carrier to the infantry battalion, but the country was extremely difficult for tracked vehicles and this officer was unable to link up with the infantry. As a result, there was no proper intercommunication and, since the tanks could not see in the scrub how far the infantry had advanced, their support of the infantry was not effective, while the support afforded by the infantry to the tanks against anti-tank guns was non-existent.

There appeared to be an aversion on the part of some infantry battalions in Tunisia to working closely with tanks, or having tanks anywhere near them, possibly because they thought that tanks attracted enemy fire. Bitter experience soon taught them differently, but there were nevertheless other instances of lack of infantry interest or cooperation before the campaign was successfully concluded. In this particular action, apart from our relatively minor losses, the East Surreys lost their CO, killed while leading his men, and all their company commanders were wounded; good liaison and cooperation might well have prevented these casualties.

After withdrawing from Djebel Djaffa, the battalion pulled back to Sloughia and the Auchinleck Avenue area, while A Squadron re-crewed and re-equipped. On 24 April it was B Squadron's turn; they were ordered up to the Banana Ridge area to support 1st Infantry Division in an attack on Point 174 (J6937) as part of a composite battalion made up of one squadron each from 142nd Regiment RAC, 145th Regiment RAC and the 48th Battalion RTR. The composite battalion was under the command of the CO of 142nd Regiment RAC. Appendix III to the Battalion War Diary for April 1943 records that the attack started at 2.00pm, when the tanks crossed the start line with 1 KSLI and 2 Foresters; the aim was for the tanks to support the infantry on to the objective from behind and the attack was both swift and successful, with a minimum of ammunition being fired by our tanks. The enemy responded immediately with a series of sharp counter-attacks, which were repulsed with the loss of five enemy tanks, including two PzKpfw III and one damaged Tiger, and many infantry captured; they showed little fight. B Squadron's casualties from mines, 88mm and mortar fire were five ORs killed (Sgt W.G. Cornish, Tprs D.L. Watts, J.L. Nagle, R.T. Jones and B. Kynaston), two seriously wounded (one of whom, Tpr S.V. Pearce, later died of his wounds) and six ORs slightly wounded; tank casualties were 5X, 6Y and 4Z (an X casualty was repairable within the unit, a Y casualty in 2nd line workshops and a Z casualty was a write-off). Tpr Ron Nicoll (see **Plate 67**), a gunner in one of 6 Troop's tanks, was awarded the Military Medal for his gallantry in saving the lives of three wounded infantrymen under small arms and mortar fire in this action.

On 25 April the battalion, less B Squadron, was ordered to move as soon as possible to the Banana Ridge area, just behind Snake Ridge, in a reserve rôle; it moved within 35 minutes, at 10.00am, harbouring at J628314 at 12.45pm and finding B Squadron already there. At 3.00pm it was again A Squadron's turn, and it moved up to take over from a squadron of 142nd Regiment RAC in support of 2 Foresters defending Point 174, in a counter-attack rôle. There it remained, on the reverse slope of Point 174 and under heavy and incessant mortar fire, until 8.00pm; incredibly, despite one or two mortar bomb strikes on the tanks, there were no personnel or vehicle casualties. Maj John Mennell, then 2IC of the battalion, wrote:

Although they were not actively engaged, they were subjected to very heavy mortar fire which made it impossible for anyone to leave the tanks during the hours of daylight. This had many obvious disadvantages.

This bombardment did not prevent the officer commanding 4 Troop, who was nominated to liaise with the Foresters' Battalion HQ, from dismounting, and he remembers:

I reported to the CO of the Foresters in his dug-out on the reverse slope of Point 174, but was curtly told to go and dig my own foxhole some way away. It was obvious that liaison would be quite difficult if I did so, but I dutifully withdrew my tank some 30 yards away down the slope, grabbed a shovel off the rear deck and scraped frantically away at the stony ground until I was all below ground surface level. With two jumper leads connecting my headset to the 19 Set, I lay in my scrape for some five hours, with no communication from, or further contact with the infantry battalion HQ. When we at last received the order to withdraw I thankfully re-mounted my tank and pulled out, without another word to, or from, the Foresters' HQ.

This was another example of the reluctance of some infantry battalions in the Tunisian campaign to work with tanks; to give the Foresters' CO his due, however, his battalion had suffered heavy casualties in the attack, and he personally had been shot up in his carrier by some of B Squadron's tanks on his return, the previous day, from a reconnaissance. Luckily he was unharmed!

Appendix IV of the Battalion War Diary records the efforts of the Battalion Technical Adjutant, Capt Geoff Thompson, and the mech staff with their two Churchill ARVs on the following three days, 26, 27 and 28 April, to recover the B Squadron tanks, as well as one belonging to 25th Army Tank Brigade, mainly in the minefield on the track between Point 151 and Point 174. Capt Thompson particularly recalled the recovery of one on the 26th, which had had its belly bulged in by a double Teller mine:

I spent the afternoon cannibalising a 25 Tank Brigade Churchill brewed up on the same minefield to get the gear change box (wasn't alone, there were two charred bodies in the turret). Then, when I got it to our tank, I found it too much bellied to take the gear change box. Enter Henry Church, A Squadron Mech Sgt; he put a tommy bar in and I stood outside and guided him very carefully back along its own tracks off the minefield.

Plate 67   Tpr R.W. Nicoll MM of B Squadron (John Walker)

Then I sat in, acting as a seat back for Henry who, with great expertise and two tommy bars, got it into top gear and we drove home in style, only to learn from Brigade Workshops that the bellying was so bad it was a Z Casualty! Nice try!

C Squadron thought that its turn had come on 26 April, when a warning order was received from 21st Tank Brigade readying the squadron to form part of the advance guard to continue the advance of 1st Infantry Division east of Peter's Corner; nothing came of this, however, and C Squadron's frustration continued. Also on the 26th, Lt C.R.G. (Chris) Hutchinson was posted in from 21st Brigade Tank Delivery Squadron to replace Capt Alan Lott as commander of 3 Troop, A Squadron.

We had all become disgusted at the callous greed of the local Arabs, who did not hesitate to rob the bodies of the dead after they had been buried, even taking the clothes in which they had been killed; it must be admitted that we, and many others, took great pleasure in booby-trapping some of them with grenades, and listening to the occasional explosion subsequently emanating from no man's land with quiet glee after darkness had fallen.

By now, Allied air superiority was virtually complete, and formations of 12, 24 and sometimes even 48 Mitchell bombers droned overhead every half hour or so heading eastwards, together with their Tomahawk fighter escort. The odd Messerschmitt Bf109 or Focke-Wulf Fw190 still managed occasionally to get through at near ground level, strafing anything that moved along Messerschmitt Alley, but such occasions were now rare; one

Plate 68 Toledo *and crews of 14 Troop, C Squadron, in Tunisia in April 1943 (Ken Stokes)*

A Squadron troop leader, who shall remain nameless, recalls with amusement one time when he was returning from a mission along Messerschmitt Alley in a Dingo scout car driven by Lt Tom Bruce, when he nearly removed Tom's head with the anti-aircraft Bren gun, on its extraordinary Lakeman mounting of springs and hooks, in his enthusiasm to down the Bf109 that was firing at them. Although the adrenalin was flowing, he failed either to down the aircraft or to decapitate Tom Bruce. Theatre orders for vehicle crews under air attack at that time were for them to halt off the road and to distance themselves from their vehicle as quickly as possible, taking the fire extinguisher(s) with them; in this case the mission was urgent, however, so they broke the rules, luckily without paying the penalty. The same troop leader, in a letter home written on 27 April, says:

> At the moment we are watching a few dive-bombers in the distance – the first Jerries we've seen for several days. Most of their raids are sneak ones by single planes, while our fighters patrol the line in dozens.

In fact, more damage was caused to our echelon by Allied aircraft than by those of the enemy. On one celebrated occasion it was very capably strafed by US Tomahawks while on its way up to replenish us; this caused some loss of food, ammunition and wheeled vehicles but luckily not of personnel.

On 27 April the 18th Army Group commander decided to change the plan for the final advance on Tunis; Eighth Army in the south had been halted at Enfidaville, 1st and 6th Armoured Divisions had similarly been held up in the hills to the east of the Goubellat Plain and most progress had been made in the Medjerda valley, with the capture by 78th Infantry Division of Longstop Hill to the north, and the advance by 1st Infantry Division in the direction of the Djebel Bou Aoukaz (The Bou) to the south of the Medjerda river. He decided therefore to concentrate all his available forces for a final and decisive drive on Tunis from the direction of Medjez-el-Bab. Regrouping was started immediately; 1st Armoured Division and an infantry brigade of 46th Infantry Division were left to contain the enemy armour east of Goubellat, while the remainder of 9th Corps, now with 4th (Mixed) Division under command and reinforced by 7th Armoured Division, 4th Indian Division and 201st Guards Brigade from Eighth Army, concentrated behind 5th Corps. This was the first time we had seen these hardened and strangely-clad warriors from the desert, with their light sand-coloured vehicles and piles of captured weapons, helmets and insignia, which they were anxious to trade for our liquor or cigarettes. We were particularly impressed by the cages of chickens carried on the backs of many of their vehicles, with which they ensured a supply of fresh eggs; we obtained ours from the local Arabs by bartering used dried tea-leaves for them.

The battalion remained in harbour near Testour, at grid reference J628314, from 27 to 30 April, while the regrouping went on around us. On the 30th, A Squadron was detached under the command of 145th Regiment RAC and was told to proceed to the area of the Gab Gab gap, a gap between a long ridge leading up to the Djebel Bou Aoukaz and the Djebel itself (The Bou). On arrival, they found that our troops had succeeded in advancing up the long ridge and were now attacking across the gap on to the foothills of the Aoukaz massif; Maj Robson was told to support an attack then being mounted by the Gordon Highlanders, which had in fact already begun. Despite starting off rather on the wrong foot, Robson made

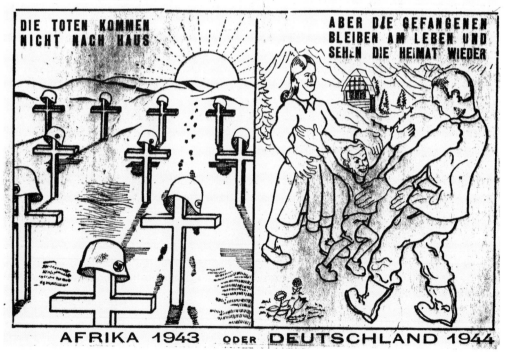

Plate 69 An example of the type of propaganda leaflet dropped on German positions in the closing stages of the war in Tunisia, to persuade Axis troops to surrender rather than fight on in a lost cause (48 RTR Assn)

all speed for Point 117, where he managed, by a stroke of luck, to link up with the Gordons' CO. A hurried plan was made for the next stage of the attack, and infantry and tanks moved off together; this phase was entirely successful and the objective, Point 212, was captured. The tanks then took up hull-down positions, looking through the gap at a large olive grove and farm in the valley beyond; the enemy, spotting the tanks, brought down heavy mortar and shell fire on them while forming up in the olive grove for a counter-attack. Despite the 'stonking', the tanks effectively broke up the counter-attack, Maj Robson personally directing our own artillery fire on to an enemy Tiger tank. The Irish Guards had by now passed through the Gordons, and from the turret of his tank Robson could see them going in with bayonets fixed. Although he did not know it until many weeks afterwards, he was witnessing an attack which was to gain two Victoria Crosses for that battalion. At dusk the squadron withdrew, the only casualty for the day being one tank which had received a direct hit from a medium artillery shell, killing the commander, Sgt J. ('Kipper') Barrett of 1 Troop.

The next day the squadron remained in harbour in a counter-attack rôle. The gap had by now been mined, and was defended by our own infantry; however, over the next three days there were constant rumours of impending enemy counter-attacks with tanks through the gap, and this meant that the squadron had, each day, to move out into hull-down positions behind the small feature known as Point 121. Although this does not, in retrospect, sound a very arduous task, the strain involved in remaining constantly on the alert in the open, under fire and in conditions of great heat and dust was very considerable. The days were long, first light being at 03.30am and last light at 11.00pm, and, after withdrawing and rallying at last light, the tanks had to be replenished and maintained and the crews fed. While most crewmen could then snatch a few hours' sleep, there were nevertheless guards to be posted and wireless watch maintained. Thus even an ordinary day when no actual fighting took place was exacting. Luckily, however, all good things come to an end, and A Squadron was withdrawn into harbour on 4 May; later the same day it rejoined the battalion, where it became obvious that big things lay ahead. The final battle for Tunis was about to be joined.

It began at 5.00pm the following day, 5 May, with a successful preliminary attack by 1st Infantry Division of 5th Corps on The Bou. The main attack, by 9th Corps, began at 03.00am the following day and was made by 4th (Mixed) Division on the right and 4th Indian Division on the left, over a frontage of 3,000 yards, supported by the Churchill tanks of the two tank brigades and the concentrated fire of over 600 guns. Behind the attacking divisions 6th Armoured Division on the right and 7th Armoured Division on the left were drawn up in an approximate order of march and feeding forward into the battle close behind the attacking infantry. The infantry attack was made in bright starlight and was completely successful. The RAF made an important contribution to the fire support by maintaining, for over two hours, light and medium bomber support on targets beyond the range of the artillery. By 11.00am the infantry had penetrated deeply enough to allow the armoured divisions to be launched through the gap; by evening they had reached a line approximately north–south through Massicault. Tunis was entered the following day, 7 May, and Bizerta fell to the Americans the same day.

The battalion celebrated 5 May in somewhat different fashion: we left the Banana Ridge area and, with our A Echelon, moved to our concentration area east of Medjez-el-Bab and in the lee of Point 151 for Operation Polegate the next day. For this operation, the final push for Tunis, the battalion was to be in support of the right hand assault brigade, our old friends 10th Infantry Brigade; B Squadron would be cooperating with 2 DCLI on the left and C Squadron, getting its chance at last, on the right in support of 1/6 East Surreys. A Squadron and 2 Beds and Herts were to be in reserve. 10th Infantry Brigade's Operation Order No 5, dated 5 May 1943, covering this operation gives a remarkably accurate summary of the enemy strength and order of battle, showing how good our tactical Intelligence was at this time.

This somewhat inopportune moment was chosen to issue khaki drill tropical kit to all ranks while under light enemy shell fire in the middle of a cornfield; it at least afforded some relief from the great heat which was now general. The whole area north of the Medjez–Tunis road was alive with the noise and dust generated by the troops and guns, and it seemed impossible that the enemy could be unaware of the vast preparations we were making. However, his air reconnaissance capability had been reduced virtually to nil by our crushing air superiority and, although we were then unaware of it, a grand deception plan had kept his attention focused firmly on the south; there was every indication that the attack in the Medjez sector was unexpected.

The CO gave out his orders at 6.00pm and, as darkness fell, the whole battalion settled for a couple of hours' sleep before H-hour. Promptly at 03.00am the following morning a single gun fired. Before the echoes had died away the sound was amplified several hundredfold as hundreds of our guns, almost wheel to wheel, opened fire simultaneously; the sight of the

Plate 70 Battalion orders group in a Tunisian cornfield, 5 May 1943. Left to right: Capt Moir (MO, with back to camera), Capt Archer (Adjt, standing), Lt Col Brooks (CO, in centre), Maj Mennell (2IC, behind him), Maj Joss (OC B Sqn), Maj Haigh (OC C Sqn, behind him) and Maj Robson (OC A Sqn, in foreground) (Author's collection)

gun flashes flickering along the whole frontage, and of the shells bursting on the enemy positions, was indescribable. At the same time we moved forward to our previously-reconnoitred positions on the Massicault Ridge, a difficult run in semi-darkness, as poor visibility was aggravated by the dense clouds of choking dust churned up by the tanks; too close to the tank in front and you were blinded, too far away and you lost your bearings. These clouds of choking fine powdery dust were reminiscent of some gas attack in the First World War; men groped, coughing, through the nauseating fog and every blade of grass was hung with its fine white particles in the early morning dew.

B Squadron had a tricky approach march across our front in the dark, but all went well and they married up with their infantry on time. Alan Gilmour, then a driver in 7 Troop, recalls:

The moon was down when the Squadron moved off at 02.30am. *Titan* led the three tanks of 7 Troop, G. R. Bartlett's tank following only seven or eight yards behind. All at once, our craft shuddered to a violent explosion. With one hand on the tiller, with the other I seized the intercom microphone: 'What's wrong?'

'A shell landed between us and the tank behind,' replied my commander, with remarkable composure. 'It's blown away your towing shackles, water cans and smoke generators . . . don't switch over to reserve fuel.'

'Why not?'

'Because you haven't got any.' The 30-gallon reserve tank at the rear (enough to take the tank 15 miles), designed to jettison on application of a lever beside my right ear, had been irretrievably jettisoned by the shell burst. Another round bursting in front of *Titan* blew in my driving visor.

B Squadron crossed its start line at 03.30am, in the wake of the DCLI, but lost one tank on our own minefield as it did so. In the meantime, C Squadron had moved up to its start line on the crest of Point 174 and waited there for the infantry; the squadron was joined there at 04.00am by our Battalion HQ. At 04.35am C Squadron was at last launched over the start line for its first encounter with the enemy. For a time silence reigned, broken only by the occasional expletive or instruction to gunner or driver as a commander forgot to switch from his A or B Set to the intercom (IC); these provided comic relief to what otherwise was a fairly tense period, until first B Squadron and then C reported that their infantry had taken their objectives. The supporting artillery had now switched from barrage to counter-battery fire, and, as it became light, some of the stage effects receded. Looking back from Point 174, the two armoured divisions could be seen stretched out in long writhing snakes of dust as far as the eye could see.

The opening battle was over as far as we were concerned, and the battalion harboured forward in a field of now-burnt corn; by now it was light, and with the first glimpse of the sun came the bombers. In tight box formations of 8–12 at a time they roared over us all day long. From our harbour we could see them make their bombing runs, see the bombs fall in a long curving trajectory, hear the rumble as the bombs burst and watch the bombers curve away, chased by the untidy smudges of the anti-aircraft fire. As one formation completed its run another immediately followed it; we could not help feeling sorry for the German troops on the receiving end of this bombardment.

Now came the inevitable waiting, which is so large a part of any battle; the armoured brigades were by now passing through and we wished them well. We might not have to fight again in this campaign, although we expected to be needed on the final ridge before Tunis. Night came and we camped where we were; the next day, the 7th, was equally uneventful, although in the late afternoon we moved forward to the little village of Massicault, where we again harboured in a cornfield. While there we heard details of how the armoured divisions had swept all before them and, listening on the wireless, we heard the leading squadron of the Derbyshire Yeomanry laconically report its entry into Tunis. Meanwhile, the Americans had also broken through to Bizerta. As an anti-climax, it began to rain!

On 8 May we moved forward again, in a rapid advance to the curious walled town of La Mahommédia, overlooking Tunis, where we harboured for the night; as we lumbered forward many new and strange sights met our eyes. Prisoners, mostly German, were streaming past, on foot and in their own transport; as Cyril Edwards recalls:

> The members of the 48th instinctively capitalised on this bonanza and took ownership of whatever took their fancy. High-ranking officers were made to join the foot-sloggers whilst their staff cars were driven off . . . especially prized were motor-cycles, with or without side-cars; half-tracks, water trucks and even field kitchens were collected, and soon it seemed that every tank crew had personal transport parked alongside their tanks.

Sometimes we passed 88mm guns overrun by the armoured divisions, with their crews spreadeagled beside their weapons; sometimes the French population ran out with bottles of wine and flowers, which they thrust into the tank crews' hands. It was an extraordinary experience. Tunis was now in our hands and we watched the gallant 78th Infantry Division being moved forward to occupy it, an honour which it richly deserved. 7th Armoured Division had swung north and were thrusting towards the Americans while 1st and 6th Armoured Divisions were directed towards the Cap Bon Peninsula, where speed was essential if the Germans were to be denied time to regroup and organise themselves in a mountainous region so favourable to defence. On the 8th, however, both divisions had come up against stiff resistance, 6th Armoured at Hammam Lif and 1st Armoured at Crèteville. On the same day we learned with great sadness that Capt Alan Lott had died of his burns.

The armoured divisions were to make one more attempt to break through on 9 May; if that failed, 4th (Mixed) Division would stage a set-piece attack, supported by our tanks. In the meantime it all seemed rather unreal as we lay by our tanks watching the puffs of smoke bursting on the hills above Hammam Lif by day and the French incautiously celebrating with fireworks by night. That night we made a night advance to Hammam Lif, where, the following morning in what must have been one of the most gallant actions of the campaign, the Lothian and Border Horse finally broke through. The chase was on again, and we quickly moved forward and joined the long queue trickling through the little town; it was dark before we finally got clear, but even so we were able to see the remains of the 88mm guns and the Lothians' tanks, mute testimony to the severity of the fighting. By midnight we were on the road and jammed nose to tail; it was armoured mobility at its most negative. Wisely, the colonel decided to pull off the road and wait for morning; all around us, smoke and flames rose from burning dumps ignited by the retreating Germans as they fled northwards. That night we were again placed under command of 10th Infantry Brigade for the pursuit up the Cap Bon Peninsula; the CO decided that C Squadron should lead it.

Several subalterns from A and B Squadrons went into Tunis in a liberated German staff car that night and celebrated the victory in suitable fashion on captured German beer and French red wine with some friendly French girls. In the words of one of them:

> The French have gone absolutely mad . . . everywhere I've been mobbed by hysterical French people, and soldiers, who, now it's all over and they can see the way the wind

has blown, are producing uniforms and hitherto immobilised cars and either strutting self-importantly round the towns or driving at breakneck speed in their cars through the country roads, hooting their horns like mad.

Very early on 11 May, C Squadron pulled out and passed through Soliman to join up with 10th Infantry Brigade, sharing the lead up the west side of the peninsula with 2 DCLI. At first the tanks and carriers led but, as resistance was so negligible, the infantry soon took over. The distance travelled and the speed at which it had been travelled formed a gruelling test of both tanks and crews. Great numbers of prisoners crowded the roads. By 2.30pm the leading elements had linked up with 12th Infantry Brigade, which had been advancing up the east coast of the peninsula, at Kelibia; Cap Bon Peninsula had been encircled.

In the meantime, the rest of the battalion had been following up by bounds, but at about 3.00pm it halted, harbouring that night near Tozegrane, a few miles from the tip of the Cape. Alan Gilmour recalls the urgency of these last few hours:

. . . at 01.30am on 11 May we were ordered to advance with all speed towards the Cape. Thirteen miles were covered before dawn (the strain of driving through rough country when you cannot see a yard in front of you beggars description). At last we halted, and the crews brewed tea in lieu of breakfast. In the early light we presented a

Plate 71   The German surrender on the Cap Bon peninsula, May 1943 (Deric Skey)

bizarre spectacle – wan, dirty, unshaven, eyes red-rimmed and bloodshot, shivering with cold.

While here, a column of Italian prisoners passed by; Cyril Edwards continues:

This was a very different scenario, with different prizes to be gained. They travelled, mostly packed like sardines, in open lorries, very happy, singing lustily to guitar accompaniments and waving Chianti bottles. The stock of wines was like a special Christmas bonus; my own tank, like most, hardly had room for the co-driver!

For us, apart from a slight brush the next day involving Recce Troop, under Capt Ken Reed, and some Germans who refused to surrender, the African campaign was over.

It was a bit of an anti-climax; we had been geared to such a high pitch and the adrenalin had been flowing so fast that it was difficult at first to realise that the fighting had stopped. The battalion concentrated back at the village of Soliman on 12 May; Soliman was a typical Arab village of whitewashed houses, both dirty and smelly. Luckily it was near the sea, and the men were able to bathe regularly, despite the large numbers of inflated German corpses which were washed up daily on the shore. Best of all, after the hectic months which had preceded this pause in the war, the battalion was able to relax; had it realised for how long this pause was to last, however, the troops might not have been so happy. Thoughts now turned, naturally, to the acquisition of creature comforts and soon, like every other unit in the First and Eighth Armies, the unit boasted captured Italian tents, German cookers, souvenir small arms, binoculars and pieces of uniform, as well as a miscellany of captured vehicles; the 2IC was particularly pleased with his Volkswagen! Greed quickly outweighed common sense, however, until military discipline stepped in and we were forced to disgorge the more obvious of our hard-won trophies.

A Brigade Thanksgiving Service was held shortly afterwards, followed by a Victory Parade in Tunis in which the battalion was represented by a small contingent under Maj Robson. The salute was taken by Gen Eisenhower and Gen Giraud. Tunis had, up to now, been out of bounds but sightseeing leave for small parties started. As the town was grossly overcrowded and had little to offer, many ignored the opportunity, preferring the quieter, cooler existence by the sea. After a few days the usual crop of rumours started; it was obvious that the battalion could not stay indefinitely in Soliman, neither would it have wanted to do so, but where was it likely to be sent? Some said back to the UK, others suggested Italy or, more depressingly, the Far East. Luckily they were not kept in suspense for long and, with mixed feelings, learned that their destination was to be Penthièvre, some 15 miles to the south of Bône, where they had disembarked only two months previously. One of the more unkind rumours had it that this was due to the brigadier's liking for the Penthièvre wines. On the 17th the battalion was visited by Maj Gen Raymond Briggs, who had commanded 10th Armoured Division in the desert and was to become Director of the Royal Armoured Corps (DRAC) in the War Office; his pulling of the brigadier's leg was much enjoyed by those of the battalion who witnessed it.

The battalion was soon on the move; battalion and squadron advance parties left for Penthièvre on 25 May and on the 27th the tanks set out by road on transporters on the 350-mile journey back to Algeria. The start was not auspicious; a stifling sirocco had blown all the previous day, and while crews huddled in improvised bivvies beside the transporters prior to a first light departure, torrential rain fell. It proved a memorable journey, by way of Béja, Ghardimaou and Duvivier; from the high Diamond-T transporters a magnificent

Plate 72   Battalion A vehicles on transporters, ready for the move back to Penthièvre in Algeria, May 1943 (Author's collection)

panorama unfolded in the clear African atmosphere while the long convoy wound its sinuous way north-westwards. Final off-loading took place at Mondovi on 30 May, whence the Churchills proceeded under their own power for the 12 miles to Penthièvre. Meanwhile the wheeled party had arrived by way of Djedeida, Mateur, Sedjenane, Tabarka, La Calle and Mondovi on the 28th, to be greeted by an air raid on Bône and a terrific display of anti-aircraft fire that night.

The battalion area was a gorse-covered slope on the coastal plain which stretched inland from Bône; it could scarcely have been more remote from civilisation. Penthièvre itself was a small featureless village a mile or two away from the camp. At the beginning of summer it was a pleasant enough spot; winter, however, would be another matter. Everyone was feeling bored after the excitement of battle, and conditions in the camp soon began to pall; lack of water, the distance of the site (17 miles) from the sea, the proximity of Brigade HQ and the scarcity of training areas added to the problems.

In spite of the location, however, years of practice in improvising creature comforts stood the battalion in good stead and ensured that no time was lost in making conditions more congenial. Two-man bivvies were soon replaced by 160-pounder ridge-pole tents, and squadron lines became reminiscent of a village street. Nissen huts housing squadron bars and recreation rooms, equipped with electric light, pianos, tables and chairs were soon erected; the B Squadron bar was known as the B-Hive, and was run by Tpr Edgar Criddle on supplies of wine, not château bottled but quite agreeable, from Bône. Criddle had a flair for writing and producing sketches and plays, and he largely devised and produced several ambitious shows by the B Squadron concert party on the stage set up in the B-Hive; he was also a talented and regular contributor to the *B-Line*, the monthly B Squadron magazine already mentioned. As the malaria season approached, mosquito net, Mepachrine and mosquito repellent cream discipline was tightened up, together with the rolling down of sleeves, changing from shorts to trousers and tucking the trousers into socks or anklets as dusk fell. The female anopheles mosquito nevertheless managed to penetrate these defences, and malaria and other diseases such as dysentery, endemic to the area, took their toll. Contact with the Arabs and their animals brought fleas and lice in its wake, and much use had to be made of AL-63, the disinfesting powder based on DDT.

On 1 June came the news that Tpr R. Nicoll of B Squadron had been awarded the Military Medal and Cpl Muchmore and Tpr Amos of A Squadron the GOC First Army's commendation for their bravery during the final stages of the Tunisian campaign. Lt Jack Dunn of C Squadron was admitted to 5 General Hospital on the 16th, having carelessly shot himself in the foot with a captured German Luger pistol. The battalion was again visited by HM King George VI, accompanied by Sir James Grigg, the Secretary of State for War, on the 18th; 'Looks very fit', was the laconic comment of Reg Heard in his diary entry for that day. The route to the camp from Mondovi was lined by the unit's tanks and crews (**Plate 74**), and the King again drove through the unit lines on his return to Bône. It seemed strange that only three months had elapsed since the 48th had held a similar parade on the occasion of his first visit to the battalion at Hoddom; so much had happened in the interim. On 4 July Lt J.P. MacGregor was posted in from 254th Tank Delivery Squadron and, on the following day, 2Lt J.B.L. Stewart, 2Lt J.M. Cruikshank, 2Lt J.R. Braun and 2Lt T.N. Fowles arrived. Further officer postings occurred in August; Lt C. Olgin was posted to the LAD from 21st Tank Brigade Workshop Company on the 2nd, while on the 6th Lt T. Ainsley, Lt G.W. Isgar

Plate 73   C Squadron officers at Penthièvre. Back row, left to right: Lts Wife, Hunter, More, Thomas, Reynolds. Front row: Capt Dunn (note injured foot), Maj Haigh, Capt Hoad (Ian More)

Plate 74   HM King George VI inspecting the battalion at Penthièvre on 18 June 1943 (IWM)

and 2Lt C. Greenwood arrived in the battalion. On the 10th, Lt G.C. Harvey was posted in from the North Irish Horse in exchange for Lt J.P. MacGregor, and Lt J.C. Dunn was posted out to 6th Battalion, 1 GRTD on the 18th. Apart from the provision of creature comforts such as beds, the battalion now began to occupy itself with training, both physical and mental, and vehicle maintenance. Vehicle maintenance at this time of the year was carried out under difficulties; tools left in the sun for a few minutes could not be handled, and at the height of summer the hulls and turrets of the tanks became unbearably hot. As far as training was concerned, the brigadier was an example of untiring energy and where he led the unit, somewhat wearily, followed. His energy seemed boundless; he organised inter-unit shooting contests (the unit's 30-yard range was opened on 13 June), ran inter-squadron tactical exercises, ran cloth model exercises of hitherto undreamed-of size and scope and even organised a bully-beef competition, to see whose cooks could produce the most palatable dish from the contents of the humble bully-beef tin. Though inwardly groaning at the time, the battalion realised later how much it owed to his keenness and enthusiasm; without them, everyone would have become stale and lazy. As well as the normal training exercises the unit carried out some less usual ones; on one occasion in mid-September the whole battalion marched, in three stages over two days, to the picturesque little fishing village of Herbillon, a distance of 35 miles. Though some fell by the wayside, for under the sweltering sun it was in the nature of an endurance test, with drinking water in the water bottles too hot to drink, most came through the unaccustomed exertion with credit. Three days were spent there, bathing and relaxing, including a swimming gala; then the return march was made in a single night. Also in September, Capt Tony Kingsford, troop leader of B Squadron's 10 Troop, was appointed Adjutant in place of Capt Barry Archer; Lt Martin Savage was the Assistant Adjutant and battalion LO. Capt Ken Reed left the battalion on posting to 272nd Forward Delivery Squadron (part of 21st Tank Brigade), and was replaced by Capt Ian More.

In addition to training, the battalion had its share (some would say more than its share!) of fatigues. It was only to be expected that the Bône Area Commander would cast covetous eyes towards the three tank battalions lying untapped at his doorstep. The tasks allotted to the battalion were many and varied; they unloaded ships in the harbour, sorted stores in the ordnance dump at Mondovi, dug trenches. Squadron commanders tore their hair in desperation as they contemplated the handful of men left over for training each day.

Despite these preoccupations, however, there was still some time for leisure and, if Bône was not completely European in its distractions, it was at least somewhere to go on the weekly day off. There was swimming and bathing for everyone, cinemas, shops and innumerable bars; there was also quite a number of French girls and a sprinkling of British nurses. The weekly day off was, therefore, the signal for another exodus, this time of liberty trucks to stream down the straight, dump-lined road to Bône. In addition, during June and July, the squadrons each enjoyed a week in the Rest Camp in Bône. ENSA provided shows of varying talent and competence, there were cabarets in the NAAFI and the selection of films available in camp, in the Rest Camp, in the town and in the hospitals in the area was such that it was possible to see a different programme on three evenings a week.

In August 1943 a number of bush fires occurred, culminating in a grand conflagration when the cork forests of Ain Mokra burned for a week; the battalion was turned out and rushed to the scene, but the combined efforts of hundreds of soldiers and civilians made little impression on the flames. Early in the month there was a tragic occurrence when members of a B Squadron troop spending a recreational day by the sea got into difficulties in treacherous currents; the troop leader, 2Lt J.M. Cruikshank, and LCpl J. Livingstone lost their lives.

There were, inevitably, more changes of personnel. In October, Lt J.A. (Jim) Trueman was posted to 142nd Regiment RAC, in November Capt M. Goldby was posted to the RAC School, North Africa, and the former Adjutant, Capt Barry Archer, left to attend Middle East Junior Staff Course No 8, while, in December, Capt (Po-Po) Chambers was posted out to No 5 AFV Maintenance Section RAC; his successor as 2IC of A Squadron was Capt R.B. (Brian) Achurch. The following day 2Lt R.J.L. Scott, 2Lt W.J.E Jones, 2Lt M.G. Reaney and 2Lt P.L. Buckley joined the battalion from 254th Tank Delivery Squadron. On 20 December, Lt Col Brooks left to attend a course in the Middle East, leaving the 2IC in command, and on the 23rd Captain Reed went to Le Khroub to inspect the US M3A3 light tank, with a view to assessing its suitability as a Recce Troop vehicle in place of the Bren carrier. On the entertainment front, the battalion received two visits from Army bands in December; on the 15th the band of the 53rd Training Regiment RAC played in the HQ Squadron canteen and on the 21st the RTR band played in the camp.

With the advent of the New Year, significant changes in battalion headquarters took place;

Plate 75   The battalion Christmas greetings airgraph for 1943 (Roger Blankley)

on 4 January 1944 the 2IC, Maj John Mennell, left for Algiers en route to the Middle East Staff College as a student. As the CO was still in the Middle East and the 2IC had been commanding the battalion in his absence, the latter's departure meant that command of the battalion now devolved upon Maj C.H. (Charles) Crowther, the commander of HQ Squadron. On the same day the Brigade Commander, Brig T. Ivor-Moore, MC, paid his farewell visit to the battalion on his appointment as Brigadier RAC, Eighth Army. Maj J.D. ('Stylo') Styles returned briefly to the battalion from the RAC Training Depot on the 11th, assuming command the following day. On the 21st came the publication of Maj Robson's Mention in Despatches, while, on the 27th, Lt Col Brooks returned from his course and reassumed command. The battalion's third Churchill ARV Mk I was received on the 28th, to complete the battalion's establishment of three, one to each tank squadron. Driving and maintenance courses on the Stuart light tank started on 1 February at the RAC Training Depôt, the first being attended by Lt Ian More.

The most significant event to occur in the battalion in March 1944 was the posting of Lt Col Gerry Brooks on promotion to colonel, as 2IC of 25th Army Tank Brigade; Col Gerry had been in command of the battalion for just over three years and, in that time, he had led it from a rather unorthodox Territorial unit to an efficient fighting battalion. His success was due, for the most part, to his outstanding ability as a trainer and leader of men. Apart from his purely military abilities, he was held in the greatest affection and respect by all ranks; possessed of a most youthful mind and body, he was as at home commanding the battalion in the field as he was at a WOs' and Sergeants' Mess party. It was with the very greatest regret, therefore, that the battalion said farewell to him; he was succeeded, on 14 April, by Lt Col John Loveday of the 16th/5th Lancers, promoted for the purpose from his previous appointment as Brigade Major of 21st Tank Brigade. After only four days in command of the 48th, he was unfortunately called to take over command of his own regiment, and was later killed in action while commanding it. There was then a hiatus in which the battalion was without either CO or 2IC, and Maj Charles Crowther, commanding HQ Squadron, again assumed temporary command.

The other main HQ Squadron appointments at this time were filled by Capt (QM) 'Eggy' Eggleton (Quartermaster), Lt Deric Skey (Intelligence Officer), Lt Ian More (who had replaced Capt Ken Reed as OC Recce Troop), Capt Tom Bruce (OC Intercomm Troop), Capt Eric Gilmour RAMC (MO), Capt Archie Scott-Gardner CF (Padre), Capt Geoff Thompson, MC (BTA), Capt Tony Kingsford (Adjutant), Capt Maurice Ladd (2IC HQ Squadron), Capt Martin Savage (Assistant Adjutant and LO), WO1 E.T. Fell (RSM), WO2 Vaughan (RQMS, formerly SSM of A Squadron) and Sgt Hector McIver (Provost Sergeant). The Orderly Room was under the hand of Sgt George Adamson as ORS, with the now Sgt Hopkinson, Cpl Sparkes, LCpl Virgo and Tpr Elsdon as his staff; the ORQMS, WO2 Tobias, was in Algiers at 2nd Echelon.

Despite all the changes and distractions, boredom was the worst enemy with which CO and squadron commanders had had to contend during the closing months of 1943. The unit was trained for war, had been blooded and yet somehow, it seemed, the battle eluded it. It is difficult to keep a unit at concert pitch for too long; furthermore there were disquieting rumours that the Eighth Army, having triumphed in Sicily and being now engaged on the

*Plate 76 Lt Col J.W.R. Loveday,
16th/5th Lancers, who commanded the
48th for only a few weeks before leaving
to take command of the 16th/5th Lancers
(John Mennell)*

Italian mainland, held a poor opinion of the Churchill tank. Impressed with the success of the Sherman tank in the desert, it was said that they despised the allegedly slower Churchill with its smaller 6pdr gun. To find out the truth or otherwise of such statements, it was decided to conduct a comparative trial of both tanks, in North Africa. The trial took place, under arrangements made by 1st Armoured Division, at Bou Farik, south of Algiers, on 6 December 1943, and involved:

> (i) Climbing a scrub-covered hill of medium gradient.
> (ii) Traversing the side of a hill intersected by small wadis.
> (iii) Climbing a steep hill on firm ground.
> (iv) Climbing up a steep bank out of a wadi.
> (v) Traversing heavy plough on dry going.

The course was about one mile in length. Tests were carried out again on 11 December, after 24 hours' rain.

The conclusions, in the report by the Brigadier RAC at Allied Force HQ, were that:

> (i) Over difficult country in dry weather the Churchill is slightly faster and more manoeuvrable than the Sherman.
> (ii) Their obstacle-crossing capacity is about the same and there is, in fact, very little to choose between them.
> (iii) Heavy mud is impassable by either tank.

While the battalion is resting, it might be appropriate here to describe briefly the US M4 medium tank, otherwise known as the Sherman (**Plate 78**), particularly as the 48th and other infantry tank units in the Mediterranean theatre were partially re-equipped with it in the spring of 1944. Its main advantage over the Churchill, and indeed over every other British tank of the period, was its 75mm gun. Not only was its calibre 18mm greater than the 57mm of the Churchill's 6pdr gun, giving it a heavier armour-piercing shot but, because of its greater calibre, it also fired a very useful high explosive shell. At this time the 6pdr had no HE shell, although one was about to enter production; but even when it became available, it would not pack the punch of a 75mm shell. Another advantage of the Sherman over the Churchill was its external gun mantlet, which gave better ballistic protection than the internal mantlet of the Churchill. In most other respects the two tanks were broadly comparable, although the Sherman caught fire more easily when penetrated; to such an extent, indeed, that it was known to the Germans as the 'Tommy cooker'. Several marks were produced during this tank's production life and details varied according to mark; the average weight was 30 tonnes, maximum road speed 25mph, road cruising range 120 miles and it carried a crew of five men. A total of 49,200 Shermans was produced between February 1942 and June 1945, in 10 factories.

Partly to improve the firepower and partly the turret protection of the Churchill, while at the same time removing any Eighth Army criticism of the Churchill's main armament, an officer of 21st Tank Troops Workshop at Le Khroub had the idea, at the end of 1943, of replacing the 6pdr gun and internal mantlet of the Churchill IV with the 75mm gun and external mantlet of the Sherman. Not only would this reduce the vulnerability of the Churchill's gun mantlet and eliminate a natural aiming point for enemy gunners, but it would also provide the Churchill with the HE round that it so badly lacked. His calculations proved the modification to be feasible, and he was accordingly given permission to modify one tank. Range trials with this prototype showed that the Churchill provided not only a steadier firing platform than the Sherman but also a longer range. Orders were therefore given for a rework programme to be started as a matter of urgency at 16th Base Workshop REME at Bône and, in the three months to June 1944, nearly 200 tanks were converted. The battalion was equipped with some in Italy the following year; they were known as the 'Tank, Infantry, Churchill IV (NA75)', and one is shown in **Plate 83**.

An even more disconcerting rumour concerning the brigade's future rôle alleged that it was to be converted to infantry, to make good the heavy losses being incurred in Italy. This rumour seemed to be confirmed when the commander of 21st Tank Brigade, Brig T. Ivor-Moore, MC, was replaced by Brig C.E.A. Firth, DSO, an infantryman who, according to his obituary in the *Daily Telegraph* of 17 October 1991, 'wished to convert [the Brigade] to infantry – more suitable to the terrain. But as it was equipped with Churchill tanks the Prime Minister objected'. This story might not be true as, in a post-war conversation with Maj Maurice Ladd, Brig Firth claimed that he had pleaded successfully for the brigade not to be converted. Whatever the truth of the matter, to the battalion all now seemed lost and there was nothing it could now do but await its fate.

The brigade had now severed its connection with 4th Division and had once more regained its independence as an Army tank brigade; there was, however, one more service to be performed for its former formation. After 4th Division had moved to Egypt for amphibious training, the brigade sent parties to dispose of its equipment at Bougie; this rather disrupted the battalion's Christmas plans, but at least those at Bougie enjoyed an unlimited supply of wine. While thus employed there, the battalion received the long-awaited news: it was to keep its tanks and would move to Italy with 21st Army Tank Brigade. To its very great relief Brig Firth would not move with them; he was to be replaced by Brig David Dawnay, DSO, a Regular officer of the 10th Hussars and until recently CO of the North Irish Horse in 25th Army Tank Brigade.

As the New Year opened, it found the battalion undertaking vehicle convoy and ferrying duties; although the tanks had been used on a number of exercises they had latterly become of only secondary interest. However, in January 1944 Recce Troop, now commanded by Lt Ian More, former commander of 14 Troop in C Squadron, acquired 16 used US M3 light tanks (otherwise known as the General Stuart, the Stuart or, colloquially, the Honey) from No 4 Vehicle Park in Bône; previously in US service, these tanks had been abandoned at Kasserine and were to replace the Recce Troop's carriers. Eleven carriers were returned to the Bône vehicle park and, of the 11 Honeys replacing them, permission was given to remove the turrets from all except four. Much time was spent in cleaning them, as they were received in a very poor state. Recce Troop at this time was organised into a HQ section of two vehicles, commanded by Lt More in a turreted Honey and his 2IC, Sgt Eric Potter, in a turretless one, and three sections, each commanded by a corporal in a turreted Honey and with two turretless vehicles in addition.

April saw renewed attention, which rapidly developed into feverish activity and preparation, being paid to the heavier tanks; on 30 April 1944 they were loaded on board ship at Bône and, on the following day, the battalion sailed for Italy, the vehicles following in a later convoy.

CHAPTER 5

Italy
(1944–45)

The battalion's move to Italy was uneventful; not that it was dull or without incident, but it arrived at its destination without interference from the enemy. It is difficult to pick out any highlights from the move so long after the event. Naturally everyone was delighted to be leaving Africa at long last for a country about which they had heard so much, and which was at least on the Continent of Europe; the majority at least was looking forward to resuming a more active part in the war. The 48th had loaded its tanks at Bône on 30 April, and the personnel embarked there the following day, on the SS *Christian Huygens*, after an orgy of farewell parties. Messes, which had taken so long to build and which had been the object of so much inter-squadron and inter-unit rivalry, were smashed to the ground and, soon after the battalion left, it would be almost impossible to tell that some 800 souls had spent nine months of their lives on that solitary hillside. On 1 May the *Christian Huygens* pulled out into Bône bay on its voyage to Naples, having been preceded there by an advance party under Maj Robson; the tanks were to follow in a later convoy and Maj Haigh, with the rear party, was to bring up the rear on the SS *Durban Castle* on 14 May.

Next morning, Sicily stood on the port beam and the Straits of Messina were safely negotiated that night. On the morning of 3 May, the *Christian Huygens* stood off Naples, with the rails thronged with men eager to get their first glimpse of Italy. Forty miles out, the vessel had passed through a thick smokescreen from the eruption of Vesuvius and, by the time the ship docked, the upper deck was covered in a layer of volcanic ash; when it emerged from the smoke, Vesuvius could be seen to be belching large columns of smoke and ash 1,000 feet into the air.

Like most ports, Naples is flattered when seen from the sea: the sweep of the bay, the turquoise of the sea and Vesuvius, billowing smoke, was a sight to be treasured, although the saying 'see Naples and die' was unfortunately to be literally true for many of those seeing it before the war's end. The spell was soon broken when, after the sweaty and confusing business of disembarkation had been completed, the men were piled into the hot lorries and bounced through the dusty and potholed streets of a very smelly Naples and along the straight Caserta road to the transit camp at Afragola, in a hot and dusty olive grove. The monotonous routine of camp life began yet again.

The tanks, meanwhile, had landed at Taranto, far away in the 'heel' of Italy; complicated arrangements were therefore needed to reunite them with their unit. Three days later, on 6 May, the unit sent a party there by rail, via Salerno and Metaponto, to collect them; all tanks had been taken over and crewed by the 15th and they then proceeded, either by transporter or rail, to join the remainder of the battalion. This was an impressive journey through Bari and Foggia to Lucera, near to which the battalion was now located and to which it had moved on 8 May. Lucera was nearer to the front, and the battalion could not be unaware of the tremendous battle then being fought at Cassino, not very far away. Formation signs appeared everywhere in profusion, telephone wires hung from every tree still standing, staff cars nosed their way past in a cloud of dust and rusting shell cases littered every olive

Map 5   Battalion moves in Italy

grove in untidy heaps. The new CO, Lt Col A.O. Hutchinson, a miller and maltster in civilian life, arrived on 15 May from the 51st Battalion RTR, where he had been 2IC; he soon earned the soubriquet 'Flash Harry' in the battalion and was not to last two months in the appointment. The battalion's new 2IC was Maj C.R. (Charles) Spencer, a 12th Lancer who soon became known as 'Two-Minute' Spencer from his habit of saying that any task given him would take two minutes to complete.

The unit had been given only until 11 June to be action-ready, and the intervening three weeks were taken up with reorganisation to the new War Establishment and the re-training entailed by partial re-equipment with Shermans, which also started to arrive on the 15th of the month. Squadrons were now reduced from five troops to four, each of three tanks. Initially, two Shermans were incorporated into each troop, together with two Churchills, but this was found to be less efficient than having two all-Sherman and two all-Churchill troops per squadron. In theory, the Churchills were intended for the assault rôle and the Shermans for fire support, although in practice little distinction was made between them. It might have been thought that the Shermans, being vastly easier to maintain and operate, would have been the more popular with the crews; this was not the case, however, many preferring the Churchill for its superior armour protection. Squadron HQs were issued with the Churchill V (CS), armed with the 95mm howitzer.

On 24 May Recce Troop received eleven brand-new Honeys, four with and the remainder without turrets (as explained in the previous chapter), but with many extras; the main armament of the turretless tanks was a 0.5in Browning heavy machine gun, mounted on the turret ring.

Plate 77 Brigadier David Dawney DSO, commander of 21 Tank Brigade 1944/5 (Author's collection)

Plate 78   A typical M4 Sherman tank (Author's collection)

Some were modified by the addition of rails on top of the hull to carry stretchers. The Honey, officially known in British service as the Stuart, was the American M3 light tank, issued in both turreted and turretless versions to the reconnaissance troops of infantry tank battalions in Italy (**Plate 79**). It carried a crew of four men in the turreted version, weighed about 14 tonnes and was armed with a 37mm gun and two or three 0.30in Browning machine guns. It had a road range of some 70 miles and a maximum speed of 36mph.

As part of the reorganisation, B Squadron's 9 Troop was disbanded, but otherwise the squadron continued the custom of numbering its troops from 6 to 10, following on from A Squadron, whose troops had formerly been numbered from 1 to 5 and were now numbered 1 to 4 by combining 4 and 5 Troops. C Squadron, on the other hand, whose troop numbers had previously followed on from those of B Squadron, starting with 11 Troop, renumbered its troops from 1 to 4. Training exercises again became the order of the day, and of these 'Gremlin' was the most notable; naturally the unit chafed at the delay in getting into operations again, but it was necessary as both terrain and tactics were so different from those encountered in Tunisia.

It was presumably this exercise, together with the brigade commander's desire to have a flash which showed that the brigade was under new management, which inspired the redesigned 21st Tank Brigade flash. The original flash, it will be remembered, had been a standard Army tank brigade diabolo in dark blue (in felt, on uniform sleeves); the new one, introduced at about this time, was designed by Capt Tom Gorringe of A Squadron, retaining the blue diabolo in a lighter shade but with a red gremlin twined round it, on a circular yellow ground, the whole embroidered in silk. Capt Maurice Ladd had these flashes made up

Plate 79   Turreted and turretless Honeys of Recce Troop, with crews (Tony Kingsford)

by a silk factory near Caserta from the original Gorringe drawing; they were issued in pairs, one right- and one left-hand, to be worn on both uniform sleeves with the gremlin facing forwards. Stencils were made up for painting the flash on unit vehicles. At about the same time, the coloured epaulette strips of the RTR battalions were reintroduced, the 48th's colours being yellow (top) and black (bottom). One final change in the signing of tank units of 21st Tank Brigade resulted from the brigade again becoming independent; the unit tactical numbers once more became 173, 174 and 175, instead of the 67, 68 and 69 allotted when the brigade had formed part of 4th (Mixed) Division. Now, however, this number was carried in white on a square in the Royal Armoured Corps colours of red and yellow, rather than the earlier brown, the square being divided horizontally into two halves of which the upper was yellow and the lower, red. The 48th was allotted '174' until 145th Regiment RAC was disbanded in early 1945 and replaced by the North Irish Horse, when, as the junior battalion of the brigade, it was renumbered '175'.

The months of July and August could be considered as the calm before the storm. Apart from training exercises, a considerable amount of sport was played and several entertainments were arranged for the troops: for instance, on 14 July the Canadian Corps military band visited and performed, on the 25th the band of the Royal Canadian Armoured Corps did likewise and on the 31st HM King George VI paid the battalion his third visit in less than 18 months. On 2 August another military band arrived, this time the band of the Royal Canadian Army Service Corps, and on the 20th the battalion was entertained by 'Rapid Fire', a Canadian concert party. The Army commander visited the battalion on 16 August, to wish it well before it again went into action later in the month.

Plate 80 The new formation sign of 21 Tank Brigade, introduced in the summer of 1944 (Author's collection)

The Italian campaign had started on 3 September 1943, when troops of the Eighth Army had crossed the Straits of Messina and established themselves on the toe of the Italian mainland at Reggio/Calabria; Italy capitulated, and the Axis forces withdrew before the Eighth Army, who were thus able to make very rapid progress through the mountainous country of Apulia. Six days later, on 9 September, the US Fifth Army assaulted the beaches of Salerno, breaking out of the beachhead on the 29th and capturing the city of Naples. Taranto, Brindisi and Bari were soon also in Allied hands, and by 8 November the Eighth Army had reached the River Sangro. The end of 1943 found the Fifth and Eighth Armies stretched across Italy from Tortona to the River Garigliano.

The winter rains that year had come with a vengeance. Most of the roads were not built to take heavy Army traffic and collapsed in the wet weather, while the fields would no longer support the weight of a vehicle; and the country in which the fighting was now taking place was broken and mountainous. On 22 January 1944, therefore, an attempt was made to turn the flank of the Axis defensive positions by landing the 6th (US) Corps at Anzio, some 30 miles south of Rome. The German forces, however, managed to contain the Allied landing within the beachhead until the end of May, when 6th (US) Corps finally managed to break out. Meanwhile, the Germans, far from relinquishing their hold along the Garigliano, constructed two formidable lines of defence. The most forward was known as the Gustav Line, and stretched from Cassino along the Garigliano to Gaeta. Behind this lay the second, the Adolf Hitler Line, in the Liri valley, the most practicable route to Rome, the entrance to which is dominated by the 1,500ft high Monte Cassino. When 21st Tank Brigade and its component battalions sailed for Naples from Bône on 1 May 1944, the Allied forces were held up on the Gustav Line, although planning to break through it very shortly.

On 5 June Rome fell to the Allies and on the 6th the Allied invasion of Normandy started. The battalion again began to wonder if it would all be over before they got into action again. On the 19th, however, 21st Tank Brigade was placed under the command of 1st (Cdn) Corps, which was then resting, and thus began an association that was to ripen into a firm friendship in the desperate battles for the Gothic Line which were yet to come. Throughout the early summer, however, training and waiting continued to be the unit's lot; gradually the fascination of a new country began to pall, so that it was with genuine delight that the order to move forward was received at the end of July. The actual move took several days, by which time the brigade had been left far behind. It was with some relief that the battalion, in early August, 'got in front of the Eighth Army Mobile Laundry and Bath Unit', as one member of the unit succinctly put it.

By the end of August, the battle for the Gothic Line had begun in earnest, and it is perhaps appropriate here to say something about the country over which the battle was being fought. In this area, the Apennines fall away at right angles to the sea and there is hardly any coastal plain; thus an advancing army is faced with a series of steep, razor-backed ridges across its front, with a river between each pair. The country is ideal for defence and particularly suited to the German delaying tactics; with a minimum number of defending troops he could hold up the Allies until they were forced to deploy at least a brigade, with tank and artillery support, to dislodge him, whereupon he withdrew to the next ridge and the sequence started again. In fact this part of Italy was not tank country, tanks being used more as mobile pill-boxes in support of the infantry rather than as armoured spearheads, with infantry in support, in the exploitation of breakthrough.

The campaign in Italy was complicated and the detail makes confusing and slow reading to anyone unfamiliar with it. It will be easier to follow, therefore, if the campaign as a whole is covered in outline only, while the operations in which 21st Tank Brigade and its component tank units were involved are dealt with in four phases.

The first phase (25 August to 21 September 1944) covers the operation for the breaking of the Gothic Line, including the capture of Rimini and the forming of a bridgehead over the River Marecchia. The second phase (11 October 1944 to 12 January 1945) covers the advance into the River Po plain up Route 9, culminating in the capture of Ravenna and the forming of a general line on the River Senio. Phase three (12 January to 1 April 1945) covers the holding of the winter line, including minor operations in the area south of Lake Comacchio. Finally, phase four (1–30 April 1945) covers the offensive across the River Reno and River Senio, the forcing of the Argenta Gap and the crossing of the River Po and the River Adige.

Phase 1 – The Breaking of the Gothic Line

21st Tank Brigade was now commanded by Brig David Dawnay, DSO (**Plate 77**), who had, until recently, been CO of the North Irish Horse in 25th Tank Brigade; command of the 48th had, from 30 July, been assumed by Lt Col E.H. ('Ted') Tinker (**Plate 81**) of the 13th/18th Hussars. On 18 August Capt Tony Kingsford had been posted to C Squadron, his place as Adjutant being filled by Capt Martin Savage.

At the beginning of August, the battalion had moved up to the Spoleto area, some by rail and some by transporter. On 22 August it started a series of road moves and cross-country

Plate 81   Lt Col E.H. Tinker, who commanded the battalion from July to 7 Dec 1944 (Mrs E.J. Tinker)

marches which were to continue for more than a week until the Adriatic sector of the Gothic Line was reached. For this phase, 21st Tank Brigade was operating under command of 1st Canadian Infantry Division throughout, with the 12th Battalion RTR under command of 1st Canadian Infantry Brigade, 145th Regiment RAC under 2nd Canadian Infantry Brigade and the 48th, under command of 3rd Canadian Infantry Brigade, in reserve. Within 3rd Canadian Infantry Brigade, A Squadron was grouped initially with the Royal 22nd Regiment (the 'Van Doos'), B with the Carleton and York Regiment and C with the West Nova Scotia Regiment.

The plan was for the 1st Canadian Infantry Division assault across the River Metauro, with 21st Tank Brigade under command, to be made at 1.00pm on 25 August; this assault was to be on a two-brigade front, with 1st Brigade on the right and 2nd Brigade on the left, the objective being the high ground south of Mombaroccio. Tanks were to cross the river one hour before first light on the 26th, six hours after the infantry assault. The task of 3rd Brigade, with our battalion under command, was to pass through 1st Brigade to assault across the River Foglia.

All personnel and vehicles had a hard and wearying journey to the concentration area. The roads were mountainous, winding and with steep gradients and, owing to bad weather in the initial stages, tanks were compelled to move long distances on their tracks, sometimes pulling transporters behind them up particularly difficult slippery hills; in addition, most moves had to be made at night, for reasons of security. Some idea of the problems faced by the 48th is given in this extract from the souvenir edition of the *B-Line*:

August 22nd: Squadron moves to Spoleto and loads on transporters. August 23rd:

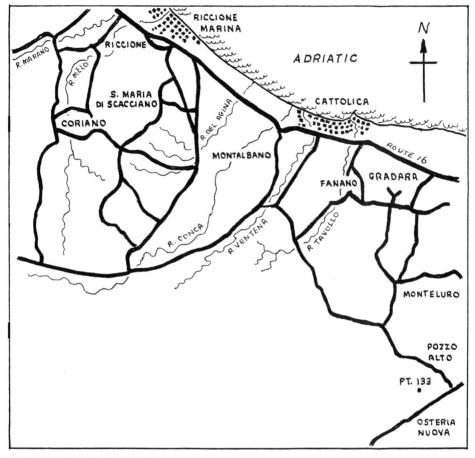

Map 6   Breaking the Gothic Line

Transporter convoy leaves Spoleto 02.30 hours, arriving Jesi at 16.00 hours. August 24th: At midnight the tanks accomplish a five-hour run, harbour at dawn, and, as night falls, move on another eight miles. August 26th: The approach continues. August 27th: The River Metauro is crossed in the course of a night march through overwhelming dust. Twelve miles covered in twelve hours. August 29th: More miles added as a cross-country run is performed in the dusk. August 30th: Twelve miles covered in the afternoon. The River Foglia was crossed on August 31st . . . On the same day two of the Squadron's tanks went up on mines. A foretaste of the opposition to come was furnished by heavy stonking by German mortars, which continued throughout the night.

21st Tank Brigade report *Operations in Italy, August 1944 – May 1945* says:

Great credit is due to the transporter companies and to the tank crews themselves for overcoming all difficulties and for achieving this concentration up to time. But the effects of this move were evident in the number of tanks which had mechanical breakdowns in the early days of the attack.

Plate 82   Battalion orderly room staff at Spoleto in August 1944. Standing, left to right: Sgt Adamson, Tpr Elsdon, Sgt Hopkinson, LCpl Sparkes. Seated: LCpl Virgo (Tony Kingsford)

On 29 August, 3rd Canadian Infantry Brigade, supported by the battalion now up to War Establishment in Churchill (42), Sherman (18) and Stuart (11) tanks, took over the divisional front; on the 30th, A Squadron was again the first into action, as it had been in North Africa, when it supported the West Nova Scotia Regiment in its crossing of the River Foglia. A Squadron's two Churchill troops were 1 Troop (commanded by Lt Reaney) and 3 Troop (commanded by Lt C.R.G. (Chris) Hutchinson); the Sherman troops were 2 Troop (commanded by Lt Rowell) and 4 Troop (commanded by Lt Tom Gorringe). Apart from a certain amount of mortaring and shelling, no great difficulty was encountered, although the squadron lost one OR killed and one wounded, as well as one tank disabled, in the action; by the 31st the brigade was over the river and A Squadron was stood down and rallied back to the battalion at about 5.30pm.

Early on the morning of the 31st, B Squadron was next into action, when it was switched to the support of 2nd Canadian Infantry Brigade. The reason for this switch was that resistance in the Gothic Line was weaker than expected and it was therefore essential to push on at once rather than wait to mount a set-piece attack. B Squadron was to support the

Princess Patricia's Canadian Light Infantry (PPCLI) attack on Point 133, a spur which dominated the River Foglia; 145th Regiment RAC, who normally worked with 2nd Brigade, was not yet forward and immediate tank support was required. Despite mines, on which two tanks were lost, and well dug-in enemy infantry and snipers, the attack was successful and by the evening Canadian troops were installed on the objective. At this time, B Squadron's 6 and 8 Troops (commanded by Lt Bruce Cottrell and Lt Henry Palmer, respectively) were equipped with Shermans and 7 and 10 Troops (commanded by Lt Braun and Lt Greenwood, respectively) had Churchills. Squadron HQ had both Churchill IVs and Churchill Vs, the latter being a close support tank armed with the new 95mm howitzer. By this time, 6pdr HE rounds had at last become available, although they were not as effective as those of the Sherman 75mm gun.

During the afternoon of 1 September, the battalion, less B Squadron, moved across the River Foglia to an area east of Osteria Nuova, on the lateral road (Route 3) beyond the river, where it received orders to capture Pieve, five miles to the north; it was to move as soon as possible, picking up a company of the Royal 22nd Regiment on the way. Enemy resistance was now unexpectedly light, so an attempt was to be made to break through with speed and push up the coast to Rimini. As time was short and speed essential, A Squadron was ordered to go straight to Pieve followed by C Squadron, which was to contact and pick up the infantry and hand them on to A Squadron on arrival at Pieve. C Squadron was then to pass through A Squadron and capture Gradara, a walled castle and village on a hill 2,550 yards to the north. A Squadron moved off with 3 Troop leading at about 01.30am, reaching Pieve at

Plate 83   C Squadron Churchill IV (NA75) and crew. Left to right: Sgt Camp, Cpl Wood, Maj Haigh, 'Taxi' Steele, Tpr Yeo (Don Hoad)

about 04.00am on 2 September. While leading through the village, Lt Hutchinson's tank was hit and caught fire, Lt Hutchinson being captured; other casualties were two ORs killed and two wounded. After a considerable amount of fire had been brought to bear on the anti-tank gun responsible by the Shermans of 4 Troop, Cpl Jupp of 4 Troop got right into the village, dismounted with his Thompson sub-machine gun, took two prisoners and reported the way clear for C Squadron. As a result of his bravery in this action, Cpl Jupp was later awarded the Military Medal. A Squadron then took up supporting positions on the high ground to the east of the village, where it remained until leaguering back at dusk.

C Squadron meanwhile had orders to get through to Gradara in order to take the high ground dominating Route 16, the main coast road. By 04.00am its infantry had been mounted and the squadron moved off. As a result of one tank slipping off the track and three others breaking tracks, however, it was unable to put in its attack at first light, as had been planned, and had instead to mount it in daylight. Quick action by the infantry after they had dismounted soon cleared Pieve and the advance on Gradara continued; after two tanks had been hit by anti-tank gun fire and a third by mortar fire, however, it was clear that Gradara was held in some strength and, being a walled town, could not be taken by tanks alone. Maj Haigh therefore ordered the squadron to withdraw to the high ground dominating the approaches to the town. Casualties in this action were: one officer killed (Lt Peter Reynolds) and one wounded (Lt Isgar), two ORs killed and three wounded, one Churchill destroyed and one Sherman damaged.

The main Gothic Line, and the Monte Luro feature behind it, had now been overrun and

Plate 84   A dug-in Panther tank turret, part of the Gothic Line defences (Deric Skey)

Plate 85   Part of the Gothic Line, showing trees felled and buildings demolished to give clear fields of fire for Panther tank turrets dug in on the ridge to the left of the photograph (Deric Skey)

the Adriatic coast was reached at Cattolica early on 3 September. The same day, with the aim of advancing along the coast with all speed, a composite squadron consisting of three troops of Shermans (2 and 4 Troops of A Squadron and 2 Troop of C) and one Churchill troop (1 Troop of C Squadron) was formed under the command of Maj Haigh, with Capt Kingsford as 2IC; Squadron HQ was made up of one Churchill from HQ Squadron, together with one Churchill and one Sherman of C Squadron. Also under command were two companies of the Hastings and Prince Edward Regiment, two troops of M10 (Wolverine) SP 3in anti-tank guns from 111th SP Regiment Royal Canadian Artillery, and our own Recce Troop, commanded by Capt Ian More. On call through a forward observation officer (FOO) was one battery of Priest 105mm guns of 24th Field Regiment (SP) RA. The aim of this force was to push north-west along the main coast road to Rimini; enemy resistance was reported to be slight as he pulled back to Rimini, pausing only long enough to blow the bridges en route.

At 10.00am on 3 September this force moved forward, and by about 2.00pm its forward elements were some 3,000 yards beyond the River Conca, with further progress impeded by a blown bridge. In efforts to find a way round the obstacle, one Honey of Recce Troop was destroyed by a defiladed anti-tank gun; a hail of mortar and machine gun fire, which wounded Lt Mike Trueman in the arm and hand, prevented further movement by the remainder. Attempts to outflank this position during the afternoon were unsuccessful, so plans were made for an advance on the village of San Maria: in the failing evening light, however, direction was lost and fire twice brought down on friendly forces. The advance was therefore called off and the tanks brought back to harbour. Casualties in this action had been four ORs missing, believed killed, and one officer (Lt Trueman) wounded. One Honey was destroyed.

At 07.30am the following morning, the composite squadron came under command of the Hastings and Prince Edward Regiment, who planned to advance along Route 16 and attack the village of San Maria Scacciano. Meanwhile, at 07.00am on the same day, B Squadron was placed under command of the 48th Highlanders of Canada, who were to be prepared to exploit through the composite squadron on the capture of San Maria. Paratroops on the San Maria ridge put up a fanatical defence; the country south-west of Rimini was excellent defensive country, and our advance was finally held up on the River Mela. In the dry weather prevailing at this time, neither this river nor the River Marano presented much of an obstacle in themselves, but the enemy held strong defensive positions on the high ground beyond them, from which they could dominate the battlefield.

The composite squadron's action was inconclusive; enemy machine gun and sniper fire was so intense that its accompanying infantry was pinned down, with heavy casualties. Although tanks managed to get into the village there was not, by this time, enough infantry left to clear it; as a result, Lt David Thomas (2 Troop, C Squadron) was killed by sniper fire and his tank put out of action by a *Faustpatrone* (the German equivalent of the bazooka) and Lt Hunter's steel helmet was pierced by a sniper's bullet, which luckily only creased his forehead. Capt Ian More, commander of Recce Troop, was severely wounded in the shoulder by a mortar bomb while taking cover under his Honey, and his gunner, Tpr Wilkinson, was killed. The command of Recce Troop was taken over by Lt K.M. (Max) Hunter, promoted to acting captain for the purpose, on 8 September. Lt T.S. (Tom) Bruce had meanwhile been appointed Assistant Adjutant and battalion LO on the 5th of the month.

The tanks were eventually called back at 9.30pm to their harbour of the previous night; casualties were one officer (Lt Thomas) and three ORs killed and one officer (Capt More) and seven ORs wounded. One Churchill and three Shermans had been destroyed. In this attack the opposing forward aid posts were within 50 yards of each other; between the two walked a German doctor under protection of the Red Cross, tending the wounded of both sides. Throughout the day the Padre, Capt D.E.A. (Archie) Scott-Gardner, was in the thickest of the fighting in the village, tending the wounded without any regard for his own safety. Cyril Edwards has this to say about him:

> . . . a real exponent of muscular Christianity, whose 8cwt, flying a red cross (sometimes) appeared in places no soft-skinned vehicle should be at. It was thought by many that he must have been as well known to the German paratroopers, who seemed to oppose us most of the way up the Italian peninsula, as he was to ourselves. [There are] several references in the War Diary to his visiting enemy positions to check on our wounded and/or prisoners.

He received a well-earned Military Cross for his actions in this campaign. The Medical Officer, Capt I.E.W. (Eric) Gilmour RAMC, also did sterling work, as did the Regimental Aid Post staff.

Meanwhile, the task of B Squadron and the 48th Highlanders of Canada was to exploit from San Maria to the River Marano; however, as already described, the village proved more difficult than expected and, despite the call for speed by the commander of 21st Tank Brigade, the exploitation was delayed. An indecisive action ensued, in which a night infiltration of the village by both tanks and infantry was attempted during the night of 4/5 September, and much sniping by tanks, SP guns and small arms of both sides took place. After an inconclusive series of engagements the fight was broken off at 3.00pm and the battalion pulled out for rest and reorganisation.

During B Squadron's inconclusive battle for San Maria, the composite squadron was ordered to be ready at 06.00am on 5 September to assist the Hastings and Prince Edward Regiment to attack and capture Ceccarini. During the night of 4/5 September, tank and personnel replacements had been received from 272nd Forward Delivery Squadron, and B Squadron now consisted of:

Squadron HQ	2 Churchills
1 Troop (Lt Reaney, A Sqn)	3 Churchills
3 Troop (Capt Harvey, A Sqn)	3 Churchills
5 Troop (Lt Buckley, C Sqn)	3 Churchills
2 Troop (Lt Rowell, A Sqn)	3 Shermans
4 Troop (Lt Gorringe, A Sqn)	3 Shermans

Thus the squadron enjoyed a return to the earlier five-troop organisation, and moved out of harbour at 04.30am with 11 Churchills and six Shermans.

The attack began according to plan and encountered no opposition; in almost no time the tanks were in a position to bring fire down on the objective, which they did with considerable effect until they saw the Royal Canadian Regiment moving up to it on their right. It transpired that, even before the attack had commenced, Ceccarini had been in our hands; this was not the first time that information about our own troops had been less than satisfactory, due presumably to the fluid nature of the operations and the reluctance of commanders to notify higher formations without delay, when otherwise engaged, of the positions of their forward elements. The squadron was therefore pulled back a short way and settled down to breakfast. However, at 08.45am it was on the move again, this time to help B Squadron, held up by the enemy's forward positions in the area of Point 70 (San Andrea). It was tasked to do this by supporting the 48th Highlanders in an attack towards San Lorenzo in Strada on Route 16, the main coast road; unfortunately, in attempting to move up to give fire support to the Highlanders, who were held up short of the objective by heavy mortar and machine gun fire, one tank of 5 Troop became bogged in a stream crossing its route and no alternative way over this obstacle could be found.

The squadron therefore finally harboured back for the night. The harbour area had, however, been subjected to heavy and accurate mortar fire during the day and the tanks had accordingly dispersed. Collecting them together again and bringing them back into harbour in the dark was no easy matter and it was midnight before all the flock had been gathered in; even then, one Sherman of 2 Troop overturned completely when it slipped off the track coming into harbour and it was left for the night standing on its turret. By now the squadron was very tired after four days and nights with very little sleep, but it bedded down in its slit trenches and under the tanks, content in the near promise of the brigade commander that it would be withdrawn for a rest as from that night. The action that day had cost the squadron no casualties in either men or tanks.

The following morning, 6 September, the squadron was formed up ready to move back for its promised rest. At 12.00 noon, however, Maj Haigh relayed over the wireless the orders he had earlier received at Battalion HQ, for two Churchill troops (3 and 5 Troops) to remain in their present location for a further task; the rest of the squadron was to return, a troop at a time at 15-minute intervals, to the new battalion harbour area at San Maria. These troops began to move at 1.00pm.

3 and 5 Troops moved back to their location of the previous night, but their attack was not due to go in until 4.00pm. The aim was to restore the situation on the 48th Highlanders' front, disrupted by an enemy counter-attack the previous night. In the event, the Highlanders were so much below strength due to the heavy and accurate shelling and mortaring to which they had been subjected that it was decided to regroup and postpone the attack; the tanks accordingly withdrew to their harbour of the previous night, where they were finally relieved at 03.00am on the 7th by two troops of the 12th Battalion RTR, guided in by Recce Troop, and rejoined the rest of the battalion at San Maria. Casualties were one OR killed, one wounded and one missing, one Churchill disabled by a heavy shell hit on the engine covers and one with a broken track.

There now followed a week of rest and refitting in the area of Cattolica, during which Maj Charles Crowther, the commander of HQ Squadron, departed the battalion, Capt Maurice Ladd taking over from him and Capt Rand replacing Ladd as 2IC of the squadron, while Capt Tom Bruce joined B Squadron in place of Maurice Rand. On 10 September, on his return to the battalion from 272nd Forward Delivery Squadron, Lt Roy Wife was promoted to captain and posted to C Squadron; Lt R.J.L. Scott was posted to A Squadron the same day. Also during this week Sgt Hector McIver was removed as Provost Sergeant, together with LCpl Freddie Parr, one of his regimental policemen; he was replaced temporarily by Cpl Frank Munns, Reg Heard being his only remaining policeman.

The battalion again became operational on 14 September, and was involved in operations until the 23rd of the month. The operational situation had changed little during this week; the enemy was short of manpower but the country was ideal for defence, consisting of a series of ridges running across our line of advance, from the high ground of the Apennines down to the sea. Each one of these ridges could be held by fire with only very few men on the ground, and the enemy was determined to delay our advance as much as possible and fight for every feature and farm if necessary. The problem was, therefore, a difficult one, as our infantry were continually held up by well-sited machine guns and snipers, and the 'going' made tank manoeuvres, except in small numbers, impossible. Life for the tanks was made even harder as anti-tank guns, both wheeled and self-propelled, and Tiger and Panther tanks were well-sited and hard to spot, while, in the very close country, the *Panzerfaust* (bazooka) men had great advantages over our tanks unless these were constantly protected by infantry, especially at night.

All these factors combined to make operations very slow and rather confused. However, the Germans were now holding the last two features before the Apennines bent away from the coast at Rimini; once these positions fell to the Allies the Plain of Lombardy would be at the mercy (or so it was thought at the time!) of our numerically superior armoured forces. It is not surprising, therefore, that the battles for San Martino and San Fortunato were among the most bitter of the whole Italian campaign.

The week of rest and recuperation had been enjoyed also by the remainder of 21st Tank Brigade and 1st Canadian Infantry Division, while making plans for the operation to capture both the San Fortunato feature to the west of Rimini and Rimini itself. The battalion began operations again in support of 1st Canadian Infantry Brigade, but it later became necessary to put squadrons in support of other brigades; at one stage there was a squadron supporting each

Plate 86   Some of the Battalion HQ officers at Presenzano, in the summer of 1944. Back row, left to right: Capt Gilmour (MO), Lt Savage, Capt Ladd, Capt D.E.A. Scott-Gardner (Padre). Front row: Lts White (HQ tank troop commander), Skey (IO) (Tony Kingsford)

of the three brigades of the division. As it is not possible to knit the operations of the three tank squadrons into a single narrative, they are described separately in the following paragraphs. Recce Troop deserves a special mention: it was not used as a troop in the reconnaissance rôle in these operations but rather to maintain contact with the enemy, to help with replenishment of forward tanks and to evacuate casualties under fire. It was often impossible for soft-skinned vehicles to get forward, and even a White scout car ambulance could have trouble; the light tanks of Recce Troop proved ideal for these rôles and were very extensively used by both day and night. Medical and recovery arrangements also worked well; the Regimental Aid Post was established centrally, well forward, so that it could service any squadron or squadrons operating, while tanks were recovered and repaired throughout the operation, with the result that there were always just enough tanks available to meet requirements.

To deal with A Squadron first, Maj W.M. ('Robbie') Robson, the officer commanding, received orders on 14 September for the squadron to be ready to take up a defensive position in support of the Hastings and Prince Edward Regiment, from which to protect the flank of 3rd Canadian Infantry Brigade while it attacked across the River Marano, supported by the

12th Battalion RTR, to capture the San Lorenzo–San Martino feature to the north. This done, A Squadron handed over to B Squadron at 6.00pm and, under cover of darkness, moved across the River Marano.

At 11.30am the following day the squadron was ordered to provide support for the Royal 22nd Regiment as its squadron of the 12th Battalion RTR had been severely reduced in numbers; the task was to capture the San Martino feature by way of the palace in the centre of the ridge, from a start line some 1,500 yards north of the River Marano. On arrival at the start line, Sgt Wilson's tank of 2 Troop was hit by anti-tank fire from Rimini airfield to the right flank, where there were two dug-in Panther turrets, and suffered two casualties. Sgt Wilson, with great courage under shell and mortar fire, got them out and away, during which time his tank was hit again. Cpl Bailess's tank, next to him, was hit twice in succession from the same area and instantly brewed up; all the crew managed to bale out without injury. At about the same time, Lt Reaney's tank, further forward in a sunken road, was hit and began to burn; the crew baled out, suffering three casualties. Cpl W. Smith assisted Lt Reaney and Tpr Collier back to safety and then made two separate efforts to get the tank back, although it was almost completely surrounded by the enemy. The tank brewed up completely shortly afterwards.

A little later, after crossing the start line, Maj Robson was not heard on the air; Lt Rowell investigated and found the OC's tank hit and brewing up, with both Maj Robson and Sgt Spicer, his operator, dead and his gunner wounded. Having assisted the wounded back he reported to his 2IC, Capt Brian Achurch, who had already taken command of the squadron. Meanwhile the advance was on; 3 Troop on the right and 1 Troop (two tanks) with Sgt Challis on the left were making good progress and finding plenty of targets; they had got ahead of the infantry, so halted in suitable positions for the infantry to catch them up. The advance then continued on to the first objective and beyond, to just short of the San Martino ridge, the final objective, where the infantry were held up by machine gun posts on the reverse slope of the ridge. To silence these posts involved the tanks leaving their hull-down positions and going forward over the crest of the ridge, but Sgt 'Plum' Warner, in the 95mm CS Churchill, did sterling work with smoke and Sgt Challis went forward over the crest to deal with the enemy posts. After silencing most of them, his tank was hit by anti-tank fire from the next ridge; it caught fire, one crew member being killed and Sgt Challis severely wounded. The rest of the crew got him out and back to safety, but he died before reaching hospital. The squadron remained in support of the Royal 22nd Regiment until released at 02.30am on the 16th; it finally reached harbour at 05.00am, having lost one officer (Maj Robson), two sergeants (Spicer and Challis) and three ORs (Tpr Kelsall, Tpr Clapper and Tpr McPherson) killed, and one officer (Lt Reaney) and six ORs wounded. Tank casualties were three Churchills and three Shermans damaged beyond repair and five Churchills and one Sherman damaged and repairable. Capt Achurch was promoted to major on 17 September, in Maj Robson's place, and retained command of A Squadron.

After a day spent licking its wounds and reorganising, A Squadron was ordered forward again at 09.30am on 18 September, this time in support of the Hastings and Prince Edward Regiment as part of 3rd Canadian Infantry Brigade Group. The group's task was to capture the San Fortunato ridge, the last high ground dominating the Rimini Gap, which led to the flat country to the north; A Squadron's task was to support the Hastings and Prince Edward Regiment on to Covignano, north of San Fortunato on the ridge. A Squadron moved by artificial moonlight at 11.00pm to an assembly area east of the River Ausa, which it crossed at first light the following morning. However, the infantry had got ahead, so the tanks did not pick them up until they were on the first objective; the initial advance, through very close country in which *Panzerfaust* men were active was therefore tricky, and one tank was lost to them. Two more tanks were lost to anti-tank guns on the intermediate objective, but the crews were unhurt. At 10.30am the squadron, by now consisting of just seven tanks, took up positions for the final assault; Lt Scott's tank was bazooka'd when only some 30 yards from the village, and the crew baled out with one man wounded. The remaining six tanks reached the outskirts of the village, but without infantry support which had been held up by intense machine gun fire. The position being untenable without infantry, the four remaining tanks of the squadron pulled back to a farmhouse just below the objective, where they immediately became subjected to very heavy and accurate artillery fire, both from the coast and from the objective. Further casualties were inflicted on both tanks and men, and Cpl Scrase of Recce Troop, in a turretless Honey, made three hazardous journeys right up to the farmhouse position and evacuated all the wounded, for which action he was later awarded a well-deserved Military Medal. The squadron by now consisted of three Shermans only, but they took up positions to support the infantry forward in a left hook on to the objective; before this could be carried out, however, Covignano was captured by the Seaforths of Canada, supported by a troop of 145th Regiment RAC; the remains of A Squadron therefore pulled out to reorganise. Three ORs (Tpr Dobson, Tpr Strange and Tpr F. Dowling) had been killed, three more (LCpl Kelly, Tpr Becker and Tpr S. Riley) died of their wounds and a further three ORs (Cpl Morrey-Jones, Cpl W.F. Smith and Tpr Hickman) had been wounded in this operation; tank casualties had been one Sherman and four Churchills damaged beyond repair and two Churchills damaged but repairable. Two Shermans had been bogged before reaching the start line.

In the meantime, B Squadron had come under command of the 48th Highlanders of Canada, in 1st Canadian Infantry Brigade, on 13 September, and was to help the Highlanders on the following day in a local operation on the low ground to the east of the San Martino feature. The country was very close and neither tanks nor infantry could make much progress; furthermore, they were under observation from the high ground and therefore suffered merciless pounding from both artillery and mortars, of which the tanks naturally attracted the lion's share.

Next day the advance was resumed, with much the same result. It was by now evident that no progress could be made until San Martino was captured. B Squadron accordingly took over from A Squadron in protecting 3rd Canadian Infantry Brigade's left flank, while A Squadron moved across the River Marano.

On 15 September, B Squadron and the 48th Highlanders were ordered to move to the area south-east of San Lorenzo; the squadron moved at 6.30pm, arrived at 7.15pm and was shelled soon after arrival. At first light the next day it again started to advance with C Company of the 48th Highlanders but was soon halted, at first by intense sniper and machine gun fire and, shortly afterwards, by equally intense and very accurate artillery and mortar fire; all tanks were forced to close down early on and if a tank opened its hatches, down came the mortar fire. Towards noon SP anti-tank guns were brought up and engaged the tanks from hidden positions; the first to be hit was Sgt Harding's of 10 Troop, the crew being machine gunned and then taken prisoner. The tank was later totally destroyed by a *Panzerfaust*. No real headway could be made; as soon as an attack was staged it was broken up, and as soon as any movement was made it was stopped. At about 4.00pm, Maj Joss decided that nothing was to be gained by remaining as an Aunt Sally, and withdrew the squadron some 150 yards to concealed positions. Casualties among the infantry had been heavy; our own consisted of one officer and five ORs wounded, one officer and one OR missing and five ORs taken prisoner. Tank casualties were two Churchills destroyed and four Churchills and one Sherman damaged but repairable; the squadron's tank strength was now two Churchill IVs, one Churchill I, one Churchill V and five Shermans, organised into SHQ (two Churchills) and two troops, one with the two Churchill IVs and the other with the five Shermans.

On 17 September, B Squadron moved before first light to the area of San Martino to support A and C Companies of the 48th Highlanders in an advance to C Pugliesi from the west. Although the squadron suffered only eight personnel casualties, six tanks were put out of action by artillery fire; by dark, the squadron had only the two SHQ Churchills and the four Shermans of 8 Troop battleworthy. After replacements had arrived the following morning, this strength was increased by one Churchill IV, two Shermans and two turreted Honeys.

Further replacement tanks arrived on the morning of the 19th, bringing the squadron tank strength up to two Churchill Vs (SHQ), one troop of Churchills and two of Shermans. At 08.30am, orders were received to cross the River Ausa, a move which was successfully carried out apart from the loss of three Shermans due to mechanical trouble; after arriving on the far side, and while the crews were improving their camouflage, an artillery stonk came down on their location, wounding Sgt Broomfield, LCpl Gilmour, Tpr Maclay and Tpr Harris, the last two seriously. By 12.30pm, however, it was obvious that the enemy was withdrawing in confusion, although leaving small pockets of resistance; by dawn the following day the objectives had been taken and at 10.00am the squadron was told that it would be relieved on 22 September. This relief in fact took place at 11.00am on the 23rd, but the squadron was not employed in the interim; it was obvious that no real progress could be made while San Martino was held by the enemy.

Plate 87   Churchill V (CS) of B Squadron HQ, with Maj Joss (OC) and crew (Tony Kingsford)

Meanwhile, C Squadron, commanded by Capt Don Hoad in the absence of Maj Haigh, with Capt Kingsford as 2IC, had entered the battle for the San Martino ridge; it had been ordered forward north of the River Marano at 09.00am on 16 September, to relieve A Squadron in support of the Royal 22nd Regiment. Two troops only, 2 and 3, were used in the attack on a spur of the San Martino ridge, and they too were followed by accurate mortar and artillery fire wherever they went. Once on the objective, their infantry asked them to remain with them during the night; this they did, the tank crews being involved in a grenade fight with an enemy patrol during their maintenance and replenishment. The morning of the 17th brought more accurate mortaring, but the accuracy was noticeably decreased when a German observation post hiding in a nearby barn was discovered and eliminated. The squadron harboured back at about 8.30pm on the 17th, south-east of San Lorenzo, to reorganise and replenish, with no personnel casualties and only two Churchills requiring repair.

On 19 September, the squadron was ordered to support the West Nova Scotia Regiment in an attack on Point 152, at the southern end of the San Fortunato feature; the enemy was believed to be holding this feature in strength, with forward elements on the west bank of the River Ausa. The plan was for Capt Wife's 1 Troop (Churchills) and Lt Fox's 2 Troop (Shermans) to move across the river immediately behind the West Nova Scotias as soon as the Carleton and York Regiment had established a bridgehead and two tank crossings had been made by the Royal Engineers. Each of these troops would support one company on to the final objective, with additional support from the two 95mm Churchill Vs of SHQ and the Shermans of Lt Buckley's 4 Troop. After some initial success, however, the attack, like that of B Squadron, ground to a halt in the face of heavy and accurate artillery, tank gun and mortar fire, much of it coming from the direction of Rimini. The tanks were pulled back at 05.00am on the 20th to replenish, having suffered one OR killed and one officer and one OR wounded; tank casualties consisted of one Churchill and four Shermans written off, two Shermans having brewed up. At about 2.30pm the squadron was ordered to pull back to replenish and reorganise.

By now Rimini had fallen, although it was not until the early hours of 21 September that the last Tiger was disposed of north-east of San Fortunato. Due to rain, no movement was allowed that day but, during the night of 21/22 September, the 1st New Zealand Division passed through our positions to continue the advance. As soon as it had taken over, 21st Tank Brigade passed into corps reserve and was given three weeks in which to refit; the brigade concentrated in the Riccione area, thus bringing Phase 1 of the brigade's operations in Italy, the breaking of the Gothic Line and the capture of Rimini, to a satisfactory conclusion.

The official Canadian account *The Canadian Army, 1939–45* says that the month of September 1944 saw the fiercest fighting of their Italian operations; it certainly saw their heaviest casualties. Yet, ironically, the victory was hollow. The plains beyond the Rimini Gap, towards which everyone had striven so valiantly, were now sodden and the rivers swollen with the early autumn rains; instead of the rolling tank country we had expected, we were faced with boggy paddy fields and flooded waterways, obstacles every bit as difficult to overcome as the alternating ridges and rivers of the Apennines. It was almost enough to break a tank man's spirit!

Phase 2 – The Advance to the River Senio

The battalion took advantage of the three weeks of rest and reorganisation to make some personnel changes. To begin with, the battalion 2IC, Maj Spencer, was posted out and the former commander of B Squadron of the 12th Battalion RTR, Maj Jim Cornwell, DCM, took

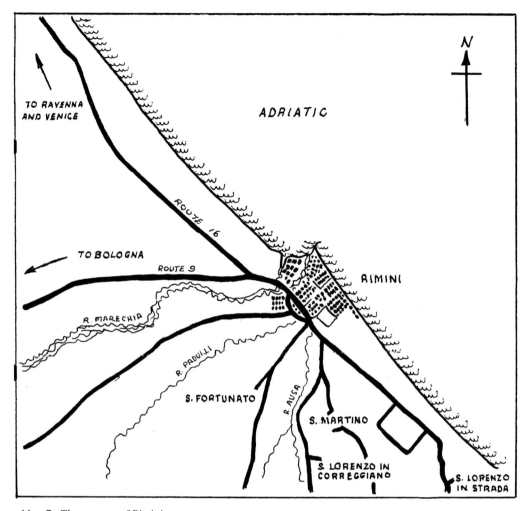

Map 7   The capture of Rimini

his place. On 22 September Capt F.D. Hoad was promoted to acting major with effect from the 20th, in place of the wounded Maj Haigh, although he had to revert to captain when Freddie Haigh returned from hospital on 12 October; on the same day Capt Wife was posted from C to A Squadron. Further officer moves occurred on the 26th, when Capt Neil Chadwick took over from Capt Savage as Adjutant, the latter going to A Squadron as 2IC; in addition, Lt R.G. (Ralph) White was promoted to acting captain, Lt T.S. (Tom) Bruce (from HQ Squadron) and Lt P.S. Vos were posted to B Squadron and Lt D.L. James to A Squadron, the latter two having come from 272nd Forward Delivery Squadron. On the 28th, Capt Kingsford was posted from C to B Squadron as 2IC and Capt E.A.A. (Alan) Harvey from A Squadron to HQ as battalion LO. On 5 October Lt Bruce was promoted to acting captain and a new EME, Lt W.G. Smith REME, arrived from 16th Base Workshop; three days later, Lt Greenwood was posted from B Squadron to HQ Squadron as OC Recce Troop in place of Lt J.M. Trueman, who was posted to C Squadron.

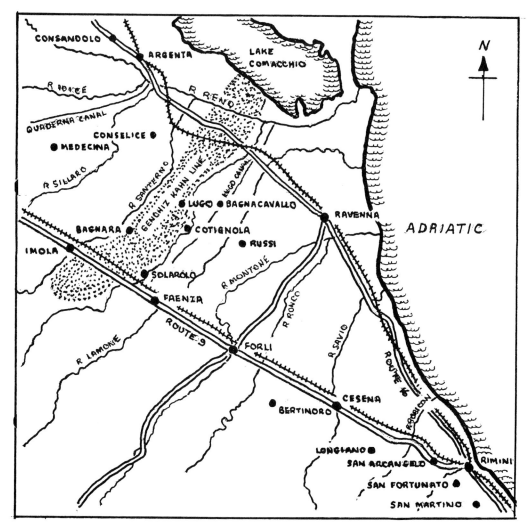

Map 8   The advance to the River Senio

Apart from the necessary re-equipment and recrewing, there were many Orders of the Day and Messages of Congratulation, which follow a successful battle as night follows day, to be read and passed on. One, which was particularly cherished and gratefully accepted by the battalion, was an invitation from the commander of 1st Canadian Corps to wear the Corps maple leaf on sleeves and vehicles. On uniform sleeves, this took the form of a brass maple leaf on a rectangle of red cloth. The opportunity was also taken, during this rest period, to organise various demonstrations and entertainments for the troops, amongst which were demonstrations of the Churchill Crocodile flame-thrower tank and of the use of the 6pdr APDS round against the Tiger, both demonstrations being held in the lines of the 12th Battalion RTR. An inter-squadron football tournament, won by A Squadron, took place on 14 October and a cocktail party in the Officers' Mess in the evening of the same day. The following day the battalion held a memorial service for those who had fallen in the campaign

Plate 88 Capt Tom Bruce, 2IC B Squadron, beside the Squadron HQ sign in 1944. Note the battalion tactical number, now 174, on a yellow/red rectangle (Jack Rockliff)

up till that time. The battalion was entertained, in B Squadron's lines, by the band of the Grenadier Guards on 24 October. In October, November and December, five ORs at a time were permitted to take leave in Florence, which helped, if only in a small way, to lift morale. Further officer promotions and postings took place: Capt Hoad was promoted to acting major and Lt Henry Palmer to acting captain on 28 October, while Lt E.D. Hall was posted on 17 November from C to HQ Squadron to take command of the scout cars of the Intercomm Troop. Lt A.F. Holtorp returned to the battalion on the same day from HQ Squadron of 21st Tank Brigade and was posted to B Squadron.

21st Tank Brigade became operational again under command of 1st Canadian Corps and in support of 1st Canadian Infantry Division on 11 October 1944. This phase belonged primarily to the 12th Battalion RTR and 145th Regiment RAC, however; our battalion played only a minimal part in operations between 11 October 1944 and 12 January 1945. Owing to the recent heavy rains the ground was in no condition for the use of tanks in large numbers, so, while the other two battalions of the brigade moved forward the 48th remained in the Riccione area for nearly two months. The opportunity was taken to organise a course on the handling and use of the PIAT (Projector, Infantry, Anti-Tank), the British equivalent of the German *Panzerfaust*, for the personnel of Recce Troop on 15 November.

On 2 December the battalion had been placed at 24 hours' notice to move forward again, to come under the command of 5th Corps in support of 43rd Gurkha Brigade. The transporter move of squadrons of the 48th began on the night of the 4th/5th; Battalion HQ opened in Forli on the 4th and, by the 6th, C Squadron was with the brigade on the line of the River

Plate 89   The Churchill Crocodile flame-thrower tank with its trailer for flame fuel (Author's collection)

Lamone, north-east of Faenza. Its was purely a holding rôle, and between 6 and 12 December only indirect shooting across the river was possible; this was remarkably accurate, however, thanks to the employment of an air OP.

At this time the battalion again underwent a change of commanding officer when, on 7 December, Lt Col E.H. ('Ted') Tinker was posted to the UK; he had been in command for less than five months, but was later appointed to command the 12th Battalion RTR in place of Lt Col H.H. Van Straubenzee. Maj Jim Cornwell, the 2IC, assumed command of the battalion the same day; it was an auspicious day for him, as it also brought news of HM King's approval of the award to him of the DSO. At the same time came news of the award of the Military Cross to Lt R.J.L. Scott and to the Padre, Capt D.E.A. Scott-Gardner, as well as the Military Medal to Cpl E.A. Jupp of A Squadron. Maj Cornwell's tenure of command was, however, of only brief duration, as the new CO, Lt Col P.W.D. (Peter) Sturdee RTR arrived to take over on the 15th of the month.

On the morning of the 11th, a troop of C Squadron registered two bridges with the help of the air OP, each tank harassing the bridges with 100 rounds of HE. A further development was the use of radar to plot the positions of roving enemy self-propelled guns, which were then engaged indirectly by tanks which had previously been registered on the routes known to be used by these SP guns. This development owed much to the fortuitous proximity of the battalion's tactical HQ to a radar detachment. On the night of the 10th/11th, 3rd Canadian Infantry Brigade finally managed to get a bridgehead across the river south-east of Bagnacavallo, and 12th Battalion RTR crossed during the following two nights.

On the 13th the 48th was relieved, pulling back to Forli in preparation for supporting 2nd New Zealand Division, together with 43rd Gurkha Brigade, in the clearance of Faenza. This operation would take place in conjunction with a 5th Corps attack south of the town, aimed at by-passing it and reaching the River Senio beyond. The 5th Corps attack started during the night of 14/15 December and, on the evening of the 16th, A Squadron was called forward; early next morning it crossed the River Lamone by Bailey bridge near Route 9 and joined the Gurkhas, who had already cleared most of the town. A new attack was launched on the 18th, in which A and C Squadrons each supported a battalion of Gurkhas and by 10.00am on the following morning it was clear that the enemy was making a small withdrawal; 2nd New Zealand Division launched a major and successful attack that night and on 22 December the 48th was withdrawn to Faenza, where it took over first a sector of the line astride Route 9 and then one just to the south of it, remaining with the Gurkhas for the rest of December. On 1 January 1945, C Squadron, in support of the 2/10 Gurkha Rifles, relieved the New

Plate 90   The jeep and driver of C Squadron commander in 1944 (Don Hoad)

Zealanders in the sector south of Route 9, 2 Troop and 4 Troop between them keeping up harassing fire on enemy positions throughout the day and night of 2, 3 and 4 January. On 5 January the battalion was relieved by the 6th Battalion RTR.

During this time, 145th Regiment RAC carried out its last operation before its much-lamented disbandment in January 1945; it was released on 23 December, following the capture of Bagnacavallo and replaced in 21st Tank Brigade by the North Irish Horse, formerly of 25th Army Tank Brigade and commanded by Lt Col A.W.A. (Tony) Llewellen-Palmer, DSO, MC, who came under command on 5 December 1944; Brig David Dawnay thus again had his own beloved regiment under his command.

Phase 3 – The Winter Line

By 5 January 1945 the River Senio had been reached, but, as it was obvious that the enemy was firmly entrenched and intended to stay and that no major attack could be launched until the spring brought drier weather, the decision was taken by the Allies to stand on the line of the Senio for the rest of the winter. The arrival of the New Year therefore found 21st Tank Brigade filling a defensive rôle on this line, a rôle which it would continue to fill for the next three months.

On 2 January further officer postings took place: A/Maj Don Hoad was posted from C Squadron to command HQ in the absence in hospital of Maj Ladd, A/Capt Tom Gorringe was appointed as A Squadron's LO and Lt R.T. Haselhurst arrived from the 2nd Battalion RTR. On 18 January the first party, consisting of Capt Maurice Rand, two corporals and three

Plate 91   C Squadron fitters and their half-track, 1944 (Don Hoad)

troopers, returned from UK leave. The battalion concluded its period of operations with 5th Corps and, on 7 January, began the planned move back into the 1st Canadian Corps area to relieve the 12th Battalion RTR squadrons supporting the Canadian brigades holding the River Senio. By first light on 11 January the relief had been completed.

The method of support to be given by the tanks to the infantry on the line had still to be decided. The Canadian corps commander at first wanted some tanks to be dug in at a few nodal points along the front. This, however, would not have made best use of the tanks as, firstly, their mobility would have been lost and, secondly, maintenance and re-supply would have proved to be a problem. It was finally agreed that the digging-in of tanks was unnecessary, and the method of support finally adopted on most sectors was for one or two troops from a squadron to take up positions in the reserve infantry company localities, on immediate call day and night to support the forward companies in case of emergency. Squadron HQ was close to the HQ of the infantry battalion or brigade it was supporting, and one or two troops of 75mm gun or 95mm howitzer tanks were placed in suitable positions to give fire support. On some occasions Honey tanks were used to give close support to the infantry or to put down harassing fire with their Browning machine guns. Together with the 12th Battalion RTR, the 48th operated in this manner with 1st Canadian Division from 7 January to 26 February, and with 8th Indian Division from 26 February to 9 April 1945.

As it was necessary to keep the enemy sufficiently busy to prevent him from withdrawing divisions to reinforce other hard-pressed fronts, while at the same time obtaining the maximum of rest for our own divisions, the greater part of the winter was spent by the

Plate 92   Lt Col P.W.D. Sturdee, who commanded the battalion from 15 December 1944 until its disbandment (1 RTR collection)

Plate 93   Churchills of the 48th Bn RTR parked up in the Piazza del Popolo, Faenza, over Christmas 1944 (Deric Skey)

squadrons of the battalion moving in and out of the villages and casas bordering the River Senio, engaging in duels with the German artillery and *Nebelwerfer* (multiple rocket launchers). The increasing use here of tanks as self-propelled artillery caused the ammunition situation to become critical; expenditure had to be carefully controlled and limited to essential infantry support in the next few weeks. Although some clashes occurred, as the enemy held so many positions on our side of the river and canal systems and his patrols were annoyingly active, the battalion's main memory of that winter was of rain, mud and snow.

At the beginning of February, the battalion was relieved by the 12th Battalion RTR in the Bagnacavallo sector and took over the duties of reserve battalion. The opportunity was now taken to carry out some further officer postings, when Maj Cornwell returned to the 12th Battalion RTR as its 2IC on 21 February, being replaced by Maj J.B. Lumby from the same unit. On the following day, Capt T.M. Gorringe was posted from A Squadron to HQ to take over the appointment of Adjutant from Capt Neil Chadwick, who relinquished the appointment on 28 February. Meanwhile, planning and preparation for the spring offensive began to be put in hand. The 12th and the 48th again exchanged rôles at the beginning of March, but this time the 48th had to cover a very extended front, supporting 19th and 21st

Plate 94 Churchill IVs (NA75) firing across the Senio during the winter of 1944 (Author's collection)

Indian Infantry Brigades of 8th Indian Division. A Squadron had the most active time, supporting 1st Jaipur Infantry in several abortive attacks on the Lugo road bridge. Again the 12th Battalion RTR relieved the 48th in the middle of the month, the battalion going back to the River Montone for training with 21st Indian Infantry Brigade in river crossing and tank/infantry cooperation. On 17 March another party of one officer (Capt K.M. Hunter, MC) and five other ranks was despatched on leave to UK (LIAP), while, on the 18th, Lt E. Liddell of A Squadron was promoted to acting captain and Lt G. Proud was posted to A Squadron. On 25 March Lt Greenwood was appointed to command Recce Troop.

It was also on the 25th that the battalion relieved the 12th Battalion RTR for the last time, covering the whole front from opposite Alfonsine to Bagnacavallo; two troops of A Squadron were, however, spared to train in street fighting with 1st Jaipur Infantry, with a view to supporting them in the forthcoming capture of Lugo. Thus ended Phase 3 of the battalion's campaign in Italy.

Phase 4 – Senio to Venice

The final offensive in Italy began on 9 April 1945, and was to be an all-out attempt to smash the German army in Italy. General Alexander's plan was again for a two-prong attack, but with a bold and carefully planned change of direction by Eighth Army at the very moment when the Fifth Army was to deliver the second blow. Once again the Germans were to be misled into expecting a major landing, this time south of Venice, and credence was lent to this deception plan by the joint operation by the Commandos and 56th Division to clear the 'spit' and 'wedge', and the islands, of Lake Comacchio, which were in fact vital to the real flanking thrust inland.

In the meantime, the whole of the Eighth Army, except for a skeleton force in the mountains, was secretly concentrated to the north of Route 9. The 5th Corps offensive was to start with an assault crossing of the River Senio astride Lugo by 8th Indian Division and 2nd New Zealand Division; but this would be no ordinary river-crossing operation. The rivers in the Lombardy plain have high flood banks, built to a height of 30 feet or more to prevent the melting snows from the Apennines spilling over the fertile black soil as they thunder down to the sea in the spring. At the time of the Allied assault the snows had not yet melted, but the Germans, with their usual ingenuity and efficiency, had honeycombed the walls of the flood banks with seemingly impregnable defences. The Allies held the near bank; the problem was to seize the far bank. To solve this problem, a new blend of the well-tried ingredients of success was used; a heavy air bombardment, a gigantic artillery programme and surprise, part of which was a trump card, not previously used in Italy, the flamethrower.

In common with other battalions in 21st Tank Brigade, the 48th had by now handed in its Shermans in exchange for Churchill VIIs, mounting the British 75mm gun. For this final phase of the campaign in Italy, squadron HQs each now had one Churchill IV and three Churchill Vs with 95mm howitzers, while each fighting troop had one Churchill VII, one NA75 Churchill IV (with the US 75mm gun) and one Churchill IV (6pdr gun), thus complicating the logistics of ammunition supply. In addition, two tanks per squadron were fitted with three-ton fascines, to be used in the crossing of small obstacles.

For the final 5th Corps offensive, code-named Operation Buckland, 21st Tank Brigade was placed under the command of 8th Indian Infantry Division's 21st Indian Infantry Brigade. The division was to assault across the River Senio on a two-brigade front, 21st Brigade being on the left and 19th Indian Infantry Brigade, with two squadrons of the North Irish Horse under command, on the right. The 21st Brigade Group was given the task of breaking

Plate 95   The Churchill VII, armed with the British 75mm gun, which replaced the Shermans in the battalion in 1945 (Tank Museum)

Plate 96   Churchill IV (NA75) (Tank Museum)

through the Senio–Santerno defences north of Bagnacavallo in order to facilitate the advance through the Argenta Gap to Ferrara and Venice. For this operation, the 48th had two troops of Crocodiles (Churchill VII flame-thrower tanks) from 51st Battalion RTR, two troops of Kangaroos (armoured personnel carriers) from A Squadron of the 4th Hussars, one troop of M10 SP anti-tank guns from 225th Anti-Tank Battery RA, two Churchill bridgelayer tanks and one Sherman dozer from F Armoured Squadron RE and one section of 3rd Field Squadron RE under command.

Shortly after midday on 9 April the Allied air forces went to work, with the medium bomber and ground-attack squadrons attacking gun positions, strongpoints and command posts on the Senio and beyond, while, in an hour and a half, 800 heavy bombers, using a line of smoke shells in the sky as a bomb line and seemingly impervious to the flak apparently bursting amongst them, saturated the German defences on the immediate front of the two assaulting corps (5th Corps and 2nd Polish Corps) with 125,000 high explosive fragmentation bombs. Then, before the enemy could recover, the four-hour artillery and mortar programme began, a programme bigger than that at El Alamein.

The initial task of the tanks was to neutralise the river banks and to support the Crocodile flame-throwers which were opening the way for the assaulting infantry: all tanks opened fire at 7.05pm. When the Crocodiles did likewise at 7.12pm, the whole front seemed to burst into lanes of fire; the infantry assault went in at 7.20pm, with about an hour to go before dark.

Plate 97   The Churchill bridgelayer tank (Tank Museum)

During the neutralising phase prior to the infantry assault, Lt J.B.L. (John) Stewart, commanding the right-hand tank of C Squadron, was wounded in the head by a sniper and had to be evacuated.

The 1/5th Mahratta on the right were counter-attacked and were unable to secure the far bank in the initial assault; this greatly delayed the construction of the bridge ('Melrose') in the centre of their sector, by which our tanks were scheduled to cross. This bridge was planned to be ready at about midnight, but in the event was not completed until 04.45am, the sappers building it being considerably hampered by snipers. As soon as it was complete B Squadron crossed, followed first by C and then by A Squadron and the supporting arms. LCpl Alan Gilmour, a long-time tank driver with B Squadron, recalls that:

> . . . in the half-light it was a weird experience. Negotiating the first flood bank, *Titan* seemed to stand on her tail and I was virtually lying on my back. Through the visor I could see only the night sky, with Ursa Major a great mark of interrogation in the heavens, while we climbed up and up, engines roaring, metal tracks clashing. The ascent was checked; for a moment our 40 tons swayed ponderously on the point of balance, and then the constellations swam in wild confusion across my window as the nose of the tank fell, and we found ourselves in precipitous descent. Now the prospect was of dark turgid waters. I had the impression that we crossed the river on two girders exactly spaced to take our tracks. The slightest deflection of the steering arm would have spelt disaster. As in many a precarious moment, drivers leaned on fate. Another blind climb, a sudden fall, and we were on the north bank of the Senio.

Plate 98   The Sherman 'dozer (Tank Museum)

B Squadron soon caught up with the 3/15th Punjabis on the right and they advanced together with little opposition until halted by a blown bridge over the San Arginello canal. C Squadron in the centre linked up with the 1/5th Mahratta and met little opposition in getting forward. A Squadron on the left with the 1st Jaipur Regiment had no trouble in capturing the walled town of Lugo, although they found it difficult to clear the cheering population; the town was finally cleared by about 1.00pm and A Squadron rallied back to C Corelli. Its only casualty had been Tpr Watson wounded. Resistance was finally met by B and C Squadrons and their infantry battalions along the line of the Lugo canal and the infantry COs decided, at about 8.00pm, to remain on the canal all night. At first light on 11 April, the attack was resumed, and by 4.30pm the squadrons and their infantry were within 200 yards of the River Santerno. Here they were relieved by 17th Brigade, and the tanks rallied back to a concentration area north-west of Lugo.

Lt Col Sturdee learned that, for the next stage of the advance, the battalion would be under command of 78th Infantry Division and in support of 36th Infantry Brigade. A Squadron was to support the 5th Buffs, B Squadron the 8th Argyll & Sutherland Highlanders and C Squadron the 6th Royal West Kents. Early on 12 April, B Squadron moved out to the infantry

Plate 99   Churchill IV (NA75) of 48th Bn RTR crossing the Senio over two Churchill ARKs, one atop the other (Deric Skey)

Plate 100   The Churchill ARK armoured ramp carrier (Author's collection)

battalion's location, and both it and the rest of the 48th were at short notice to move all day. The plan was for the Argylls, with B Squadron in support, to cross the River Santerno and to attack north-west to enlarge the bridgehead already gained by 17th Indian Infantry Brigade and 12th Battalion RTR, to allow 38th Irish Brigade and 2nd Armoured Brigade to assemble for their breakthrough to the north. The attack started at 6.00pm, and an hour and a half later the infantry were on the objective, with no casualties and no resistance. This lack of resistance, coupled with local civilians' reports that the Germans had pulled back, decided the infantry commander to exploit forward and capture Conselice if possible. The light was failing as B Squadron, moving in line ahead, made a dash through hitherto unpenetrated country and little opposition, and the village of San Patrizio was soon in our hands; B Squadron even managed to capture intact a *Nashorn* (Rhinoceros) 88mm SP anti-tank gun (**Plate 101**) completely equipped and in running order when the crew dismounted in San Patrizio near B Squadron HQ. The Germans had been told to take up a position in the village from which to prevent Allied armour passing through it and were surprised and indignant to learn that San Patrizio was already in British hands.

On the following morning, 13 April, the 6th Royal West Kents, accompanied by C Squadron, passed through the Argylls' position at first light to attack Conselice. Considerable opposition was met in this town, which was not finally cleared until 14 April; by this time Lt A.H. ('Freddie') Fox, together with his operator, Tpr G. Pigott and his gunner, Tpr A. Curtis, had been killed by two anti-tank guns firing from near the town on the left after he had knocked out another hidden in a haystack; his driver, LCpl F. Abbott, was wounded and taken prisoner. Capt Ian More, commander of 1 Troop, Cpl J. Maffet and LCpl W.J. Bird were seriously wounded by a mortar bomb, Cpl Maffet later dying of his wounds. It was a Black Friday the 13th indeed for C Squadron, although Sgt Catchpole was awarded

Plate 101   The German SP 88mm anti-tank gun 'Nashorn' (Rhinoceros), based on the chassis of the PzKpfw IV medium tank (Author's collection)

SHOT-UP TANK WAS DECOY

THE troop commander's tank had been knocked out. There were two tanks left and both were under fire from a German self-propelled gun, south of Conselice over the Santerno river, writes *Daily Sketch* War Correspondent, Maurice Watts.

Sgt. A. E. Catchpole and Cpl. E. Smith, the two remaining tank commanders, had to deal with the S.P. But Cpl. Smith's tank was hit. His gun was put out of action, his wireless silenced.

Nevertheless, he drove forward into the fire of the S.P. while Sgt. Catchpole crept off to the right to deal with it from the flank.

Sitting there in his tank, Cpl. Smith could, with his fellow tank crew of C Squadron 48 Royal Tank Regt., do nothing but sweat it out.

Eventually Sgt. Catchpole got near enough to fire at the German gun. One round was enough. The S.P. baled out of its position, retired behind a house and fled.

Plate 102   A cutting from the Daily Sketch, *mentioning the action in which Sgt Catchpole won his DCM (John Walker)*

the DCM and Sgt Paice the MM as a result of their bravery in this action; Sgt Catchpole had located and knocked out the SP gun which had killed his troop leader, a fact duly reported in the *Daily Sketch* (**Plate 102**). While the Padre, Capt Archie Scott-Gardner, MC, was, with German permission, removing Lt Fox's body in the Red Cross carrier, a German jumped into the tank and drove it away.

In the meantime, A Squadron with 5th Buffs had moved up to San Patrizio, and Battalion HQ, with HQ 36th Infantry Brigade, to farmhouses north of Zeppa. This left Battalion HQ rather exposed, as the enemy had not been cleared from the area north of Zeppa and east of Conselice. When two companies of the Buffs and 1 and 2 Troops of A Squadron were sent out to clear this area, Battalion tactical HQ cheered them past, feeling a little more comfortable with someone else between them and the enemy.

A combined attack to clear Conselice was planned for the night of 13/14 April, supported by concentrations of field and medium artillery. C Squadron attacked on the left, supported by a company of 6th Royal West Kents, at 9.00pm, while B Squadron, with 8th Argyll & Sutherland Highlanders, secured the left flank and A Squadron, with the Buffs, attacked northwest of the town. No opposition was met and no prisoners taken; civilians told the troops that the Germans had left half an hour previously. After pressing on to Chiesanova, which was reached at 03.00am, the battalion was concentrated in the area of Conselice–San Patrizio, where it remained until 16 April. Advantage was taken of this relatively peaceful interlude to fit the tanks with all-round vision cupolas and with 'Tabby' (active near infra-red night vision) equipment, 30 sets of which had just become available. Capt Kingsford recalled that:

> . . . we were not very successful in getting the 'Tabby' equipment to work. I suppose it was very primitive – at any rate, we never used it to any good purpose.

At 12.30pm on 14 April Lt Greenwood, with four Honeys, a scout car of Recce Troop and accompanied by a sapper section, moved off to reconnoitre the road north from Conselice and to clear mines; they had reached the village of Lavazzola, south of the River Reno, by 4.40pm and returned after making contact with 38th Infantry Brigade, who had cleared the south bank. On the 15th, A Squadron, in conjunction with 5th Buffs, was tasked with crossing the River Sillaro north-west of Conselice and capturing positions north of it on the edge of the flooded area south-west of Argenta; 2nd Commando Brigade was to pass through later, to take Argenta on the flank. For this operation flail tanks, a Churchill bridgelayer, a Sherman dozer, two ARVs and a RE section were attached to A Squadron; at last light 2 and 3 Troops of A Squadron moved up, with two companies of the Buffs, through the positions held by 56th Reconnaissance Regiment north of Chiesanova. At 8.30pm on the 16th, A Squadron provided a half-squadron, consisting of 1 Troop (Lt James) and 4 Troop (Lt Hall) under the command of Capt F. Liddell in a Squadron HQ tank, on immediate call to 2nd Commando Brigade in the area north-west of Conselice; tank support was called for by the Commando Brigade on the 17th but, owing to the difficult terrain, it did not arrive in position until first light on the 18th, having started out at 10.30pm the previous evening.

By this time 43rd Commando had pushed through 2nd Commando along both banks of the Fossa Zena and 1 Troop, supported by 4 Troop, attempted to push on to join it; unfortunately, 1 Troop's leading tank struck a previously undetected mine, brewed up and blocked the approach ramp to the bridge west of Argenta. The leading elements of 43rd Commando were therefore forced to withdraw, and Capt Liddell withdrew his tanks south of Argenta. The following day the half-squadron gave supporting fire to a limited attack by 43rd Commando and, on the 19th, to a similar attack by 2nd Commando. Capt Liddell and his scout car driver had been wounded when the vehicle struck another mine in the area of the Argenta bridge; Lt James took command of a composite four-tank troop, with Lt Hall acting as rear link to the CO of 2nd Commando. The tanks withdrew at first light on 20 April and were released by 2nd Commando Brigade at midday the following day, when they moved to rejoin A Squadron north of the River Reno.

On 17 April the rest of the battalion had been moved north of the Reno, this time to support 36th Infantry Brigade of 78th Infantry Division in its part of the assault on the Argenta Gap. Argenta itself was captured that evening, by 5th Northants Regiment of 11th Infantry Brigade supported by C Squadron; it had already been outflanked by the advance of 56th (London) Infantry Division from its landing on the south-west shore of Lake Comacchio. 36th Infantry Brigade passed through and across the Fossa Marina. On the 18th there was tough fighting as one battalion after the other, supported by their affiliated squadrons of the 48th, pushed up Route 16 against strong opposition. Boccaleone was reached in the morning and Consandolo was secured by last light; during the night, the third battalion group passed through to capture Benvignante. B Squadron lost Sgt W.J. Broomfield, Cpl E. Moore, Tpr E. Wright, Tpr B.F. Holmes and Tpr F.A. Smith killed in this action, while Tpr Hughes, Tpr Morgan, Tpr Summers and Tpr Duffort were wounded: Hughes later died of his wounds. It seemed particularly sad that men should have to die with the end so obviously near.

The enemy made strong counter-attacks on this village during the morning of 19 April, but the infantry held firm with the help of C Squadron and, at about 7.00pm, elements of 6th Armoured Division passed through to take up the advance. Both B and C Squadrons had had sharp brushes with the enemy, losing five and two tanks respectively; C Squadron's personnel casualties consisted of Cpl H. Jones, Tpr Sullivan, Tpr Astbury, Tpr Luxton and Tpr Dewey wounded in action. C Squadron was released at first light on the 20th and concentrated south-east of Benvignante; during the day, A Squadron concentrated near Boccaleone and B Squadron remained in Consandolo, near Battalion HQ.

The battalion was still in support of 36th Infantry Brigade, 78th Infantry Division's objective now being the line of the Po di Volano, east of Ferrara. On 21 April the squadrons were ordered to support their infantry battalions in the advance to the River Po, A Squadron moving to Benvignante in the afternoon to marry up with 5th Buffs, C Squadron moving during the evening to join 6th Royal West Kent and B Squadron moving off with 8th Argylls at 4.00pm. The advance was contested in a half-hearted fashion, the extent of the demolitions rather than the resistance offered by the enemy regulating its speed. The Po di Volano was reached, south-east of Ferrara, during the night of 21/22 April; the tanks had covered some 20 miles during the night. B Squadron's Cpl F. Attridge and Tpr H.T. Imber were wounded during this advance. Meanwhile, 8th Indian Division was coming up Route 16 to the west; on the morning of the 23rd it by-passed Ferrara to the west and the first troops reached the River Po to the north of the town at 10.45am that morning. The following day all resistance in the Ferrara area came to an end.

On the morning of 23 April, the 48th had been switched from the Ferrara area to the area of Copparo, now coming under command of 56th (London) Infantry Division and in support of 169th (Queen's) Infantry Brigade for the crossing of the River Po. During the battalion's advance in support of 36th Infantry Brigade, 56th Division had been pressing north towards the River Po on the right of 78th Division, with 12th Battalion RTR in support. Forward elements of 24th Guards Brigade on the right and 167th Infantry Brigade on the left were held up some 3,000 yards south of the Po; as soon as it reached the river, 169th Infantry Brigade was to make an assault crossing and the 48th was to follow it across in support.

The battalion concentrated north of the Po di Volano in the neighbourhood of Formignana; here the tank squadrons were ordered to maintain and repair their tanks which, in the preceding fortnight, had covered about 100 miles as well as being almost continuously in action. Within half an hour of arriving, however, A Squadron was standing by to move at short notice to support 24th Guards Brigade in pushing up to the Po. It remained on standby throughout the day and at nightfall was ordered to be ready to move, if called for, at first light. The squadron was by this time complete, with the exception of one tank, which was having engine repairs carried out at the previous location. However, no order to move was received, and at 08.00am a composite force consisting of two Honeys and two HQ tanks under command of Lt Greenwood, took over A Squadron's responsibilities; again, it was not called for.

Squadrons now began to link up with the infantry battalions of 169th Infantry Brigade, A with 2/5th Queen's, B with 2/6th Queen's and C with 2/7th Queen's; the morning of 25 April was spent in reconnaissances and conferences, squadron commanders going with battalion commanders to the river bank, which had been reached that morning. All along the bank were signs of the devastating attacks which the RAF had been making in the previous few days on the enemy attempting to escape across the River Po. There was a great deal of enemy

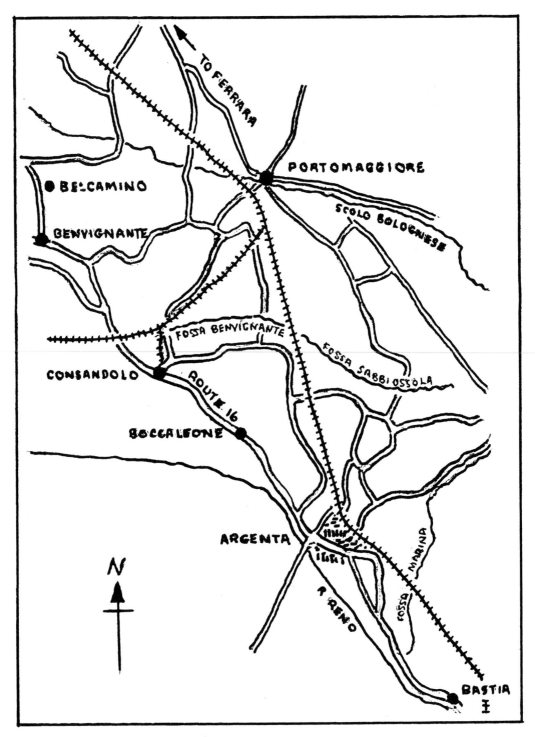

Map 9   Forcing the Argenta Gap and the advance to the River Adige

Safe Conduct

The German soldier who approaches the Allied positions without arms and with this SAFE CONDUCT is to be well looked after, to receive food, and be removed from the danger zone as soon as possible.

PASSIERSCHEIN

Deutsche Soldaten, die sich mit diesem Passierschein und ohne Waffen den alliierten Linien nahern, sind anstandig zu behandeln, zu verpflegen und unter Bewachung zurückzuschaffen.

Zur Vermeidung unnötigen Risiko, dieses Flugblatt oder etwas Weisses überm Kopf schwenken! 8-26

Plate 103 Allied air-dropped propaganda leaflet, offering safe conduct through the Allied lines if the finder surrendered (Les Burnham)

equipment abandoned intact, as well as large numbers of horses and cattle left behind and roaming about untended. All bridges over the river had been blown. The original plan was for 2/6th Queen's to cross in Fantails, due north of Copparo; it was then to form a bridgehead west of Crespino supported by a squadron of the 7th Hussars in amphibious tanks (Duplex Drive (DD) Shermans). They were to be followed by the other two battalions of the brigade, supported by their tank squadrons, ferried across on rafts. 24th Guards Brigade on the right and 167th Infantry Brigade on the left would then pass through and push on to the River Adige; 78th Infantry Division would cross on the left of 56th Division. Each tank was to carry 12 tins of petrol and as much additional ammunition as possible; a section of Royal Engineers, a Churchill bridgelayer and a Sherman dozer were to move with A Squadron.

These plans were modified, however, when, after reaching the Po early in the morning, both 24th Guards Brigade and 167th Infantry Brigade pushed troops across the river during the day and secured bridgeheads on the north bank with very little opposition. During 25 April, the 48th had been concentrated a few hundred yards from the crossing point, but there was a long delay in getting the rafts working after the Queen's Brigade crossed the river during the evening of the 25th and early morning of the 26th. In fact it was not until the morning of the 26th that the first tanks began to cross, and only A Squadron was across by last light that day; a crossing rate of about one tank per hour was all that could be achieved by the Royal Engineers. Alan Gilmour remembers:

Plate 104   A Sherman Duplex Drive (DD) tank, for amphibious operation, entering the water (Author's collection)

For days the enemy had bombarded us with canisters which dispensed leaflets, luridly illustrated, showing the folly of attempting the crossing. 'The war is nearly over,' said these documents, 'why get killed now?' In brilliant moonlight we crossed slowly and sideways at four o'clock in the morning. There was no opposition.

Meanwhile, the infantry had pushed on, meeting only very light opposition and finding many bridges left intact by the enemy. A Squadron caught up with them north of the town of Rovigo and supported the whole brigade front in mopping up the banks of the River Adige. C Squadron joined them about noon on the 27th, by which time patrols were already making their way across the Adige; although all the Adige bridges were blown, opposition was still very light but the weather was appalling, with heavy rain, thunder and lightning. B Squadron was across the River Po by dawn on the 28th, whence it went into billets in Rovigo for the night. Again Alan Gilmour's descriptive pen paints a graphic picture:

We bowled into Rovigo to discover that our billet was an infants' school. We had our evening meal at tiny desks, too small to get our knees under, and gazed at sentences some well-meaning teacher of English had written for the children to learn. 'The weather is very dump', 'Henceafter I shall let you know it', 'The sister of the teacher has long ears' (a daring one, that), and 'He often advices me to be more carefully'. Growled the *B-Line* in a dour editorial 'We advice these teachers to be more carefully still!'

Plate 105   Officers of B Squadron at Lungo Brenta in May 1945. Left to right: Lt Holtorp, Capt Kingsford (2IC), Lt Cottrell, Maj Joss (OC), Lts Braun and Palmer (Tony Kingsford)

The crossing of the River Adige was planned for the night of 28/29 April. All went as planned, except that, as there was little or no opposition, the artillery programme was cancelled at the last moment; by 04.00am the 2/5th Queen's had occupied Stanghella and work had started on the construction of a Class 40 pontoon Bailey bridge near the Route 16 river bridge. The 2IC gave orders for the battalion to be lined up on Route 16, with B Squadron in the lead, by 1.30pm, so that they could cross the river as soon as the bridge was complete, estimated to be at about 3.00pm. However, after the battalion had done this, Brig Dawnay, the commander of 21st Tank Brigade, ordered all of it, less B Squadron, to turn back to Rovigo, as there was a general stand-fast order in operation and the battalion was no longer in support of 169th Infantry Brigade. After discussion, it was decided that the battalion should cross the Adige after all and concentrate in Stanghella instead of Rovigo; all except B Squadron got themselves fixed up in billets there as soon as they were across the river.

B Squadron, however, having crossed first and assembled to the north, then began the best gallop of its career – 50 miles in five hours to Lungo Brenta, a few miles south-east of Venice, through Conselve, east to Candiana and Correzzola and north through Codevigo. Alan Gilmour again:

> . . . we roared after them following the high road north which, mile after mile, was lined by groups of civilians and, at one point, by partisans who discharged a feu-de-joie, frightening us considerably. The pace was maintained when dusk fell and fireflies began to signal in the twilight. Grim old *Titan* settled down to a steady roar and a consistent roll, like a ship in a swell.

Plate 106 The Churchill ARV I of B Squadron with its crew at Lungo Brenta in May 1945 (Tony Kingsford)

Carried away by the excitement of the pursuit, Maj 'Bill' Joss mixed his metaphors and, taking the bit between his teeth and turning a blind eye to the wireless, pressed on hard for Venice. Ned Cook, who was the wireless operator in his tank, continues the story:

We resumed our way along the road towards the city so aptly named 'The Queen of the Sea'. At last, coming near the coast, we could see its buildings rising from the haze of the lagoons – a wonderful and tantalising sight, Venice, the city of the winged lion. Just at that moment I caught a very indistinct voice on my (rear) link set, only just discernible above the roar of the 350bhp Bedford engine and the noise of the tracks pounding the road. I heard the voice calling B Squadron commander with instructions to halt and return to rendezvous with the battalion somewhere near Rovigo. Without acknowledging, I passed the message to the major, and we both gazed across the lagoons at that enticing sight of Venice . . . We had come a long way that afternoon, about 35 miles as the crow flies and probably nearer 50 by road – a remarkable feat for the Churchills in the column – and the prospect of not being allowed our prize of entering Venice after all that was rather more than our major could stomach. 'Don't acknowledge it,' he said to me with a grin, 'we must surely be out of wireless range by now.' So off we went again, and every minute the voice of the caller, whom it appeared was at Brigade HQ and working on our frequency, became fainter and fainter until it disappeared completely in the background 'mush' of the set. We arrived eventually at a place called Lungo Brenta, a few miles from the causeway linking the mainland with Venice. Here we found, to our dismay, that we were on the wrong side of a small river or canal which, as it was crossed only by a wooden bridge that would certainly not take our weight, forced us to call a halt . . . Venice was still, as it were, just around the corner but it could as well have been a thousand miles away.

In the event, Venice was taken by 169th Infantry Brigade, the honour falling to 2/5th Queen's. The CO and LO of the 48th moved into the city, with HQ 169th Brigade, on 30 April and thus ended the battalion's part in the defeat of the enemy in Northern Italy. The battalion had been in the forefront of the battle from the Senio to the Adige and had supported no fewer than three divisions in the process, and every tank had done the whole journey on its tracks. On 1 May the commander of 21st Tank Brigade received the following message from the Army commander:

My best congratulations on the part 21 Tank Brigade has played in the present operation. Your support of the infantry in the face of the great natural difficulties of the terrain has been a decisive factor in the success of the offensive to date. All ranks have shown a splendid fighting spirit and determination to close with the enemy. Well done indeed. I know that, as we advance, you will continue to contribute to the total destruction of the enemy forces in Italy, which was our aim and which is already largely achieved.

It was apparent that German resistance in Italy was ending, and in fact, on the following day, 2 May, came the announcement of unconditional surrender. Alan Gilmour recounts:

. . . that evening Bartlett and I sat in the tank, tuned in to the BBC and a moment later learnt of the unconditional surrender of the German forces in Italy. Across the breech of the 6pdr we shook hands. Our six-year crusade had ended.

B Squadron spent about a week in Lungo Brenta during which its members were able to visit a tourist-free Venice and Venetians were able to witness the unusual spectacle of gondolas filled with tank types wearing their tank oversuits (**Plate 107**). Then, on 8 May, the day on which the German capitulation in Europe was announced, the squadron joined the rest of the battalion at Stanghella, just north of the River Adige. A week later, on the 15th, the battalion moved in trucks back to Rimini, leaving its tanks behind in the care of a small rear party for disposal.

In Rimini the battalion was billeted in sea-front hotels and, for several weeks, led an almost idyllic holiday life in this Adriatic resort. Those entitled were able to take UK leave in the form of 'Python', LIAP (leave in addition to Python) or LILOP (leave in lieu of Python), while others took local leave in the form of visits to Rome, Florence, Padua and other cultural centres. In beautiful weather, those remaining in Rimini were able to spend hours on the beach, swimming or playing tennis, cricket or basketball. Duties were minimal, consisting mainly of POW camp guard duties.

On 15 May Maj J.F. Reynolds was posted in as 2IC of the battalion, Capt F.D. (Don) Hoad was again promoted to acting major and Lt Henry Palmer to acting captain. On the 25th, Maj C.A. Joss was posted to 21st Tank Brigade HQ, Capt Tony Kingsford assuming command of B Squadron in his absence. On 7 June Maj Joss returned to the battalion, going to HQ Squadron as senior major; also that day came the announcement of immediate awards by Field Marshal Alexander of the Military Cross to Maj C.A. Joss, Capt H.D. Palmer and Lt M.G. Reaney, the Distinguished Conduct Medal to Sgt A.E. Catchpole and the Military Medal to Sgt R. Paice. This was followed by an immediate Mention in Despatches for Capt

Plate 107   B Squadron gondola crew in Venice, May 1945 (Ned Cook)

Kingsford on 16 June. On the 10th of the month Lt A.F. Holtorp was posted back to HQ 21st Tank Brigade. The RSM, E.T. Fell, left the battalion on release on the 24th, after having very successfully filled the appointment of Regimental Sergeant Major since July 1942. The Quartermaster, Capt (QM) 'Eggy' Eggleton, also due to leave on release the same day, was not so lucky; having been injured in an accident the previous day, he was instead admitted to 66 General Hospital.

On 27 June the battalion was visited by the Army commander, Lt Gen Sir Richard McCreery, accompanied by Brig Dawnay, the brigade commander. With the departure on leave of the CO, Lt Col Peter Sturdee, and the Adjutant, Capt Tom Gorringe, Maj F.A. Haigh, MC, assumed command and Capt Harvey, the LO, took over temporarily as Adjutant on the 29th. The following day Harvey too left for 28 days' leave in the UK and Capt R.G. (Ralph) White assumed the Adjutant's mantle. Lt F.W. Skey, who had been the Intelligence Officer virtually ever since his arrival in the battalion, was promoted to acting captain and posted to A Squadron the same day. Peter Sturdee returned from leave and reassumed command on 8 July; on the 19th, Lt Bruce Cottrell was posted to the 6th Battalion RTR as BTA, while on the 23rd, two officers and 67 ORs were posted to the 8th Battalion RTR for duties in the Far East theatre of operations.

On 4 July, A Squadron opened its attractive new canteen and invited members of B Squadron to use it. But such things did little to relieve the boredom that was beginning to set in; this was not helped by the lowering of morale caused by the gradual disintegration of the battalion due to postings out and demobilisation. Those with high demobilisation numbers saw their friends of five years disappearing at an increasing rate while themselves having little chance of a change of scene. Those with wives and families or jobs waiting at home became increasingly impatient with life on the Adriatic coast, the last straw being the posting out of 140 men to various cavalry regiments in August to make up their numbers.

The last issue of the *B-Line* in August reckoned that, within a month, there would be no B Squadron left; Capt Henry Palmer was the last remaining officer who had come overseas with the squadron three years previously. On 3 August the battalion took part in the parade in Rimini stadium to bid farewell to Brig David Dawnay, who had commanded 21st Tank Brigade throughout its participation in the Italian campaign. The battalion dance band under Sgt Al Potts broadcast from the BFS Adriatic on 18 August, with Vic Chesterton on piano and Johnny Walker on double bass and vocals; that same evening, Ronnie Hatch, Neil Chadwick and Eric Gilmour, the MO, represented the 48th in a general knowledge competition against the RASC and won by 9 to 7. A further nail was hammered into the battalion's coffin with the posting out, to various cavalry regiments, of one officer and a further 96 other ranks on 27 August; and, with the end of August 1945 and the end of the war, the War Diary ceased to be compiled.

It seemed that, like the old soldiers in the song, the 48th was doomed not to die but just to fade away. As Alan Gilmour put it in the souvenir edition of the *B-Line*:

If that means that old campaigners live increasingly in the past, will we have memories

Plate 108 Brig Dawnay, commanding 21 Tank Brigade, and Lt Col Peter Sturdee at the farewell parade in Rimini's stadium (Don Hoad)

enough to ensure that we go down, rose-crowned, into the darkness? As the years pass we will forget much of the good, and most of the bad, of those 70 eventful months. 'I record only the sunny hours', reads the inscription on the sundial; so it is with human memory. . . . As the mind searches its recesses a variety of pictures is produced; work and leisure, fighting and playing. Swimming, in Croydon baths, off the South Coast during wireless schemes, in the North Sea between outpost duties, in the Mediterranean and the Adriatic; in the Volturno and, of course, the river at Stanghella. Nights spent in billets, empty houses, ruined houses, stables, sheds, tents of all shapes and sizes, bivvies, ditches, decks, holds, tank turrets, underneath tanks, on transporters; on English beds, Scottish beds, Italian and German beds, Arab – well, hardly! Varieties of mud, notably in the original tank park at Wickham Market, where each time a squadron moved out at least two Valentines could be relied on to belly and shed tracks, and at Linney Head, where the tanks steered themselves in the grooves leading to the battle practice site; Hoddom mud, Riccione mud and the mud at Santone.

The mind flashes back over six Cambrai Day celebrations and six Christmases spent in strange places. We remember queues – we queued for pay, for NAAFI and issues of equipment; we queued for food and medical inspection. Sometimes we just queued. We came to terms with the phenomenal world, for we lived close to nature – so close indeed that at Penthièvre we shared couch and crust with the ants, the spiders and the beetles – and, sleeping under the sky, came to know the heavens; those magnificent sunsets behind the Apennines and the brilliant constellations of the Algerian night, with the Milky Way a vivid ribbon overhead. Each of us will retain his indelible impression – maybe the first glimpse of Vesuvius and Capri, or the sight of the rubble that was Cassino; St Peter's, St Mark's, or perhaps just a farmhouse in Umbria. These are the incidentals, the sum of which forms our background to war.

Tanks! Gross, insatiable beasts which demanded slavish attention, which wallowed in filth and devoured vast quantities of sustenance – and yet, and yet, for so long virtually our homes and the focal point of our endeavours. Tanks, spitting rapid death or thundering measured destruction; tanks, a lurching column of them, more massive and more formidable in the African moonlight, or decked with vine leaves and branches advancing in carnivalesque procession among the Apennine foothills. The distant clatter of tracks in an Algerian olive grove, the angry glow of red-hot exhausts in the night. And dust – spirals of dust, blankets of dust, moving clouds of dust surmounted by black berets. Vivid impressions of darkness relieved by graceful arcs of tracer fire, or dispelled by flares or burning dumps. Ships – Landing Craft on Loch Fyne; troopships bursting with human cargoes; swaying hammocks; cursing and loss of equipment. Fishing craft off Riccione, and Venetian gondolas. Trucks in endless convoys, creeping up fissures in the Atlas mountains, winding through Tunisia, exploring every route from Taranto to Turin; ammo trucks, petrol trucks, liberty trucks. Prisoners – hundreds of thousands trudging the roads and filling enormous compounds. Rain and wind – the hot sirocco which scorched in Cap Bon and Penthièvre. Exotic shrubs and fantastic reptiles, scorpions and centipedes and the infuriating cigala. Inoculations, drill parades, guards, fatigues – ah! the enchantment dies.

We disperse and go our ways. From time to time, God willing, we will meet; perchance we will see our own transitions to sedate and greying citizens reflected in each other. But when this happens, we will not be thinking of what we are then but of what we were during the testing time of active service, and we will delve into the wealth of experience which is ours. The remembrance of these things, the fellowship

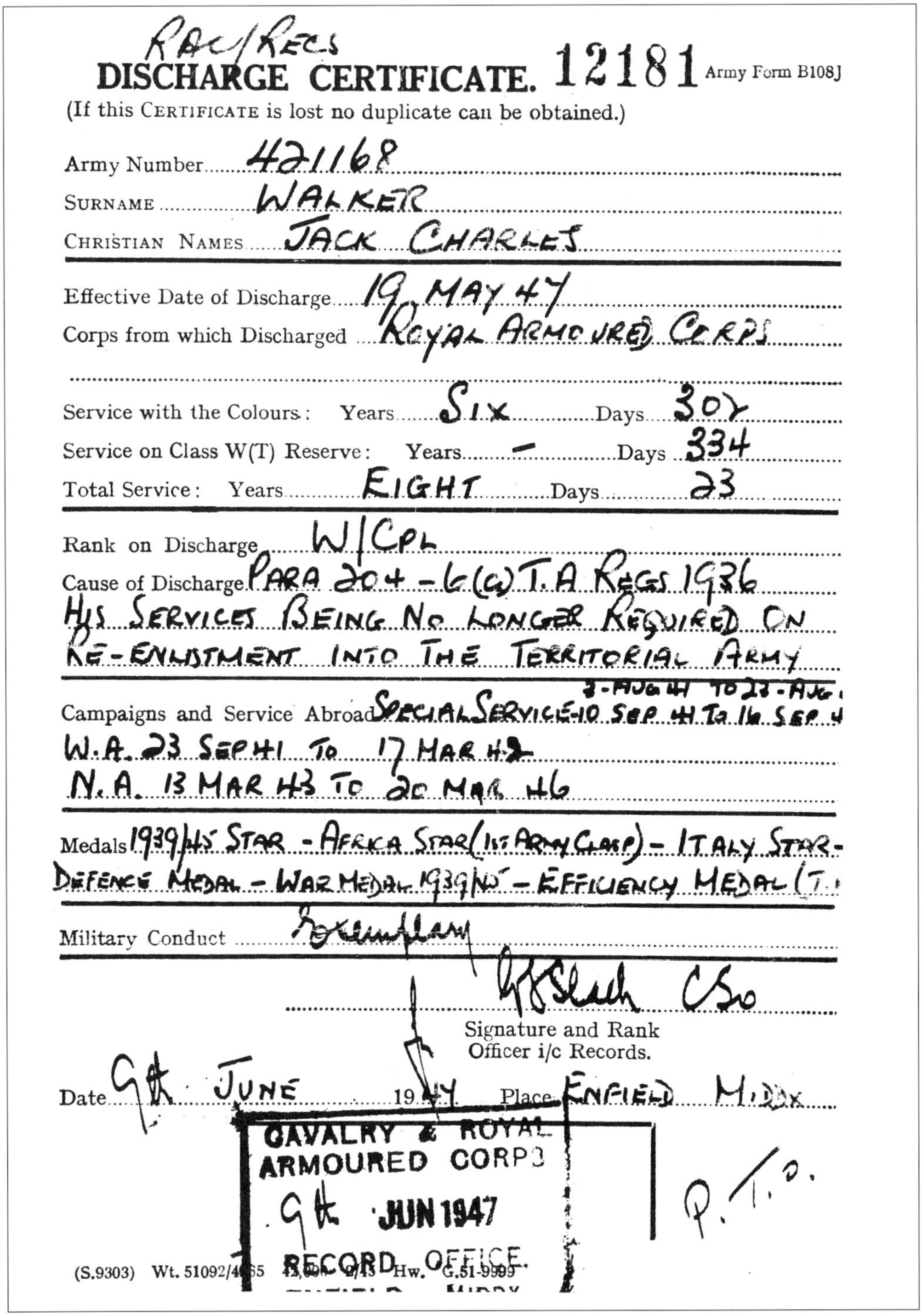

RAC/RECS

DISCHARGE CERTIFICATE. 12181 Army Form B108J

(If this CERTIFICATE is lost no duplicate can be obtained.)

Army Number......*421168*

SURNAME......*WALKER*

CHRISTIAN NAMES......*JACK CHARLES*

Effective Date of Discharge......*19 MAY 47*

Corps from which Discharged......*ROYAL ARMOURED CORPS*

Service with the Colours: Years......*SIX*......Days......*302*

Service on Class W(T) Reserve: Years......*—*......Days......*334*

Total Service: Years......*EIGHT*......Days......*23*

Rank on Discharge......*W/CPL*

Cause of Discharge......*PARA 204 – 6(C) T.A. REGS 1936*
HIS SERVICES BEING NO LONGER REQUIRED ON
RE-ENLISTMENT INTO THE TERRITORIAL ARMY

Campaigns and Service Abroad......*SPECIAL SERVICE 10 SEP 41 TO 16 SEP 41*
3-AUG 41 TO 23-AUG
W.A. 23 SEP 41 TO 17 MAR 42
N.A. 13 MAR 43 TO 20 MAR 46

Medals......*1939/45 STAR – AFRICA STAR (1ST ARMY CLASP) – ITALY STAR –*
DEFENCE MEDAL – WAR MEDAL 1939/45 – EFFICIENCY MEDAL (T.

Military Conduct......*Exemplary*

GR Slach CSO

Signature and Rank
Officer i/c Records.

Date......*9th JUNE*......19*47*......Place......*ENFIELD MIDX*

CAVALRY & ROYAL
ARMOURED CORPS
9th JUN 1947
RECORD OFFICE

P.T.O.

(S.9303) Wt. 51092/4065 43,000 4/43 Hw. G.51-9999

Plate 109 Other ranks' discharge certificate (John Walker)

and the hardship, will not fade away; and while the remembrance endures the Battalion will live on.

But the disintegration process continued, until the final two men and a boy were demobilised in 1946. The official disbandment of the battalion in the middle of that year was merely a belated confirmation of something that had already occurred. Its final appearance was in the Victory Parade held in London in June 1946, in which it was represented by Maj Maurice Ladd who said,' I was the longest-serving member of the battalion available in London, so they picked on me!'

Its life might have been short but it had been full of incident, and the battalion had played its full part in the greater scheme of things; its going was regretted by all who had shared its comradeship and hardship. It had created a record of which it could be, and was, justly proud.

Although known unofficially in Italy, and officially when abbreviated in operational and administrative documents, as '48 RTR', the battalion's official title throughout its brief life was '48th Battalion, Royal Tank Regiment'. In this form, the Royal Tank Regiment followed British Army tradition in having its component units as battalions of a regiment; under Army Order 42 of 1946, issued on 31 March that year, however, the battalions of the RTR were, from 18 September 1945, to be known as 'regiments'. Thus, had it still existed, the 48th would finally have been officially entitled '48th Royal Tank Regiment'; this was not to be, however, and at its disbandment it was still known by the title with which it had been born – the 48th Battalion, Royal Tank Regiment (TA).

Postscript

The 48th may have been dead but it refused to lie down. As might be expected with a body of men of such mixed talents and abilities, thrown intimately together under circumstances of shared hardships and relaxation for six years, they could not see a future in which they did not meet up regularly with their former mates, to discuss shared experiences and individual achievements.

Accordingly, the 48th Battalion RTR Reunion Society (later to become the 48th Royal Tank Regiment Association) was formed immediately after the war, with the avowed aim of keeping all former members of the battalion in touch with each other and arranging at least one annual get-together in London, as well as looking after the less fortunate of its members suffering ill-health. The first Hon Sec/Treasurer was Edmund ('Ned') Cook. It had a quite extraordinarily strong membership of some 90 per cent of those of all ranks who had served in the battalion, such was the spirit of this very happy unit; in 1985, nearly 50 years after its formation, its membership still stood at some 500 former members of all ranks, a tribute to the comradeship, loyalty and pride in their unit felt by these men.

The ranks of the association are naturally, if unfortunately, being thinned by the ravages of time; each issue of the Association Newsletter seems to contain ever more names of those who have passed 'to the green fields beyond'. Memories too are dimming, the author's not

Plate 110   The Gradara War Cemetery of the Commonwealth War Graves Commission, in which many of the battalion's dead are buried (Tony Kingsford)

Plate 111 The 48th Bn RTR Roll of Honour, photographed at the Tank Museum, Bovington, beside a Churchill tank on 14 May 1992 on the occasion of its re-dedication (John Walker)

least, and this history has suffered from both of these failings as key members have passed on or their memories have failed them at crucial points. This cannot be helped, and it is felt that, despite the passage of some 50 years since the events related in this history took place, the essential facts and chronology are correct. If any former member of the battalion reading this history feels that justice has not been done or due attention paid to some person or event which he well remembers, let him take the blame for not having responded to the author's pleas in the Newsletter and in personal correspondence for help in the compilation!

Apart from the formation of the 48th RTR Association, the battalion left its mark on various places in England, Scotland, Algeria, Tunisia and Italy. The most obvious, and at the same time the most tragic, are the headstones in the Commonwealth War Graves Commission war cemeteries in Tunisia and Italy, at Massicault, Gradara (**Plate 110**), Faenza, Coriano and Argenta, to which the association has led pilgrimages since the war. The names of those 84 members of the battalion killed in action or who died of wounds and are buried in these cemeteries are listed in Appendix D. The Battalion Roll of Honour (**Plate 111**) hangs in the Tank Museum at Bovington and was reconsecrated in a small but moving ceremony on 14 May 1992.

On a more cheerful note, one other memento of the battalion lingers on in the Tank Museum at Bovington: this is the Tiger tank knocked out by A Squadron and captured intact and in running order in the Djebel Djaffa action on 21/22 April 1943. After capture, this tank, the Platoon Commander's tank of 3 Platoon, 1 Company, of 504 Heavy Tank Battalion, was recovered, tested, given a preliminary examination and refurbished by 104 Tank Workshops REME before being put on show in Tunis; there, bearing the First Army shield and the 21st Army Tank Brigade dark blue diabolo front and rear (**Plates 65 and 66**), it was examined by HM King George VI and Winston Churchill in June 1943 before being shipped back to the UK for detailed examination. As a result of this examination it was no longer a 'runner' when placed in the Tank Museum. At the time of writing (1995), however, it was being refurbished and put back into running order, as well as being restored to its original colour scheme and markings.

Hoddom Castle became a caravan park, 'the perfect centre' according to the report in the Annandale Series for 9 October 1975, 'Best Camp in Scotland' (sic!) according to the first entry in the visitors' book, reported in the same issue. The coach-house has become an English-style pub.

Sanderstead changed very little, recovering well from the shock of providing temporary homes for such a mixed, talented and unconventional bag of temporary soldiers and avoiding much of the reconstruction which has changed Croydon beyond recognition. West Lavington and Wickham Market too recovered quickly, and are comparatively little changed today. Tunisia quickly reverted to its former state, so that it is difficult for the soldier returning to the scenes of his battles to find where they took place; apart from the war cemeteries of the Allies and the Axis forces, little trace remains of the hundreds of thousands of troops stationed there for so long, while the tourist holiday centres have changed beyond recognition. In Italy, however, the picture is different; Venice was a let-down to the 84 members of the 48th RTR Association and their wives who made a pilgrimage there to coincide with the association's 40th reunion, but the features for which they had battled in 1944 and 1945 were still clearly to be seen, as were many of the landmarks.

Little remains to be said; the battalion was disbanded in mid-1946, although its progenitor, the 42nd Battalion RTR (TA), was re-formed at St John's Hill, Clapham in 1947 as the 42nd Royal Tank Regiment (TA). The 42nd had only a brief second life, however, before it was converted back to the 23rd London Regiment in 1956 and combined with the 6th Battalion

Plate 112   Glevering Hall as it is today (C.B.W. Hurlock)

Plate 113   San Maria Scacciano after the war (Tony Kingsford)

East Surrey Regiment (TA) to form the 4th Battalion Queen's Royal Surrey Regiment (TA) in 1961. This in turn was combined with the 3rd Battalion to form the 6th Queen's Royal Surreys in 1967.

Meanwhile the 48th RTR Association carries on, its numbers shrinking increasingly with each year that passes. In 25 years' time probably none will be left to remember the good times and the bad, the triumphs and the disappointments, the zest for life and the courage with which death was faced, of a battalion formed out of the patriotism, loyalty and cheerfulness in shared adversity so characteristic of the young Londoner. It is to perpetuate the story of this battalion that this history has been written, in the hope that it will serve as an example to be followed by those who follow us.

Organisation and equipment of the infantry tank battalion

1940

The initial organisation at the outbreak of war consisted of:

HQ Company	Bn HQ	2 'I' tanks
		4 light tanks
		2 carriers
Three Tank Companies each of:	Coy HQ	1 'I' tank
		1 light tank
Five Sections each of:		3 'I' tanks

1941

HQ Squadron	Bn HQ	4 'I' tanks
Three Tank Squadrons each of :	Sqn HQ	1 'I' tank
		2 CS 'I' tanks
Five Troops each of:		3 'I' tanks

1942

HQ Squadron	Bn HQ	4 'I' tanks
		8 AA tanks
	Recce Tp	10 scout cars
	Intercomm Tp	9 scout cars
Three Tank Squadrons each of:	Sqn HQ	1 'I' tank
		2 CS 'I' tanks
Five Troops each of:		3 'I' tanks
Total A vehicles in battalion:		
		52 'I' tanks
		6 CS 'I' tanks
		8 AA tanks
		19 Scout cars

1943

HQ Squadron	Bn HQ	4 'I' tanks
		2 OP tanks
		6 AA tanks
	Recce Tp	11 light tanks
	Intercomm Tp	9 scout cars
Three Tank Squadrons each of:	Sqn HQ	1 'I' tank
		2 CS 'I' tanks
Five Troops each of:		3 'I' tanks

Total A vehicles in battalion:

'I' tanks	52
CS 'I' tanks	6
AA tanks	6
OP tanks	2
Light tanks	11
Scout cars	9

In fact, Recce Troop was formed in August 1942, with 11 Bren carriers and 26 ORs, commanded by a captain; it was organised into three sections, each commanded by a corporal and each comprising three carriers. The section commander's vehicle had a crew of three (commander, driver and wireless operator) while other vehicles had commander and driver only. Recce Troop HQ section consisted of two carriers, each with a crew of three, one commanded by the troop leader and the other by the troop sergeant.

1944 (North Africa)

Recce Troop re-equipped with 11 Stuart (M3A3) US light tanks in place of 11 carriers. Troop organisation remained as before, but personnel increased as tanks required a crew of four.

Tank squadrons were reorganised on a four-troop basis, each of three gun tanks; SHQ troops consisted of four tanks, two gun tanks and two close support (CS) tanks, battalion HQ troop of four tanks.

Total A vehicles in battalion:

I tanks	46
CS I tanks	6
AA tanks	6
OP Tanks	2
Light tanks	11
Scout cars	9

1944 (Italy)

Recce Troop Stuarts modified; six had turrets removed and 0.5in Browning MGs installed on the turret ring, which had a protective plate of armour installed around it. Troop HQ and section commanders' were turreted, remainder turretless.

Tank troops in squadrons were re-equipped, initially with two Shermans and two Churchills each. This was found not to be satisfactory and was later changed, two troops per squadron having three Churchill IVs (NA75) each; the other two having three Shermans each. In 1945 the Shermans were exchanged for Churchill VIIs, armed with the British 75mm gun.

Squadron Nominal Rolls

A Company

ORs only, as at September 1939

CSM G.H. Charlton
CQMS W.E. King
Sgt J. Barrett
Sgt F. Esdale
Sgt R. Howe
Sgt J.H. Jones
Sgt E.Le M. Latrielle
Sgt C.H. Noyce
Sgt J.E. Sergeant
Sgt R.C.J. Smalldon
Sgt F.H. Swain
Sgt N.C. Venables
Sgt A.C. White
L/Sgt S. Earle
Cpl L.B. Adams
Cpl E. Binning
Cpl C. Chart
Cpl F.J. Fisk
Cpl A.R. Gibbs
Cpl D.S. Goldsmith
Cpl K.E. Goldsmith
Cpl D. Hamilton
Cpl F. Harrison
Cpl A.S. Jaeger
Cpl V.V. Kenward
Cpl J.G.W. Munns
Cpl K.H. Price
Cpl P.C. Reynolds
Cpl E.R.A. Rice
Cpl T.S.H. Turner
Cpl S.A.J. Warren
LCpl P. Blair
LCpl J. McCombe
LCpl P. Muchmore
LCpl W.O. Nunn
LCpl A.E. Taylor

LCpl R.H.L. Tyler
Tpr F.C. Andy
Tpr B.J. Bailess
Tpr H.B. Baker
Tpr W. Baker
Tpr A. Bates
Tpr S.J. Birchenough
Tpr R. Blankley
Tpr J.A. Bottell
Tpr E.S. Burgess
Tpr M.A. Caulfield
Tpr B.R. Chaplin
Tpr E.T. Christian
Tpr R.H. Christian
Tpr M.G. Daly
Tpr L. Dury
Tpr P.T. Earwicker
Tpr C.D. Evans
Tpr C.O.O. Faithful
Tpr F.D. Featherstonhaugh
Tpr R.M. Fletcher
Tpr W. Flynn
Tpr J.L. Fry
Tpr A.G. Gale
Tpr R.N. Garrard
Tpr R.W. Greenwood
Tpr W.G. Haines
Tpr R.W. Hall
Tpr R.J. Hamilton
Tpr S.P. Hardiman
Tpr F.W. Harris
Tpr A.F. Jordan
Tpr A.C.S. Julius
Tpr H. Kempson
Tpr K.J. Kenwood
Tpr D.J. McCarthy

Tpr J. McKenney
Tpr L. Manley
Tpr J.R. Martin
Tpr K.W. Mason
Tpr E.G. Maxwell
Tpr G.G. Morrey-Jones
Tpr J.D. Nubley
Tpr H. Olivier
Tpr F.S. Patten
Tpr R.G. Perry
Tpr P.E. Perry
Tpr B.D. Pilgrim
Tpr R.H.J. Rees
Tpr K.B. Rice
Tpr J.P. Rockcliffe

Tpr J.H. Seabrook
Tpr B.J. Shaw
Tpr G.L. Sickel
Tpr F.G. Smith
Tpr F.W. Smith
Tpr S.C. Spicer
Tpr W.G. Stringer
Tpr L. Swain
Tpr J.F. Tellam
Tpr B.C. Thorne
Tpr R. Vacher
Tpr D.G. Wheston
Tpr S.D. Wilks
Tpr R.S. Williams
Tpr H.J. Wootley

Tpr W.L. Yarnton

B Squadron
All ranks, from March 1943 to summer 1945

Cpl F.W. Abbott
Cpl A.F.W. Alexander
Cpl F. Attridge
Tpr H.B. Baker
Tpr T.W. Baker
Tpr A.E. Bailey
Tpr T. Barron
Cpl G.R. Bartlett
Tpr L. Batchelor
LCpl G. Beard
Tpr W. Beaven
Tpr F.W. Belfield
Tpr E.E. Bird
Tpr W.E. Blackmore
Tpr C.M. Blythman
Tpr A.B. Blythman
LSgt S.G. Booth
M/Sgt P.J. Boswell
LCpl B.B. Boulter
Lt J.R. Braun
Sgt W.J. Broomfield
Pte W.H. Brown
Capt T.S. Bruce
Tpr G. Bryant
Tpr E.D. Buckenham
Sgt E. Buckland
LCpl A.G. Burton

Tpr W.H. Rye
Cpl D. Campbell
LCpl H.B. Cannon
Tpr J.H. Carmalt
Tpr W.H. Cavalli
Cpl B.R. Chaplin
M/Sgt W.L. Challis
Cpl V.E. Chesterton
Capt N.R.M. Chadwick
Tpr A. Chamberlain
Sgt C. Chart
Tpr W. Chugg
LCpl S.G. Clark
LCpl E.J. Clarke
Tpr G.L. Clarke
Tpr L. Clay
LCpl H.J. Cloake
Tpr B. Cohen
LCpl J.E. Coleman
Tpr S.J. Coleman
Pte W. Coleman
Tpr F.S. Collins
Cpl J. Coniff
Tpr J.W. Cock
Cpl E. Cook
Tpr H.N. Cook
LCpl R.W. Cooke

Sgt W.G. Cornish
Tpr A.E. Cory
Lt B.W. Cottrell
Tpr T. Couper
Sgt F. Cox
Sgt J.M. Cox
Tpr C.W. Coates
Tpr E.A. Crane
S/Sgt D.B. Cremer
Tpr E. Criddle
Cpl C.L. Crohill
2Lt J.M. Cruickshank
Sgt A.V.A. Cummins
Pte L. Daly
LCpl P. Daly
Tpr C.H. Darley
Tpr A.H. Darvill
Tpr H.L. Davey
Tpr G.T. Davies
Sgt J.D. Davies
LCpl G. Davis
Tpr W. Day
Tpr A.J. Dennis
Sgt D. Denny
LCpl H.F. Dixon
Tpr F.F. Duffort
Tpr E. Duffy
Tpr R.P. Eley
Tpr H.H.G. Elford
Tpr R.W. Embling
Tpr A.A. Evans
Tpr A. Fiddy
Tpr S.R. Finch
Tpr J.A. Flight
Tpr A.P. Flint
Tpr R.E. Fly
LCpl J.E. Ford
Lt T.N. Fowles
Tpr W. Gallop
LCpl H.S. Gardner
Tpr H. Garner
LCpl A.J. Gilmour
SQMS J.E. Girdler
Sgt H.G. Gunton
Capt M. Goldby
Tpr W. Goss
Lt C. Greenwood
Tpr H. Hagon

Tpr C.F. Hall
Tpr J.W. Hall
Sgt F. Harding
Tpr R. Harris
Pte S. Harris
Tpr E. Harrison
Tpr J.L. Hasler
Tpr R.H.L. Hatch
Tpr A. Hegarty
Tpr E.H. Hellyar
Cpl W.G. Hernig
Sgt J.F. Hill
Lt R.W. Hitchings
Maj F.D. Hoad
Cpl C.G. Hodges
Tpr A.E. Holliday
LCpl C. Holmes
Tpr B.F. Holmes
Tpr L.O. Holmes
Lt A.F. Holtorp
Tpr R. Howe
LCpl E.J. Howell
Tpr S.J.T. Howes
Tpr J. Hughes
Tpr K. Hughes
Tpr S.W. Hynds
Tpr H. Imber
Tpr A. Jacobs
Tpr T. Jarvie
Tpr E. Jennings
Tpr R.T. Jones
Maj C.A. Joss MC
Tpr B. Keane
Tpr W.J. Keane
Pte J.E. Keenan
Tpr S.F. Kelsall
Tpr E.G. Kemp
LCpl E.W. Kemp
LCpl W.A. Kent
Tpr A.E. Kentleton
Pte A. Keogh
Lt J.R. Kerridge
Tpr F. King
Tpr P.W. King
Capt A.F. Kingsford MC
Tpr B. Kynaston
Tpr W.T. Lamb
Sgt B. Lane

Tpr B. Langley
Tpr J.L.H. Langstaffe
Lt J.L.C. Larcombe
Tpr W. Lawrence
LCpl A.C. Lennard
Tpr J. Little
LCpl J. Livingstone
Cpl B. Lord
Tpr C.J. Lynch
Tpr D. Maclay
Tpr L. Manley
Tpr R.L. Manwaring-White
Cpl A.G. Martin
Tpr A.G. Martin
Tpr J.F. Martin
LCpl W.T.H. McCarthy
Tpr T. McDowell
Cpl B. McKeown
LCpl R. Meachen
SQMS L.H. Merton
Cpl E. Moore
LCpl S.G. Morgan
Tpr G. Morris
Tpr D.W. Munro
Tpr J.L. Nagle
Pte G. Naylor
Tpr W. Naylor
Tpr A.N. Neave
Tpr E. Newson
LCpl H.J. Nickels
Tpr R.V. Nicoll MM
LCpl L. Norman
LCpl R. Norman
LCpl P.T. Norvill
Cpl P.A. Oldfield
Tpr R.S. Owen
Cpl D. Palmer
Capt H.D. Palmer MC
Tpr S.H. Parish
Cpl J.H. Paul
Tpr J.A. Peace
Tpr S.V. Pearce
LSgt C.F. Peebles
Sgt W.H. Peet
Sgt R.G. Perry
Tpr R. Phillips
Tpr A.E. Phillpot
Tpr W. Pitfield

Pte K.G. Pooley
Sgt D.W. Powell
LCpl I. Powles
LCpl J.W. Presky
Lt G. Proud
Tpr R. Rainey
Capt M. Rand
Pte J.S. Rann
Tpr A. Ray
Sgmn T. Reed
Cpl H.G. Reeve
Tpr L. Richmond
Tpr M.A. Robbins
Tpr P. Roberts
Tpr R. Robertson
Tpr A.H. Ross
Tpr J. Ross
LCpl H.N. Rumsey
SSM J.E. Ryan
Tpr E.R. Sibbick
Tpr C.A. Simmers
SSM H.L. Simpson
Cpl W. Slater
Tpr A.H. Smith
Tpr C.O. Smith
Tpr E.B. Smith
Tpr F.A. Smith
Tpr J.F. Smith
Tpr M. Smith
Tpr H. Smithers
Tpr A. Snipe
LCpl J. Stainforth
Lt M.M.M. Standage
Tpr R.A. Stobbs
Tpr F.H. Strong
Pte C.M. Sturman
Tpr W. Styles
Tpr A. Sustin
Tpr A.G. Taylor
LCpl S.B. Taylor
Tpr D.J. Teagle
Tpr J. Thomas
LCpl G.G. Thomason
LCpl G. Thomson
LCpl L. Thorne
Tpr W. Thornton
Tpr K. Tierney
Tpr D.W. Tillman

Tpr G. Timms
Tpr A. Tobin
Tpr H.R. Tock
Tpr V. Tozer
Tpr A.W. Turner
Capt G.H.P. Tyrrell
Lt P.S. Vos
Tpr J.R. Walker
Tpr J. Walling
Cpl F.E. Ward
Tpr J. Warrior
Tpr C. Wassell
Sgt J. Watson
Sgt P.M. Watson

Tpr D.L. Watts
Sgt D.H. Weeks
LCpl R.F.T. Wells
Tpr R.H. Wells
Cpl G. Welsby
Cpl B.C.H. White
Tpr R.C. Whittington
LCpl G.S. Williams
Tpr D. Willsher
Sgt E.S. Wilson
Tpr K.D. Willetts
Tpr E. Wright
Cpl J.W. Yates

C Squadron
Tank Crew Lists, early 1944

SHQ Troop

Cdr	Maj Haigh	Capt Hoad	Capt Buckley
Dvr	Tpr Steel	Tpr R.H. Smith	Tpr Cooper
Op	Sgt Camp	Cpl Wootley	Tpr Windeatt
Gnr	LCpl Yeo	Tpr Keyes	L/Sgt Sherborne
Co-dvr	Tpr Prust	Tpr Ellicott	Tpr Simmons

11 Troop

Cdr	Lt Stewart	Sgt Spackman	Cpl Studholme
Dvr	LCpl Hardiman	Tpr Hastings	Tpr Howell
Op	Tpr W.J. Wood	Tpr Oswin	Tpr Outhwaite
Gnr	LCpl Smellie	Tpr Bray	Tpr Murphy
Co-dvr	Tpr Phillips	Tpr Jones	Tpr Swift

12 Troop

Cdr	Lt Hunter	Sgt Paice	Cpl Maxwell
Dvr	Tpr Bird	Tpr Lattimer	Tpr Griffen
Op	LCpl Currie	Cpl Maffett	Tpr Edgar
Gnr	Tpr Lomas	Tpr Browne	Tpr Sampson
Co-dvr	Tpr Woodhams	Tpr Kirkin	Tpr G. Smith

13 Troop

Cdr	Lt Reynolds	Sgt Bond	Cpl Mason
Dvr	LCpl Diggens	Tpr Harding	Tpr Hewitt
Op	Tpr McKinnell	Tpr Sones	Tpr Bruce
Gnr	Tpr Mee	Tpr Nicklin	Tpr R.C. Taylor
Co-Dvr	Tpr Inman	Tpr Beesley	Tpr Fender

14 Troop

Cdr	Lt Isgar	Sgt Gerrish	Cpl Webb
Dvr	Tpr Evans	LCpl Gage	Tpr Watson
Op	Tpr Creagh	Tpr Oden	Tpr Bolton
Gnr	Tpr Beak	Tpr Baltzer	Tpr Titterton
Co-dvr	Tpr Althorpe	Tpr Langan	Tpr Wathen

15 Troop

Cdr	Lt Thomas	Sgt Catchpole	Cpl Clinton
Dvr	Tpr Abbott	Tpr Norris	Tpr Ward
Op	Tpr Astbury	Tpr Moutrie	Tpr Cross
Gnr	LCpl Sullivan	LCpl Kembury	Tpr W. Taylor
Co-dvr	Tpr Wakefield	Tpr Annable	Tpr Foster

Spare Crews

11 Troop: Sgt Macpherson, Cpl Attridge
12 Troop: Tpr Heron, Tpr Thompson
13 Troop: Tpr Reekie
14 Troop: Tpr T.A. Wood, LCpl Stokes, Tpr Barker
15 Troop: Tpr A.B. Smith
SHQ Troop: Cpl Creagh, Tpr Spinks, Tpr Clark, Tpr Cockburn

Echelon

Vehicle	Driver	Cdr	Crew
Staff Car	Tpr Hughman		
Jeep	Tpr Wright		
15cwt QM	Tpr Wellington		
15cwt Water	LCpl Stone		
3ton Ammo 1	Tpr Ansell		
3ton Ammo 2	Tpr Daniels	SSM Harrington	
3ton Ammo 3	Tpr Cooke	Tpr Welsh	
3ton Ammo 4	Tpr Lyons		
3ton Ammo 5	Tpr Jones		
3ton Pet 1	Tpr Tallon	LCpl Cunningham	
3ton Pet 2	Tpr Jenkins	L/Sgt Cole	
3ton Pet 3	Tpr Halford	Tpr Singleton	Tpr Carmalt
3ton Baggage	Tpr Arnold	SQMS Law	LCpl Fox
			Tpr Price
3ton Cooks	Tpr Northam	Pte Sullivan	Pte Leyland
3ton Tech Stores	LCpl Croston	Cpl Girdler	
½-track	Tpr Roughley	S/Sgt Bowman	Sgt Winterman
			Tpr Yates
			Tpr Anderson
			Tpr Cummings
			Sgmn Redford
½-track	Tpr Reekie	Cpl Furst	LCpl Benfield

Vehicle	Driver	Cdr	Crew
			Tpr L. Taylor
			Tpr Cartwright
			Tpr Massie
½-track	Tpr Waite	Pte Blythman	Cpl Earl
			Pte Woods
Scout Car	Tpr Oxley	Capt Hunter	
ARV	Tpr Prescott	Sgt Bonnett	Tpr Limbert
			Tpr Rule
Slave Carrier	LCpl Smith	Tpr McIntyre	
Batman	Tpr Vacher		
Spare	Cpl Beagle		
	Tpr Jones		
	Tpr Howell		
	Tpr Langan		

Honours and Awards

Distinguished Service Order

Maj J. Cornwell, DCM   HQ Sqn (2IC)

Military Cross

Maj C.A. Joss   B Sqn
Maj F.A. Haigh   C Sqn
Capt A.F. Kingsford   B Sqn
Capt K.M. Hunter   C Sqn
Capt D.E.A. Scott-Gardner   HQ Sqn (Chaplain)
Capt G. Thompson   HQ Sqn (BTA)
Capt H.D. Palmer   B Sqn
Lt M.G. Reaney   A Sqn
Lt R.J.L. Scott   A Sqn

Distinguished Conduct Medal

Sgt A.E. Catchpole   C Sqn

Military Medal

Sgt R. Paice   C Sqn
Sgt L.A. Scrase   HQ Sqn (Recce Tp)
Cpl E.A. Jupp   A Sqn
Tpr R.W. Nicoll   B Sqn

Mention in Despatches

Maj W.M. Robson   A Sqn
Capt A.F. Kingsford   B Sqn
Lt H.D. Palmer   B Sqn
Sgt P. Camp   C Sqn
Tpr J.L. Hasler   B Sqn

Roll of Honour

7951664 Tpr J. Acklaw
7901246 LCpl W.F. Aspinall
14388635 Tpr M. Azzopardi
7910188 Sgt T. Bailey
4032265 LCpl F.H.E. Ballinger
7880469 Sgt F. Baron
420428 Sgt J. Barrett
14329508 Tpr E.F. Booker
420684 Sgt W.J. Broomfield
7925751 Tpr H.C.E. Browne
3862485 Tpr N. Burdaky
7885941 Cpl D.B. Campbell
420691 Tpr W.E. Chadwick
316932 Sgt J.F. Challis
14288245 Tpr J. Clapper
14505629 Tpr G.L. Clarke
421061 Sgt W.G. Cornish
420694 Tpr C.F. Craddock
P/271911 Lt J.M. Cruikshank
14381978 Tpr A. Curtis
7017776 Tpr H. Dobson
3384554 LCpl J. Dooley
7940769 Tpr F. Dowling
420192 Cpl P.T. Earwicker
7908442 Tpr F.D. Farman
P/292649 Lt A.H. Fox
7934323 LCpl R.E. Gage
— Tpr E. Gibbs
3389788 Tpr W. Gray
3389788 Tpr W. Gray
7892510 Sgt F. Harding
5441955 Tpr J.P. Higgins
2063550 Tpr B.F. Holmes
14265472 Tpr K.W. Hughes
420722 LCpl W.C. Humphrey
420282 Tpr R.E. Hunter
2980315 Tpr T.G. Jarvie
7910528 Tpr R.T. Jones
7897315 LCpl T.G. Kelly
3390308 Tpr S.F. Kelsall
7924708 LCpl E.W. Kemp
421107 Sgt A.T.G. Kimber

7945782 Tpr B. Kynaston
P/293717 Lt L.J.C Larcombe
— Lt R. Leon
7943619 LCpl J. Livingstone
P/172912 Lt A.O. Lott
— Lt McDonald
14399571 Tpr W.A. McPherson
421116 Cpl J.H. Maffett
7903089 Tpr B. Marriott
420454 LCpl E.E. Martin
4893564 Sgt P.H. Mason
7947958 Tpr A. Mee
420732 Cpl E. Moore
7905710 Tpr J.L. Nagle
420458 Tpr R.V. Nicoll, MM
7915315 Tpr E.G. Northam
4538370 Tpr H. Outhwaite
7927219 Tpr S.V. Pearce
7902996 Tpr P. Pearson
6481600 Tpr G.H. Pigott
— Capt G.H. Rawlins
P/232650 Lt P.G. Reynolds
— Tpr E. Rich
7947880 Tpr S. Riley
P/79966 Maj W.M. Robson
4271876 Cpl J. Scott
421142 Tpr E. Simpson
7957874 Tpr F.A. Smith
7944920 Tpr R.H. Smith
421145 Sgt S.C. Spicer
14383988 Tpr G.W. Strange
421148 Tpr W.G. Stringer
7902755 Tpr J. Terry
P/255301 Lt D. Thomas
P/242344 Lt J.A. Truman
420765 Tpr D.L. Watts
7902719 LCpl M. Watts
2050301 Sgt W.G. Wayman
421171 Tpr J.H. Wilkinson
— Tpr R. Williams
421174 Cpl K. Woodruffe

Tank Markings and Names

Tank Names

HQ Squadron
Bn HQ
    CO   *Tusker*
    2IC
    Adjt
Recce Tp
    Carriers or Honeys   *Tweed*
Intercomm Tp
    Dingoes   *Tyne*
A Sqn
    OC   *Tarzan*
    2IC
     1 Tp
     2 Tp
     3 Tp   *Talisman*
                         Texan
                         Tumult
                         Tangerine (1944)
     4 Tp   *Tessa* (North Africa, 1943)
     5 Tp   *Tempest*
                         Typhoon
                         Tornado
   (5 Tp became 4 Tp mid-1944)
    ARV
B Sqn
    OC
    2IC
     6 Tp   *Tipperary*
     7 Tp   *Tinker*
                         Titan
                         Tilly
     8 Tp
     9 Tp   *Tito*
                         Titania
                         Tikki
    10 Tp   *Tiber*
                         Tigris
                         Timor
    ARV   *Tredegar*

C Sqn
- OC
- 2IC
- 11 Tp — *Terrific*
  Terrible
  Tremendous
- 12 Tp — *Tolworth*
  Tidworth
  Tadworth
- 13 Tp — *Tonbridge*
  Today
  Tonight
  Tomorrow
- 14 Tp — *Toledo* (in North Africa)
- 15 Tp — *Tollemache*
  Tolly Light (at Wickham Market)
  Tolly Dark
- ARV

Markings

Squadron signs:
Placed on turret sides and rear, in yellow, these were the standard British Army symbols, consisting of an equilateral triangle for A Company/Squadron, a square to denote B, a circle to denote C and a diamond for HQ Squadron. Symbols and figures reduced to 0.5in width in August 1942. Troops per squadron reduced from five to four in 1944, three tanks per troop. Tank names all began with 'T' but were otherwise at the whim of the vehicle or troop commander. The above is a typical selection, by no means either complete or contemporaneous.

21st (Army) Tank Brigade formation sign:
Placed on left track guard, front and rear. From 1942 to 1944 this was an army tank brigade diabolo in dark blue. From mid-1944 to the war's end it consisted of the diabolo in a lighter blue with a red gremlin entwined around it, on a circular yellow background.

Unit tactical number:
Placed on hull lower nose plate and tail plate, '174' or '175' (depending on the battalion's seniority in 21st Tank Brigade) in white numerals on a brown rectangle with a white bar across the bottom, when the brigade was independent as Army or corps troops.

From late 1942 to end 1943, when 21st Tank Brigade was part of 4th (Mixed) Division, its units took the tactical numbers allocated to the infantry brigade it had replaced, i.e. 67, 68 (48th Battalion RTR) and 69; these numbers were again in white on a brown rectangle, but without the white line at the bottom. In Italy, from May 1944 to the war's end, when the brigade was again under Army command, the brown rectangle was replaced by one in the red and yellow RAC colours; the square was divided horizontally, the upper half being yellow and the lower half red, and the unit tactical number reverted to either '174' or '175', according to the battalion's seniority within 21st Tank Brigade.

Divisional formation sign:
Placed on the other trackguard, front and rear, when the brigade formed part of 4th (Mixed) Division; this consisted of a red circle with the upper left quadrant displaced.

National markings:
Red-white-red stripes on both hull sides, hull front and rear jettison tank.

Air recognition markings:
Allied five-pointed white star on turret roof in North Africa.

Tank name:
In white on each side, either on track guards, air louvres or hull side plate.

25 Army Tank Brigade Technical Intelligence Summary No. 1: PzKpfw VI Tiger

The following information has been received from examination of a captured PzKpfw VI in the field, 25 February 1943.

Armour (machineable quality)

		mm	in	angle
a.	Front:			
	Lower Nose Plate	102	4.01	20°
	Upper Nose Plate	62	2.44	80°
	Driver's Front Plate	102	4.01	10°
	Small base plate below lower nose plate	62	2.44	60°
b.	Turret: sides and rear	82	3.22	Vertical
c.	Sides:			
	Upper	82	3.22	Vertical
	Lower behind bogies	62	2.44	Vertical
d.	Rear	82	3.22	20°
e.	Floor	26	1.02	
f.	Top	26	1.02	

Armament

One 88mm gun with double baffle muzzle brake, one MG coaxially mounted on left of gun. One MG on right of driver

Ammunition

Marked on base 8.8cm Flak 18

Tracks

Width 2 ft 4.5 in

Penetration performance of British anti-tank guns

6 pdr Mk II & III (HVAP)

102 mm	(4.01 in)	Normal	220 yds
82 mm	(3.22 in)	"	920 "
		10°	770 "
		20°	620 "
		30°	475 "
62 mm	(2.44 in)	Normal	1680 "
		10°	1540 "
		20°	1400 "
		30°	1260 "

6 pdr Mk IV & V (HVAP)

102 mm	(4.01 in)	Normal	450 yds
		10°	250 "
		20°	100 "
82 mm	(3.22 in)	Normal	1150 "
		10°	1000 "
		20°	860 "
		30°	725 "
62 mm	(2.44 in)	Normal	1910 "
		10°	1770 "
		20°	1630 "
		30°	1490 "

2 pdr

62 mm	(2.44 in)	Normal	750 "
		10°	530 "
		20°	320 "
		30°	100 "

Bibliography

Published Sources

Chamberlain, Peter and Ellis, Chris. *British and American Tanks of World War II*, New York, Arco Publishing Co Inc, 1969
— *The Churchill Tank*, London, Arms & Armour Press, 1971
Churchill, Winston S. *The Second World War*, 6 Vols, London, Cassell & Co Ltd, 1948
Fletcher, David. *Mechanised Force – British Tanks between the Wars,* London, HMSO, 1991
Forty, George. *The Royal Tank Regiment – A Pictorial History*, Tunbridge Wells, Spellmount Ltd, 1989
— *M4 Sherman*, Weapons & Warfare Series, Poole, Blandford Press, 1987
Gilmour, Alan. 'Titan Goes to War', *British Army Review* (1986), December No 84
Gudgin, Peter. *The Tiger Tanks*, London, Arms & Armour Press, 1991
— *Panzer Armee Afrika*, Tanks Illustrated series No.8, London, Arms & Armour Press, 1988
— 'Phantom British Tank Regiments of World War II', *RUSI Journal*, December 1980
Hart, B.H. Liddell. *The Tanks*, 2 Vols, London, Cassell, 1959
Hinsley, Prof F.H., et al. *British Intelligence in the Second World War,* London, HMSO, 1981
Jackson, Gen Sir William. *The North African Campaign, 1940–43,* London, Batsford, 1975
Mowat, Charles Loch. *Britain Between the Wars, 1918–40*, London, Methuen, 1968
Perrett, Bryan. *The Churchill Tank*, London, Osprey Publishing Ltd, 1980
Playfair, Maj Gen I.S.O., et al. *History of the Second World War*, London, HMSO, 1966
Spragge, Cdr H.E., RN. *Hoddom Castle & the Western Gateway into Scotland,* Observer Press, Annan
Williamson, Hugh. *The Fourth Division, 1939–45*, London, Newman Neame, 1951

Unpublished Sources

(a) Official Papers
War Office. *Notes from Theatres of War No.16: North Africa, November 1942–May 1943*, 1943
21st Tank Brigade. *Operations in Italy, August 1944–May 1945*, 1945
48th Battalion RTR. *General Account of Operations, 28 Aug–23 Sep 1944*
— *General Account of Operations, 9 Apr–30 Apr 1945*
— *Planning Note No.1 (Operation Buckland)*, 6 April 1945
— *Operation Order No.1 (Operation Buckland)*, 9 April 1945
10th Infantry Brigade. *Operation Order No.5 (Operation Polegate)*, 5 May 1943
RAC School, N. Africa. *Firing Tests – 75mm M3 Gun & 0.30in Browning MG Mounted in Churchill*, RAC/S/A/10 dated 10 April 1944
RAC Training Depot, N. Africa. *Recommendations for conversion of Churchill Tanks to 75mm gun*, TD/1012/839, undated
25th Army Tank Brigade. *Report on Churchill Tanks in N. Africa*, 24 March 1943

— Technical Intelligence Summary No.1, 25 February 1943

(b) Privately Published
B Squadron 48th Battalion RTR. *The B-Line*, various issues
Thomason, G.G. (ed). *Lines From A War*
Hurlock, Michael. *History of Glevering Hall, Woodbridge*

(c) Private Papers and Manuscripts
Mennell, John S. Personal Diaries
Draft History of the 48th Battalion Royal Tank Regiment (incomplete)
Blankley, Roger. Short History of the 48th Royal Tank Regiment
  48th RTR (TA) – Early days & UK Training
Heard, Reg. Personal Diaries

(d) Letters to the Author from:
Barry Archer, Bill Bayly, Roger Blankley, Gerry Brooks, Les Burnham, Ned Cook, Arnold
    Cummins, Cyril Edwards, 'Pop' Fenwick, Dennis Gable, Alan Gilmour, Tom Gorringe,
    Reg Heard, Don Hoad, Peter King, Tony Kingsford, Maurice Ladd, Gerry Letchford, John
    Mennell, Ian More, Peter O'Flynn, Henry Palmer, Eric Potter, Ken Reed, Jack Rockliff,
    Pat Russell, Arthur Spackman, Geoff Thomason, Geoff Thompson, Mrs Tinker, John
    Walker and Jackie Wykes.

Index

1 ABD, 64
1 Armoured Division, 97–8, 102, 111
1 Army Tank Brigade, 37
1 Canadian Corps, 119, 135–6, 139
1 Canadian Infantry Brigade, 131
1 Canadian Infantry Division, 120, 128, 136, 139
1 GRTD, 6 Battalion, 107
1 Heavy Armoured Brigade, 22
1 Infantry Division, 86, 94, 96–7, 99
1 Jaipur Infantry, 142, 146
1 KSLI, 94
1 New Zealand Division, 133
1/5 Mahratta, 145
1/6 East Surreys, 86, 99
2 Armoured Brigade, 147
2 Bedfs and Herts, 100
2 Canadian Infantry Brigade, 120, 122
2 Commando, 150
2 Commando Brigade, 149–50
2 DCLI, 99, 103
2 Foresters, 94–5
2 New Zealand Division, 137, 143
2/5 Queen's, 151, 155, 157
2/6 Queen's, 151, 153
2/7 Queen's, 151
2/10 Gurkha Rifles, 137
2 Polish Corps, 144
3 Canadian Infantry Brigade, 120, 129–31, 137
3 Field Squadron RE, 144
3 Infantry Brigade, 84–5
3/15 Punjabis, 146
4 Division, 114
4 Indian Division, 98
4 Infantry Division, 48
4 (Mixed) Division, 48, 63, 68–9, 86, 98–9, 102
4 Vehicle Park, 112
4th Hussars, 144
5 Buffs, 146, 149, 151
5 Corps, 48, 63, 83, 85–6, 98–9, 136–7, 139, 143–4
5 General Hospital, 106
5 Northants Regiment, 150
6 Armoured Division, 80, 83, 99, 151

6 Royal West Kent, 146, 148, 151
6 (US) Corps, 118
7 Armoured Division, 98–9, 102
7th Hussars, 153
8 Argyll & Sutherland Highlanders, 146, 148, 151
8 Indian Division, 139, 142–3, 151
9 Corps, 83, 98–9
10 Armoured Division, 104
10 Infantry Brigade, 53, 86–7, 99, 102–3
10th Hussars, 38, 112
11 Armoured Division, 43
11 Corps, 33–4, 36–7, 40
11 Infantry Brigade, 150
12 Infantry Brigade, 103
13/18th Hussars, 22
14/20th Hussars, 19
15 (Scottish) Division, 25, 33–4
16 Base Workshop, 134
16th/5th Lancers, 23
17 Indian Infantry Brigade, 146–7
17th/21st Lancers, 23, 25, 80
18 Army Group, 83, 97
19 Indian Infantry Brigade, 141, 143
21 Army Tank Brigade, 19, 22, 25, 28–9, 31–4, 36–7, 40, 45, 48, 112, 165
21 Indian Infantry Brigade, 142–3
21 Tank Brigade, 48, 52, 70, 85–6, 96, 108, 112, 117, 119–21, 127–8, 136, 138, 143, 155, 147–9
21 Tank Brigade Workshops, 106
21 Tank Troop Workshops, 44, 111
24 Field Regiment (SP) RA, 125
24 Guards Brigade, 151, 153
25 Army Tank Brigade, 37, 79, 84, 91, 95, 112, 138
29 Independent Brigade, 38
36 Infantry Brigade, 146, 148, 150–1
38 Infantry Brigade, 149
38 Irish Brigade, 147
43 Commando, 149–50
43 Gurkha Brigade, 136–7
45 Infantry Brigade, 23, 25, 27
46 Infantry Division, 85, 98
48th Highlanders of Canada, 126, 131

51 (Highland) Division, 25
53rd Training Regiment RAC, 45, 108
54th Training Regiment RAC, 25
55th Training Regiment RAC, 19, 37
56 (London) Infantry Division, 142, 150–1
56 Reconnaissance Regiment, 149
57th Training Regiment RAC, 19, 45
60th Training Regiment RAC, 45
66 General Hospital, 158
72 Anti-Tank Regiment RA, 92
78 Infantry Division, 80, 97, 102, 146, 150–1, 153
101 OCTU, 34
104 Tank Workshops REME, 92, 165
111 Regiment RAC, 70
111 SP Regiment, Royal Canadian Artillery, 125
142 Regiment RAC, 94–5, 108
144 Regiment RAC, 53
145 Regiment RAC, 37, 45, 52, 74, 94, 98, 117, 120, 123, 131, 136, 138
165 Infantry Brigade, 33–4
167 Infantry brigade, 151, 153
169 (Queen's) Infantry Brigade, 151, 155, 157
201 Guards Brigade, 98
225 Anti-Tank Battery RA, 144
254 Tank Delivery Squadron, 106, 108
272 Forward Delivery Squadron, 108, 127, 134
501 and 504 Heavy Tank Battalions, 86
501/504 Heavy Tank Battalion, 91
504 Heavy Tank Battalion, 92, 165

'A' Special Service Squadron RAC, 38
Abbott, LCpl F., 148
Achurch, 2Lt (later Capt) R.B. (Brian), 53, 71, 108, 130
Adamson, Sgt George, 17, 110, 122
Adige, River, 119, 153–5, 157
Adolf Hitler Line, 118

187

Afragola, 113
AFV Schools, 17, 40
Ain Mokra, 108
Ainsley, Lt T., 106
air OP, 137
airfield protection, 23
airgraph, 79, 81–2, 109
Alexander, Gen (later Field Marshal), 83, 142, 157
Alfonsine, 142
Algiers, 77, 80
ammunition, HE and AP, 82
Amos, Tpr, 106
Annan, 52–3, 70
annual camp, 4, 6–11
Anzio, 118
Archer, 2Lt (later Capt) B. (Barry), 19, 28, 32, 63, 71, 100, 108
Ardrossan, 53
Argenta, 149–50
  bridge, 150
  Gap, 119, 144, 150
ARK, 44, 147–8
Artemus Ward, SS, 79
ARVs, Churchill, 44, 95, 149, 156
Astbury, Tpr, 151
ATS camp, 49, 51
Attridge, Cpl F., 151
Attwood, 2Lt C.H.M., 23
Auchinleck, 47
Auchinleck Avenue, 86, 94
Auchterarder, 39
Ausa, River, 130, 132–3
Autodrome, 21, 23
Aylesbury, 42
Ayr, 47

'B' and 'C' Special Service Squadrons, 38
B-Line, The, 70–1, 120, 151
'Babes in the Wood' pantomime, 20
Bagnacavallo, 137–8, 141–2, 144
Bailess, Cpl, 130
Bailey bridge, 137, 155
Bald Hill, 75
Banana Ridge, 94–5, 99
Banfora, HMT, 73
Barber, Lt John, 66
Bari, 113, 118
Barnett, 2Lt Paul, 6, 38
Barrett, Sergeant J. ('Kipper'), 99
Bartlett, GR, 101
Barton, Sgt, 22
Basford, Sgt, 63
Batory, SS, 38
battalion, infantry (I) tank, 2
Battalion key party, 9
Battalion Roll of Honour, 165

battledress, 4, 48, 78
bazooka, 126
Becker, Tpr, 131
Bedford, 40
BEF, 19–20, 22–4
Béja, 104
Bell, Lt (later Capt) G.G. ('Ding-Dong'), 6, 22, 28, 30–1, 45
Benvignante, 150–1
Biggin Hill aerodrome, 23
Bird, LCpl W.J., 148
Bizerta, 75, 80, 102
'Blade Force', 80
Blankley, Roger, 15–16, 29
Bletchley, 42
Boccaleone, 150–1
Bône, 77–9, 105–6, 108, 112–13
  Area Commander, 108
Bou Arada, 83–5
  Farik, 111
Bouchier, Colonel, 85
Bougie, 77–8, 80, 112
Bovington Camp, 17, 40
Braun, 2Lt (later Lt) J.R., 106, 155
Briggs, Maj Gen Raymond, 104
Brindisi, 118
Bristol, 70
British Expeditionary Force, 19–20, 22–4
British Legion Club, 40
Brooke, Lt Gen Sir Alan F., 31
Brooks, Lt Col G.H. (Gerry), 38, 40, 44, 63, 71, 87, 100, 108–9
Broomfield, Sgt W.J., 132
Bruce, Lt (later Capt) T.S. (Tom), 72, 97, 126, 134, 136
Buckley, 2Lt (later Lt) P.L. (Paul), 108, 127, 133
Bushell, Sgt R.H., 7, 9

C. Corelli, 146
C. Pugliesi, 132
Caldwell, Lt, 28
Cambrai, Battle of, 2
Cambrai Day, 20, 35, 157
Cameron, Maj, 37–9
Candiana, 155
Cap Bon peninsula, 102–3
Cardwell, 2Lt (later Lt) J. (Jimmy), 38
Carleton and York Regiment, 120, 133
Carlisle, 52
Carpenters of Clapham, 11–12
Carr, Lt S.A., 4, 6
carrier, armoured personnel, 144
  Bren gun, 18, 23, 53, 108
Casablanca, 80

Caserta, 113, 117
Cassino, 113, 118–19, 160
Castlemartin Ranges, 35, 42
Catchpole DCM, Sgt A.E., 148, 150, 157
Catchpole, Sgt George, 53
Cattolica, 125, 128
Ceccarini, 127
Chadwick, Capt N.R.M. (Neil), 72, 134, 141
Challis, Sgt, 130
Chamberlain, Neville, 2, 12
Chambers, Lt (later Capt) C.C. ('Po-Po'), 37, 45, 72, 108
Charlton, George, 16
Cheesewright, Sgt Bill, 18
Chesterton, Vic, 159
Chiesanova, 148–9
Christian Huygens, HMT, 113
Church, Mech Sgt Henry, 95–6
Churchill tank, 39, 43–50, 52–3, 64–5, 68, 79, 90–1, 105, 111, 122, 125, 127, 130–1, 133, 143–4, 156
  95mm CS, 44, 115, 123, 132, 143
  ARK, 44, 147–8
  ARVs, 44, 95, 149, 156
  bridgelayer, 145, 149, 153
  I, 43, 132
  II, 44, 68
  III, 44, 47, 97
  IV, 44, 66, 86–7, 92, 123, 132, 143
  IV (NA75), 44, 123, 142–4, 147
  V, 44, 115, 132
  VI, 44
  VII, 44, 143
  VIII, 44
Churchill, Winston, 23, 27, 38, 51, 92, 165
Churchmans of Ipswich, 40
Clapham High School for Girls, 3
Clapper, Tpr, 130
Clark, Maj J.O. ('Joe'), 6, 7, 19, 23, 39, 45, 53, 64
Clark, Maj P.H. ('Pip'), 64
Codevigo, 155
Colchester, 24–5, 28–9, 40
  Sobraon Barracks, 23
Collier, Tpr, 130
Collins, 2Lt (later Capt) J.C. ('Olly'), 22, 28, 34
Combined Operations Training Centre, 46
Combined Training Centre, 53
Commandos, 142, 149–50
Conca, River, 125
Consandolo, 150–1

Conselice, 147–9
Conselve, 155
Constantine, 80
Cook, Edmund ('Ned'), 163
Copparo, 151, 153
Cornish, Sgt W.G., 94
Cornwell DSO, DCM, Maj Jim, 133, 137, 141, 175
Correzzola, 155
Cottrell, 2Lt (later Lt) B.W. (Bruce), 70, 72, 123, 155, 158
Covenanter tank, 43
Covignano, 130–1
Creagh, Wally, 16
creosote, 49
Crespino, 153
Criddle, Tpr Edgar, 105
Crocodile flame-thrower tank, 44, 137, 144
'Cromwell', 32
Crouch, Maj L.P. ('Pip'), 19, 22, 25, 32, 37
Crowther, Lt (later Maj) C.H. (Charles), 15, 6, 28, 39, 45, 72, 109, 128
Croydon, 15, 21
  Empire, The, 15–16
Cruikshank, 2Lt J.M., 106, 108
Crusader, 64
Cummins, Sgt A. (Arnold), 7, 49
Cumnock, 47
cupola, all-round vision, 148
Curtis, Tpr A., 148

Dalmally, 46
'David', 39, 43
Dawnay DSO, Brig David, 112, 115, 119, 138, 155, 158–9
DD Sherman amphibious tank, 153–4
Deighton, Revd H.S., 4, 6
Derbyshire Yeomanry, 102
Devizes, 29
Dewey, Tpr, 151
diabolo formation sign, 16, 48
Diamond-T transporter, 104
Dieppe, 51
Dingo scout car, 38, 67, 92, 97
Djebel Bou Aoukaz ('The Bou'), 98
Djebel Djaffa, 86, 90, 93–4
Djebel-el-Mehirigar, 86
Djedeida, 92, 105
Dobson, Tpr, 131
Dragon, 18
  Light, 18, 28
Drake-Brockman DSO, MC, Brig G.P.L., 19, 22, 31–4
Drumlanrig Castle, 53

Duffort, Tpr, 151
Dumfries, 47, 52–3
  House estate, 47
Dunn, Lt (later Capt) J.C. (Jack), 37, 64, 72, 106–7
Duplex Drive (DD), 153–4
Durban Castle, SS, 113
Duvivier, 104
Duzerville, 79

'E-Boat Alley', 78
Eagle Squadron Competition, 40
East Surrey Regiment, 7th (TA) Battalion, 2, 4
East Surreys, 94
East Surreys, 23rd London Regiment, 4
Eastern Command, 34
Ecclefechan, 73
Eden George, Maj J., 6, 23, 28
Edwards, Capt D.B., 6, 34
Edwards, Cyril, 17, 102, 104
Eggleton, RQMS (later Capt (QM)) 'Eggy', 37, 72, 110, 158
Eighth Army, 80, 83, 91, 97–8, 104, 110–11, 118, 142
Eisenhower, Gen Dwight D., 104
El Alamein, 80
El Aroussa, 84–5
Elliott MC, MP, Col The Hon. Walter, 40, 44
Elsdon, Tpr, 110, 122
engine, AEC petrol, 64
  GMC diesel, 64
Ericson, 2Lt, 28
Ettrick, SS, 46
Exercises: Bumper, 40
  Dryshod, 53
  Gremlin, 116
  Scorch, 45
exhaust extensions, 53

F Armoured Squadron RE, 144
Faenza, 137, 141
Fantails, 153
Faustpatrone, 126
Fell, WO I (RSM) E.T., 53, 110, 158
Ferrara, 144, 151
Fifth Army, 142
First Army, 48, 53, 63–4, 68, 80, 83–4, 104
  shield, 165
Firth DSO, Brig C.E.A., 112
flame-throwers, experimental, 49
Fletcher, LCpl Bob, 91
Florence, 136
Focke-Wulf FW-190, 96

Foggia, 113
Foglia, River, 120–3
Foley, Capt, 19
Fondouk Gap, 83
Forli, 136–7
formation signs, 16, 51, 118
Formignana, 151
Forward Delivery Squadron, 91
Foss, 2Lt C.A., 34
Fossa Marina, 150
Fossa Zena, 149
Fowles, 2Lt T.N., 106
Fox, Lt A.H. ('Freddie'), 133, 148
Framlingham, 34, 40
Freetown, 38
French Foreign Legion, 84

Gaeta, 118
Gafour, 84
Gafsa, 82
Gage, Lt J.W.J. (John), 45, 66, 73
Garigliano, River, 118
George, Maj J. Eden, 9, 23, 28
German medium tanks, 80
Ghardimaou, 79, 83, 85, 91, 104
Gilmour, LCpl Alan, 2, 39, 101, 103, 132, 145
Gilmour RAMC, Capt I.E.W. (Eric), 110, 126, 129
Giraud, Gen, 104
Glasgow, 70
Glevering Hall, 33–5, 163
Gobblecock Hall, 39
Goldby, Capt M. (Maurice), 72, 108
Gordon Highlanders, 98
Gorringe, Lt (later Capt) T.M. (Tom), 72, 116, 122, 127, 138, 141, 158
Gothic Line, 119–20, 122, 124–5, 133
Govan, 73
Gradara, 123–4
  War Cemetery, 163
Grant Bros. of Croydon, 13
Green, Cpl 'Gunner', 16
Green Dragon, The, 15
'Green Hill', 75
Greenwood, 2Lt (later Lt) C., 107, 123, 134, 149, 151
Gremlin, Exercise, 116
Greyhound, The, 15
Grigg, Sir James, 106
Groupement Bouchier, 84
Guards, 49
Gudgin, 2Lt (later Lt) P.L. (Peter), 64, 66, 72, 87–8, 90
guns: 2pdr, 21, 31, 39, 43

2pdr anti-tank, 18
3pounder, 18
37mm, 116
50mm, 82
6pdr, 31, 44, 47, 53, 68, 111, 143
6pdr anti-tank, 92
75mm, 31, 82, 111, 123, 139
88mm, 88, 91
88mm anti-aircraft, 91
88mm SP anti-tank, 147
American M3 75mm, 44, 143
British 75mm, 44, 143
M10 SP anti-tank (Wolverine), 125, 144
Priest 105mm, 125
Gustav Line, 118–19

Haigh MC, 2Lt (later Maj) F.A. (Freddie), 37, 53, 64, 72, 100, 106, 123–5, 133–4
Hall, Lt E.D., 149–50
Hammam Lif, 102
Hancock, Sgt John, 9, 13, 16, 31
Harding, Sgt, 131
Harland, 2Lt, 25, 28
Harris, Tpr, 132
Harvey, 2Lt (later Capt) E.A. (Alan), 37, 72, 85, 89, 127, 134, 158
Harvey, Lt G.C., 107
Harwich, 23
Haselhurst, Lt R.T., 138
Hastings and Prince Edward Regiment, 125–6, 129–30
Hatch, Ronnie, 159
Hawick, 47, 69
Hawkesworth DSO, MC, Maj Gen, 63, 70
Hawkinge aerodrome, 23
Heard, Reg, 106, 128
Heavey, Lt W.J., 6, 22
heavy tank battalion, 91
Herbillon, 108
Hermann Goering Division, 86
Hickman, Tpr, 131
Hitler, Adolf, 1, 80
Hoad, Capt F.D. (Don), 63, 72, 106, 133–4, 136, 138, 157
Hoddom Castle, Ecclefechan, 38, 51, 64, 73
Hogshaw, Brig, 87
Holmes, Tpr B.F., 151
Holtorp, 2Lt (later Lt) A.F. (Alan), 64, 66, 72, 136, 155, 158
Home Guard, 23
Honey light tank, 115, 126, 131–2, 149, 151

Hooton, Lt Col Ted, 40
Hopkinson, Tpr (later Sgt), 17, 110, 122
howitzer, 3in, 43–4
  75mm, 82
  95mm, 44, 115, 123, 139, 143
HQ London District, 22–3
Hubert Dees Ltd, 21
Hughes, 2Lt (later Lt), 28, 38
Hughes, Tpr, 151
Hunter MC, Lt (later Capt) K.M. (Max), 72, 106, 126, 142
Hutcheson, W.J.S., 70
Hutchinson, Lt Col A.O., 115
Hutchinson, Lt C.R.G. (Chris), 96, 122

Imber, 29–30
Imber, Tpr H.T., 151
inoculation, typhus, 85
Inverary, 38, 46
Ipswich, 28, 40
Irish Guards, 99
Isgar, Lt G.W., 106, 124
Isle of Wight, 32, 49
Iver-Moore MC, Brig Thomas, 40, 43, 109, 112

Jackson RTR, Lt Col A.C., 74
Jägerregiment Hermann Goering, 91
James, Lt D.L., 134, 149–50
Jeffrey, Tpr (later Col) W.M.S. (Mike), 20
Jesi, 121
Jones, 2Lt W.J.E., 108
Jones, Cpl H., 151
Jones, R.T., 94
Joss MC, 2Lt (later Maj) C.A. (Bill), 6, 9, 13, 23, 28, 53, 70, 72, 100, 131–2, 155–7
Jupp, Capt Tommy, 38
Jupp MM, Cpl E.A., 124, 137
Jupp, Lt E. (Eric), 22, 28

Kairouan, 83
Kangaroo, 144
Kasserine, 83, 112
Kelibia, 103
Kelly, LCpl, 131
Kelsall, Tpr, 130
Kenchington DSO, MC, Brig A.G. ('Kench'), 2, 19
Kenley aerodrome, 23
key party, 10, 12
khaki drill tropical kit, 78, 100
King George VI, 1, 70, 92, 106–7, 117, 165

Kingsford MC, Capt A.F. (Tony), 37, 72, 108, 110, 119, 125, 133–4, 155, 157
Kynaston, B., 95

La Calle, 105
La Mahommédia, 102
Ladd, 2Lt (later Maj) M.P. (Maurice), 6, 9, 28–9, 72, 110, 112, 116, 128–9, 138, 162
Lagonda Works, 49
Lake Comacchio, 119, 142, 150
Lakeman mounting, 97
Lamone, River, 136–7
Landing Craft, Tank (LCT), 46
Langholm, 52
launcher, multiple rocket, 141
Lavazzola, 149
Law, Sgt, 17
Le Khroub, 108
Le Krib, 83
League of Nations, 1
Lean, Sir David, 40
Leggett, 2Lt, 28
Letchford, Gerry, 17
Liddell, Capt F., 149–50
Liddell Hart, Capt B.H., 30
Liddell, Lt E., 142
Light Squadron, 10, 38–9, 53
Lindsay, Maj Gen George, 31
Linney Head, 35
Livingstone, LCpl J., 108
Llandaff House, 13
Llewellen-Palmer DSO, MC, Lt Col A.W.A. (Tony), 138
Loader, 2Lt R.A.C., 6, 28
Local Defence Volunteers (LDV), 23
Lockerbie, 47, 52
Lockwood, WOI (RSM) W.J. (Bill), 7, 19–20, 22
'Long Plantation', 39
'Longstop Hill', 76, 86, 97
Lothian and Border Horse, 102
Lott, 2Lt (later Capt) A.O. (Alan), 37, 49, 72, 84, 87–91, 96, 102
Love, Jack, 9
Loveday 16/5 Lancers, Lt Col John, 110
Lucera, 113
Lugo, 142–3, 146
  canal, 146
Lugton, 53
Lulworth, 17
Lumby, Maj J.B., 141
Lungo Brenta, 155–7
Luton, 42
Luxton, Tpr, 151

M & V rations, 46
MacGregor, Lt J.P., 106–7
machine gun, 0.30in Browning, 116, 139
0.5in Browning heavy, 115
7.92mm Besa, 21, 43
Bren light, 22
Thompson sub–, 124
Maclay, Tpr, 132
Madagascar, 38, 73
Maffett, Cpl J., 148
Marano, River, 126–7, 129–31, 133
Marecchia, River, 119
Mareth Line, 83
Martel, Lt Gen G. leQ., 36
Martlesham Heath airfield, 27–8, 35
Massicault, 99, 101–2
Mateur, 82, 105
Matilda infantry tank, 21, 27, 30, 32, 43
McCreery, Lt Gen Sir Richard, 158
McIver, Sgt Hector, 7, 110, 128
McKenna, CSM, 9
McPherson, Tpr, 130
Mechanisation Board, 21
Medjerda river, 75
Medjez-el-Bab, 66, 69, 75, 77, 80, 82–3, 93, 98–9
Mela, River, 126
Melrose, 38
Mennell, 2Lt (later Maj) J.S. (John), 6, 9, 22–3, 28–9, 31–2, 34, 39–40, 43, 45, 64, 68, 71, 95, 100, 109
Mepachrine, 85
Merrion Camp, 42
'Messerschmidt Alley', 97
Messerschmidt Me-109, 96
Metaponto, 113
Metauro, River, 120–1
Minterne Magna, 32
mobile column, 23
Moffat, 47
Moir RAMC, Capt J.H. ('Doc'), 39, 72, 100
Mombaroccio, 120
Monte Cassino, 113, 118–9, 160
Monte Luro, 124
Montone, River, 142
Moore, Cpl E., 151
More, Lt (later Capt) I.P. (Ian), 53, 72, 106, 108–10, 112, 125–6, 148
Morgan, Tpr, 151
Morrey-Jones, Cpl, 131
Muchmore, Cpl, 106
Munns, Cpl Frank, 128
NAAFI ration, 79
Naesmyth, Brig R., 32, 34, 36, 40

Nagle, J.L., 94
Naples, 113, 118
'Nashorn' (Rhinoceros), 147, 149
nebelwerfer, 141
Nehring, Gen, 80
Newbury, Berks., 40
Newcombe, Lt, 28
Nicoll MM, Tpr Ron, 95–6, 106
No. 4 Transit Camp, 78
North Irish Horse, 37, 107, 112, 117, 119, 138, 143

O'Flynn RAMC, Capt Peter ('Paddy'), 28, 38–9
Olgin, Lt C., 106
Operation Buckland, 143
Operation Fliederblüte (Lilac Blossom), 86, 91
Operation Polegate, 99
Operation Seelöwe (Sealion), 25
Operation Supercharge, 80
Operation Torch, 68, 80
Ordnance Depôt, Chilwell and Handforth, 70
Osteria Nuova, 123

Paice MM, Sgt R., 148, 157
Paice MM, WOII WA (Bill), 7, 22
Palmer MC, Capt H.D. (Henry), 66, 72, 123, 136, 155, 157, 159
Panther turrets, dug-in, 130
Panzerfaust (Bazooka), 128
Para Regiment 5, 91
Parr, LCpl Freddie, 128
Payne, WO1 (RSM) Freddie ('Pinocchio'), 20
Peace Ballot, 1
Pledge Union, 1
Pearce, Tpr S.V., 95
Penthièvre, 104–5, 160
Peter's Corner, 86, 96
Philippeville, 77
PIAT, 136
Pieve, 123–4
Piggot, 'Piggy', 17
Pigott, Tpr G., 148
Po di Volano, 151
Po, River, 119, 151, 153–4
Point 70, 127
Point 117, 99
Point 121, 99
Point 133, 123
Point 151, 95, 99
Point 152, 133
Point 174, 94–5, 101
Point 212, 99
Potter, Sgt Eric, 53
Potts, Sgt Al, 159

PPCLI, 123
Princess Patricia's Canadian Light Infantry, 123
Proud, Lt G., 142
Purley, 13, 15, 24
Arms, The, 15
Beeches, 12–13, 19–20
Downs Golf Club, 13, 15
PzKpfw III, 80, 82–4, 86, 88, 91, 94
PzKpfw IV, 82, 86, 91
PzKpfw VI Tiger, 88

RAC OCTU, Sandhurst, 64
RAC School, N. Africa, 108
Rackowe, Capt S.S.A.P., 4
radar, 137
Radcliffe, Lt, 28
rafts, 153
Rand, Capt Maurice, 72, 128, 138
RASC, 11, 13
Ravenna, 119
Rawlins, Lt, 28, 32
Reaney MC, 2Lt (later Lt) M.G., 108, 122, 127, 130, 157
Reconnaissance Troop, 87
Red Deer, The, 15
Red Lion, The, 15
Reed, Lt (later Capt) Ken, 39, 72, 87, 104, 108, 110
Reggio/Calabria, 118
reinforcement (R) squadrons, 77
Reno, River, 119, 149–50
Reunion Society, 163
Reynolds, Lt Peter, 72, 106, 124
Reynolds, Maj J.F., 157
Riccione, 133, 136
Richmond Park, 49
Riley, Tpr S., 131
Rimini, 119, 123, 125–6, 128, 133, 157
airfield, 130
Gap, 130, 133
stadium, 159
Robson, Lt (later Maj) W.M. ('Robbie'), 45, 64, 72, 84–5, 87, 98–9, 104, 109, 129–30
Rogers, Maj George, 3
Roll of Honour, 164–5
Rome, 118–19
Rommel, 80, 82
Rota-trailer, 53, 64–5, 79
Route 3, 123
Route 9, 137, 143
Route 16, 124, 126–7, 150–1, 155
Rovigo, 154–6
Rowell, Lt, 122, 127, 130
Royal 22nd Regiment, 120, 123, 130, 133

Royal Armoured Corps (RAC), 2
Royal Canadian Army Ordnance Corps, 53
Royal Canadian Regiment, 127
Royal Tank Corps, 2
Royal Tank Regiment (RTR), 2
Royston REME, Capt D., 72
RTC, 42nd (TA) Battalion, 2, 37
RTR:
  2nd Battalion, 2, 138
  4th Battalion, 19, 63
  5th Battalion, 19
  6th Battalion, 138, 158
  7th Battalion, 2, 31, 44
  8th Battalion, 19, 23, 158
  12th Battalion, 37, 52, 64, 69, 74, 120, 128, 130, 133, 135, 137, 139, 141–2, 147, 151
  38th Battalion, 30
  39th Battalion, 30
  42nd Battalion, 3–4, 18–19, 29, 32, 165
  43rd Battalion, 31, 37
  44th Battalion, 29, 37
  45th Battalion, 38
  51st Battalion, 79, 83–5, 115, 144
  60th Battalion, 30
  62nd Battalion, 30
  65th Battalion, 30
  99th Battalion, 30–31
  100th Battalion, 30–32
  101st Battalion, 30
  102nd Battalion, 30
  124th Battalion, 30
  band, 108
Ryan, Paddy, 16
Ryan, SSM 'Buck', 28

St John's Hill, 2
Salerno, 113, 118
Salisbury Plain, 39
San Andrea, 127
San Arginello canal, 146
San Fortunato, 128, 130, 133
San Lorenzo, 130–1, 133
San Lorenzo in Strada, 127
San Maria, 126–7
San Maria Scacciano, 126, 166
San Martino, 128, 130–3
San Patrizio, 147–8
Sanderstead, 12–13, 15–17, 20, 22, 24–5
Sangro, River, 118
Santerno, River, 146–7
Savage, Lt (later Capt) M.C., 72, 108, 110, 119, 134
Saxmundham, 39
School of Tank Technology, 93

Scott-Gardner MC, CF, Capt D.E.A. (Archie), 72, 110, 126, 129, 137, 148
Scott MC, Lt R.J.L., 108, 128, 131, 137
scout car, 149–50
  White, 129
Scrase MM, Cpl (later Sgt), 131
Seaforths of Canada, 131
Sedjenane, 82, 105
Senio, River, 119, 133, 137–9, 141, 143
Shapter, C/Sgt F., 7, 9
Sherman tank, 111, 115–16, 122, 125, 127, 130–3, 143
Sherman 'dozer, 144, 146, 149, 153
Shillinglaw, Lt D. (David), 45
Shorten, Capt, 28
Sidi Ayed, 85
Sillaro, River, 149
Simmonds, 2Lt John, 28, 38
Simpson, SSM Don, 16, 28
Skey, Lt F.W. (Deric), 45, 71, 110, 129, 158
Sloughia, 94
Smaldon, St R.C.J., 7, 10
Smallwood, 2Lt (later Capt) V.R.B. ('Chips'), 19, 28, 46
Smith, 2Lt, 28
Smith, Cpl W.F., 130–1
Smith REME, Lt W.G., 134
Smith, Tpr F.A., 151
Sobraon Barracks, 25
Soliman, 103–4
Souk Ahras, 79
Sparkes, LCpl, 110, 122
Spencer-Smith, 2Lt, 28
Spencer, Maj C.R. (Charles), 115, 133
Spicer, Sgt, 130
Spoleto, 119–20
Stanghella, 155, 157
Steamroller Farm, 79
Stephenson, Cpl, 73
Stevens, Acker, 9
Stewart, 2Lt (later Lt) J.B.L. (John), 106, 145
Stobs Camp, Hawick, 52
Strange, Tpr, 131
Strong, Lt Gerald, 3
Stuart light tank, 116, 122
Sturdee RTR, Lt Col P.W.D. (Peter), 137, 140, 146, 158–9
Styles, Capt (later Maj) J.D. ('Stylo'), 19, 22–3, 28, 31, 45, 53, 64, 109
Sullivan, Tpr, 151
Summers, Tpr, 151
Sutton Common, 39–40

Swain, Len, 17
Swan & Sugarloaf, The, 15

TAB, 22
Tabarka, 82, 105
'Tabby', 148
tanks: American M3 light, 108–9, 111–14, 116–17, 139, 169
  American M4 Sherman, 108, 111–13, 116
  amphibious, 153
  Churchill, 39, 43, 45, 48–50, 52–3, 66, 68, 70, 86–7, 97, 99, 111–12, 132, 143–4, 147
  Churchill bridgelayer, 144–5
  Crocodile flame-thrower, 135, 137, 144
  cruiser, 21, 43
  'dozer, 146
  flail, 149
  Infantry, 20–1, 23, 25, 31, 39, 43
  Infantry, Churchill IV (NA75), 108–9, 112, 170
  Infantry, Mark III (Valentine), 30–2, 36–9, 41–6, 64, 67–8, 70
  light, 2, 5, 13, 18, 21, 23, 25, 27, 31, 38, 129
  Mark IV, Infantry, 39
  Matilda, 20–1, 24–5
  medium, 2, 5, 9, 12, 18–19, 21, 23, 25, 39, 80
  Panther, 128
  PzKpfw III medium, 80, 82–4, 87–8, 90–1, 94
  PzKpfw IV medium, 79, 85, 91–4
  Tetrarch light, 38
  Tiger, 81, 87–94, 99, 131, 137, 165
  Vickers Medium, 5, 12, 19, 21
Tank Corps, 36
Tank Delivery Squadron, 96
Tank Museum, 93, 165
Taranto, 113, 118
Tebourba, 82
Teboursouk, 85
Teller mine, 95
Testour, 85, 98
tetanus toxoid, 22
The B-Line, 70–1, 120
'The Bou', 76
'The Tanks', 30, 142
Thetford training area, 40
Thomas, Lt David, 70, 106, 126
Thomason, LCpl Geoff, 70
Thompson MC, Lt (later Capt) Geoff, 71, 95, 110
Tiger tank, 81, 87–94, 99, 131, 137, 165

Tinker, Lt Col E.H. (Ted), 119–20, 137

Tobias, Cpl (later WOII), 16, 110

Tortona, 118

Toward Point, 53

Tozegrane, 103

track, manganese steel, 37

Tractor, Vickers Utility, 18

Truman, Lt J.A. (Jim), 66, 72, 108

Trueman, Lt J.M. (Mike), 126, 134

Tunis, 68, 75, 78, 80, 83, 97–9, 101–2
Victory Parade in, 104

Tunisia, 69

turrets, cast, 44, 47
welded, 44, 47

'Two-Minute' Spencer, 115

'Tympson's Horse', 25

unit signs, 48

US 6 Corps, 118

US Fifth Army, 118

Valentine tanks, 30–2, 36–9, 41–6, 64, 68, 70
Mk I, 31, 37
Mks I to VII, 31
Mk II, 31, 37, 39
Mks III and V, 31
Mk V, 64, 67–8

Mks VIII, IX and X, 31
Mk XI, 31

Van Straubenzee, Lt Col H.H., 137

Vaughan, WOII, 110

Vauxhall Motors Ltd, 39, 43–5

Venice, 142, 144, 155–7

Versailles, Treaty of, 1

Vesuvius, 160

Vickers Armstrong Ltd, 31

Victoria Cross, 99

Victory Parade, London, 162

Virgo, LCpl, 110, 122

Vos, Lt P.S., 134

Walker, John, 10, 117, 161

Walker, Johnny, 159

War Establishment, 53, 115, 122

war flats, 34

War Office Film Unit, 40

War Weapons Week, 39

War Workers' Tattoo, 40

Warlingham, 15, 19

Warminster, 29, 32–3

Warner, Sgt 'Plum', 64, 88, 91, 130

Warwick, CSM (later Lt (QM)) A.W.F. (Freddie), 7, 16, 28

waterproofing, 53

Watney, Capt N.N., 6, 28

Watson, Tpr, 146

Watts, Tpr D.L., 94

Webber, Lt R.B., 72

Weeley, 23

Wemyss Bay, 38

West, Capt, 28

West Lavington, 28, 32

West Nova Scotia Regiment, 120, 122, 133

White, Lt (later Capt) R.G. (Ralph), 71, 129, 134, 158

White Hart, The, 40

White Lion, The, 15

Wickham Market, 33–5, 37–40, 42, 46–7

Wife, Lt (later Capt) Roy, 72, 128, 133–4

Wilkinson, Tpr, 126

Wilson, Capt D.W.N.F. ('Tug'), 4, 6–7, 9, 22–3, 28, 34,

Wilson, Sgt, 130

wireless set, no 19, 84

Woburn Abbey, 40

Woodall, Revd, 69

Woodbridge, 34

Woodgate DSO, MC, Maj A.B., 4, 6, 23

'Woodlands', 13, 17

Wright, Tpr E., 151

Wykes, Lt Col W.J. (Jackie), 4, 6–7, 9, 28, 31, 37

Zeppa, 148